Explorations in World Ethnology

ROBERT B. EDGERTON and L.L. LANGNESS
University of California, Los Angeles

General Editors

New Women of Lusaka

ILSA M. GLAZER SCHUSTER

Hebrew University

 Mayfield Publishing Company

To Richie, Ben and Ruth
and to the memory of
Florence Kasanda

Copyright © 1979 by Mayfield Publishing Company
First Edition 1979

Library of Congress Catalog Card Number: 78-051540
International Standard Book Number: 0-87484-428-2

Manufactured in the United States of America
Mayfield Publishing Company
1240 Villa Street
Mountain View, Ca. 94041

This book was set in VIP Aster and Phototypositor Jana
by Chapman's Phototypesetting and was printed and
bound by Malloy Lithographing.

Sponsoring editor was Alden C. Paine, Carole Norton
supervised editing, and Cheryl Smith was manuscript
editor. Michelle Hogan supervised production, the book
was designed by Nancy Sears, and Jim M'Guinness
designed the cover from a painting by Phyllis Holder.

Contents

Foreword

The rapid growth of large towns and cities in many countries of the Third World, particularly in the years following World War II, is a striking phenomenon: from one point of view a reflex of the wider forces of social transformation at work, the new urban centers themselves count among the most potent factors making for change and are a major source of its momentum. Anthropologists have made a notable contribution to the study of urbanization and its attendant problems, which they have approached from a variety of different theoretical perspectives, focusing on many different aspects of urban social life. One important area of inquiry however has not received the attention it merits. This area concerns the adjustments that women have had to make to changed circumstances. What seems plain even on the most cursory inspection is that in many parts of Africa women have experienced urbanization in ways fundamentally different from those of men. This is a situation that surely needs to be documented and its implications fully explored. Ilsa Schuster's vivid and fascinating account of the *New Women of Lusaka* is therefore to be welcomed as an important step in this direction; it offers rich material and much food for thought for all those interested not only in the question of urbanization, but also in the much wider issue of the changing role of women in the developing countries.

Who, then, are the new women of Lusaka—and what is new about them? During the early fifties—the period when I carried out my own field researches on the Copperbelt—Africans who had been drawn to the towns lived in segregated housing areas, referred to as compounds, in the mine townships and locations where they were under the control of a municipality. From these areas the menfolk sallied forth each day to seek their livelihood in a white-dominated wage economy. From that economy the women still remained effectively insulated; with the exception of an almost negligible number of primary school teachers, nurses and welfare assistants, opportunities for paid employment simply did not exist for African women, and in a very real sense their experience of town life remained largely confined to the encapsulated existence of the African housing areas. In the context of the colonial town, women were in certain respects even more dependent on men than they had traditionally been under tribal conditions. Changes of course had been taking place, but promise of more radical developments came only with the achievement of Zambian independence in 1964. Government policy now was to harness the human and material resources of the country to the task of national development. With the advent of this policy Zambian girls, hitherto left far behind in the education stakes, were encouraged to embark upon and to complete secondary schooling, and even to go on to University; nowadays they seek and follow careers at every level of the occupational hierarchy.

Dr. Schuster's study deals mainly with the category she dubs the subelite—the young women of the nation's capital who are employed in junior positions in administration, in the para-statal organizations, in company offices, and the like. Her theme is the way they have adapted to their new social and occupational status within society, as seen in the problems they have to cope with in acquiring housing accommodations, in the contexts of work and leisure, and above all in their relations with men, both within the framework of marriage and outside. The contradictions that attend this process are brought out beautifully in two chapters at the end of the text which describe the public image that has been built up of these young women through the local media.

Dr. Schuster tells her story far too well for me to rehearse it here, and I will confine myself to a few comments of a more general kind. The study itself developed as a survey using standard questionnaire methods, but in fact the resulting data have not been presented quantitatively; indeed, much of the richest and most interesting material is drawn from a relatively limited number of persons with whom Dr. Schuster came to enjoy very close personal relations over a number of years. Clearly there are a number of contexts in which one would have welcomed some "hard" data. For example, in any situation of flux such as we find in Lusaka, knotty problems are almost bound to arise about the relationship of expressed attitudes to actual behavior; quantitative data can go some way toward resolving such problems.

Yet in my view such losses have been more than offset in the present instance by the gains brought by Dr. Schuster's less formal approach. Consider the following as an example. It has happened, we are told, that a woman at a party will see a complete stranger wearing her own new dress. Yet it does not seem to matter, for the woman in question is herself wearing the new dress belonging to a friend. Observations of this kind, and the analysis they make possible, are not ordinarily made in the course of the conventional questionnaire survey. There is moreover a second and more important point: there are many complex and sensitive areas in an inquiry of this kind where formal interviewing is likely to draw a complete blank or at best a stereotyped response. But when the approach is so subjective, how is one to assess the accuracy or validity of the fieldworker's report? Some may feel that questions of this kind are raised, for example, by Dr. Schuster's seeming preoccupation with sexuality and the part that sexual fears appear to play in the lives of her subjects. Surely her account is exaggerated at a number of points, a projection perhaps of her own anxieties or else a reflection of an ideological stance? I simply want to comment here that what Dr. Schuster has reported in these regards appears to me to be wholly consistent with the picture presented by the late Hortense Powdermaker in her book *Copper Town*, based on her research in the mid-fifties, and with my own observations for the same period, for the most part still unpublished. Indeed, reading *New Women of Lusaka* I have been struck time and time again by the persistence of old attitudes and the way in which response to certain kinds of situations tends to repeat itself. Dr. Schuster is of course quite right to stress what it is that differentiates what she observed from what passed before. The independent and hardened young woman referred to in today's Lusaka slang as *toughu* is certainly not to be equated with the *kapenta* or *champion*—the "good-time girl" of the Copperbelt in the fifties—but even after a generation the family resemblance is not difficult to discern. And from my point of view it is precisely this element of continuity which gives to so much of what Dr. Schuster reports its ring of authenticity and authority. It is many years since I last visited Lusaka and without question the local scene has changed much in the meantime, but somehow through the pages of Ilsa Schuster's book it has all become familiar and alive again.

A. L. Epstein
University of Sussex

Acknowledgements

My thanks to the National Institute of Mental Health for Predoctoral Research Grant Number 1 F0-1 MH 47323-01 CUAN in 1971 and 1972 and to the University of Zambia for a Senior Staff Research Grant in 1973 and 1974. The present manuscript was prepared under a grant from the Ministry of Absorption in my capacity as Research Fellow of the Harry S Truman Research Institute of the Hebrew University of Jerusalem. Professors A.L. and T. Scarlett Epstein of the University of Sussex, and Dr. Bonnie Keller of the University of Zambia, made excellent comments on earlier drafts. I thank Ilana Bat Ami, Cheryl Smith, and Dr. L.L. Langness for their editorial help. The maps were prepared by the Department of Geography of the University of Zambia under the direction of Professor Geoffrey Williams, and the photography is the work of my husband, Dr. Richard Henry Schuster.

It is difficult to express thanks to the young women of Lusaka who were friends and informants at once. I owe a special debt of gratitude to Florence Kasanda, tragically knifed to death in July 1977 in a lovers' quarrel. Beautiful Florence was full of life and joy and pain, a little sister to me. I mourn her loss and can only hope that this book, which Florence and so many other Zambian women wanted to see published, will serve them and Florence's daughter Maureen, in some small way.

My deepest gratitude goes to my husband and my children; Ben and Ruth, who helped at every stage of the work, from fieldwork to data analysis to editing. In addition they were a constant source of moral support as the four of us were forced by circumstances to scatter over four continents and endure long months of separation.

Editors' Preface

The most recent years have witnessed a remarkably accelerating rate of publication of materials bearing on women in non-Western societies. Much of this publication has been stimulated, of course, by the Women's Liberation Movement, much by the realization that anthropology has too long centered its research on male-oriented activities. In spite of this increased activity there remains only a handful of truly detailed and intensive ethnographic treatments of women as they actually live their lives on a day-to-day basis. And although the changing roles of women have been a particular focus of study for some years, few accounts in that sphere, if any, offer the in-depth perspective of Ilsa M. Glazer Schuster's *New Women of Lusaka*. What is perhaps all the more remarkable is that Dr. Schuster's study was not, as the author herself points out, stimulated by the women's movement, which had barely started when she left America and has since been transported very slowly and with much difficulty to Africa and other developing areas of the world.

New Women of Lusaka combines sociological and anthropological methods and perspectives to give us an understanding of just how difficult and painful the process of culture change can be for individuals who become caught up in it through circumstances largely beyond their control. It documents to an unusual degree the persistence of traditional attitudes and values in the face of rapidly changing circumstances, and the forced and pernicious ambivalence that men and women alike experience as a result of the process of change. We believe this is one of the most revealing books to date on the subject of women caught between two worlds and trying, however impossibly, to meet the demands of both. Most tellingly, it records the insensitivity of men to the problems of educated young women, just as it shows how these young women can become increasingly estranged from the men in their lives.

New Women of Lusaka carries on in a new socio-political context the tradition of the colonial Rhodes–Livingstone Institute, whose work in the past has proven of great value not only to anthropologists but also to Zambians themselves.

Ilsa M. Glazer Schuster received her B.A. from Brooklyn College, her M.A. from Brandeis University, and her Ph.D. from the University of Sussex, England. This, her first book, is the culmination of a long-standing interest in Africa, and is the result of her more than three years of fieldwork in Zambia. She was Lecturer in African Studies at the University of Zambia in Lusaka from 1972 to 1974 and is currently a Research Fellow at the Harry S Truman Institute of The Hebrew University in Jerusalem. Dr. Schuster is presently completing a second book that deals with the uneducated women of Zambia.

Robert B. Edgerton

L. L. Langness

Fieldwork
with a New African Woman

1

A new type of African woman is making her appearance throughout politically independent sub-Saharan Africa. She is a young pioneer in the
capital cities: a teacher, a nurse, a university student, a stenographer, a
typist—in fact, all the conventional occupations of western women and
more. She works in administration, broadcasting, entertainment, fashion
modeling, journalism, law, medicine, politics, and publishing. She sym-
bolizes modernity, achievement, the competence of black people, a new
black aesthetic and pride. She is the role model for younger girls not only
in the towns but in those rural areas in contact with the cities. As Africa
develops economically in the future, the place of this new type of African
woman is assured, and she will be joined by thousands of others.

This book focuses on the educated young women of Lusaka, the capital city of the Republic of Zambia, and how they have adapted to their
new social and occupational status in society. The women studied were
born between 1945 and 1953.[1] They all had a minimum of nine years of
formal schooling; some had additional training, up to and including university educations and advanced degrees. The position of these educated
Zambian career women reflects social, political, and economic changes
that have taken place in modern, independent Zambia, not the least of
which is a change in their position relative to Zambian men. This dra-

matic change in the status of educated women has had a major impact not only on their own lives but on the quality of life in their society.

The status of women in traditional and colonial Zambian society was almost invariably inferior to that of men, although old age, membership in a royal lineage, or inheritance of a chieftaincy enhanced the position of a few. Ordinarily, however, young women were at the bottom of the social scale. Now, as social classes develop in modern, independent Zambia, the position of some women is becoming equal and sometimes superior to that of some men.

The philosophical underpinning   Anthropological research is necessarily based on a view of the nature of humanity, society, and culture, whether that view is made explicit by the anthropologist or remains only implied. A tension exists in anthropological theory between particularistic and universalistic orientations. Both orientations share the basic premises of mankind's psychic unity and the plasticity of infant human nature, which is molded by the members of a society through the medium of culture. *Particularism* focuses on the uniqueness of each culture and sometimes each individual ("the study of the odd by the peculiar," as a wit observed in my early student days). It is relativistic, and vividly describes the differences separating human groups, looking for exceptions to all generalizations, and suspending evaluations of human institutions, except, perhaps, on issues like complexity of economic and technological organization of a particular human group. *Universalism*, on the other hand, emphasizes shared elements among cultures, societies, and individuals. These are the universals of human existence and experience into which differences are woven and because of which judgments and evaluations can be made. (The wit at my undergraduate university described this kind of sociology and anthropology as "the painful elaboration of the obvious.")

I believe both approaches are valid, being different ways of responding to field situations and trying to interpret them to oneself and one's colleagues. However, in describing and analyzing issues carrying a heavy emotional load for the reader and writer alike, I think it is especially imperative that one's point of view be clearly defined. My own inclination is toward universalism. In *The Sane Society* (1956: 12–15), Eric Fromm expounds this point of view, which he calls "normative humanism":

> To speak of a "sane society" implies a premise different from sociological relativism. It makes sense only if we assume that there can be a society which is *not* sane, and this implies that there are universal criteria for mental health which are valid for the human race as such, and according to which the state of health of each society can be judged. . . . There are right and wrong, satisfactory and unsatisfactory solutions to the problems of human existence. . . . The fact that millions of people share the

2

same vices does not make these vices virtues, the fact that they share so many errors does not make the errors to be truths, and the fact that millions of people share the same forms of mental pathology does not make these people sane. . . . [This is] a *socially patterned* defect.

It should be accepted fact that human females are not inferior to human males. We all, male and female, enter this world with the potential for personal development of our minds and emotions. To develop this potential to the fullest is, in my opinion, a basic human responsibility. Yet societies throughout the world are structured to deny this basic human right to females, and cultures give societies the reasons why this should be. The extent to which human cultures and societies deny the female sex the potential for personal development, growth, and enrichment—and, most important, the public expression and social affirmation of these qualities—is one measure of their sickness, presenting a socially patterned defect. Male domination worldwide continues largely unchallenged. In adapting, adjusting, and learning to live within the cultural constraints of their respective social systems, many women have accepted the masculine view and evaluation of their humanity. In many cultures, the woman's primary concern is to get and keep her man. Few are able to reach beyond this narrow focus and achieve a state of mind that recognizes as a primary concern their personal dignity and integrity.

This socially patterned defect manifested itself in Zambian society. This defect was in some ways unique, since it took its shape and form in a particular time, context, and place. Times, contexts, and places change, and the form and shape of a socially patterned defect also changes. It may seem to disappear, yet all too often it remains and is simply manifested differently. In other ways the manifestation of Zambia's defect was not at all unique. The position and problems of educated Zambian women have similarities and parallels in other societies. In some ways Zambian women are worse off than women in other societies. In other ways they are not.

Getting to the field   As long as there are people who think and feel differently from each other and communities that operate under different rules and constraints than those of their neighbors, there will always be problems for anthropologists to study, whether near or far away. Although it is now becoming increasingly difficult to work freely in the third world, and tomorrow's students of anthropology may have little choice but to work close to home, I was raised in the old tradition: a "real" anthropologist had to do fieldwork far away. Throughout the long years of undergraduate and part-time graduate course work, I was highly motivated to plunge into the mystery and adventure of field research. For me to study social change in Africa seemed the height of fantasy, however—I was the wife of an experimental psychology graduate student and the mother of two small children.

But to everything there is a season. While my husband was doing post-doctoral research, we hit upon a plan. He applied to universities in English-speaking black Africa for a teaching position, while I applied for fellowships. Eventually he was offered a two-year contract with the University of Zambia and I was awarded a two-year National Institute of Mental Health fellowship. Lusaka had chosen us as much as we had chosen Lusaka.

I could find a variety of literature on other African cities, such as Lagos, Accra, Kampala, and Dar es Salaam, but almost nothing on Lusaka. Further, I could find no one who had lived there. This was a puzzle. Lusaka is the capital city of a country that had been the subject of much theoretical and practical fieldwork on African urbanization during colonial times. But all that work had been done on towns elsewhere in Zambia than Lusaka. Why had Lusaka been neglected? What should we expect when we got there?

Along with the contract and air tickets came a pamphlet from the university called "Welcome to Lusaka." It would have been useful were we millionaires going on safari, warning us to bring all manner of "soft household goods" and clothes. We had little information and understood less. We sold most of the clutter accumulated over ten years of marriage, stored some, and airfreighted the rest. In January 1971 the four of us flew off to what was still little more than a dot on the map.

Choice of subject My research proposal was flexible, but influenced by my long-standing interest in how social change affects peoples' lives. The interest derived, in no small part, from observing generational changes within my own large extended family in its various migrations. I was attracted to urban Africa because the changes taking place there seemed even more dramatic than anything I had personally observed or experienced. Although the anthropological literature at the time was still dominated by accounts of tribal societies, something new and exciting obviously was happening in urban Africa with the coming of political independence and economic development. I felt that anthropologists should not bemoan the loss of tribal isolation, but should welcome change and study its impact.

I wanted to study women in particular—an interest also stemming from a combination of personal and professional factors. Ironically, it developed outside the context of the women's liberation movement, which was still new when I left America. I had grown up in a world of traditional women within my own extended family and was at ease in such a world. I felt that with a husband and children of my own I would "make sense" as a person to African women.

4

The literature on urbanization and social change in Africa presented many puzzles. I found very little written on women, apart from West African market mammies. Some anthropologists did suggest that women in town were emancipated, then went on to describe prostitutes or mistresses. By emancipation, they meant that women in town were free to have sexual intercourse with different men. To me this was hardly emancipation. Other anthropologists hinted that women in town suffered a loss of status, since they now had to depend on wage-earning men for money. These writers suggested that the agricultural labor of a village woman made a major contribution to the production process, thereby affording her social clout. Yet this does not inevitably follow. Slaves in America made major contributions to the production process without having social clout.

Obviously the various accounts and theories I read were inconsistent and unsatisfying. I was anxious to see what actually was happening to women in African cities.

IN THE FIELD

It took me a long time after I got to Lusaka to figure out what "the field" actually was. What I faced was the anonymity of a city and the desire to study an amorphous subject: its women. I had no wish to construct artificial barriers by confining myself to a particular African neighborhood of the city, and I was equally determined not to fall into the slow and easy world of white expatriate cocktails-by-the-poolside society. Cities are paradoxical places, at once very public and very private. Social relationships depend on networks, and a person shunning "natural" networks—those developed at work or those based on kinship—has to exercise patience and reserve in order, ultimately, to be accepted where she does not "naturally" belong.

During the first few months, I spent a great deal of time driving around the various neighborhoods of the city, going through the markets, learning a bit of Chinyanja (theoretically the *lingua franca*[2] of the city), reading every statistic and historical reference I could find about the city, having an appendectomy, and nursing my family through malaria. Everything and nothing was "the field."

In order to cover a broad range of issues and concerns, it was necessary to become familiar with women of varied income and educational levels, living in different parts of the city in different sorts of life styles, some of which duplicated the life styles of the recent colonial period. Only after becoming familiar with the range of alternative life styles of Lusaka's young women did I feel it would be possible to interpret that of elite and subelite segments of the population.

Interviews   The initial phase of the research was an attempt to become familiar, in the rather limited superficial way typical of sociological survey research, with the main patterns, trends, and features of the lives of young women. Starting in April 1971, I conducted a survey utilizing open-ended, in-depth questionnaires. I began with a random representative sample of 55 black Zambian female students at the University of Zambia. Next I studied 50 young housewives in a ward of a quasi-legal shantytown called Mutendere. Following completion of these interviews, I went back and forth between educated and uneducated young women in Lusaka. The students and housewives were at the extreme end-points of an adaptive continuum of urban life. Since the Mutendere housewives' way of life was not substantially different from the African woman's way of life under colonial conditions, it seemed an important baseline from which to evaluate what had changed in the position and problems of the educated women, and what had remained the same.

Following the Mutendere interviews, I agreed to direct a family planning survey of 200 low-income women in Matero, a town council housing estate, and George, an adjacent shantytown. This was a continuation of a brilliant study in community pediatrics conducted by Dr. Felicity Savage King, who had also collected socioeconomic data on households, which she kindly allowed me to share.

By this time our two years in Zambia were nearly over. I had accumulated a great deal of factual data and impressions, but I still felt a relative stranger to African social life. We made a family decision to stay on. I was accepted by the university, where I organized and taught an interdisciplinary social science course on black Africa, and continued research until August 1974 with support from University of Zambia grants.

Still alternating educated and uneducated women, I turned to 50 student nurses. Next, I interviewed 78 market women in six areas of Lusaka. The marketeers were as poor and uneducated as the Mutendere, Matero, and George housewives, but, as earners of incomes, they were more positively adapted to urban life in independent Zambia. The gap between marketeers and nurses was not nearly as wide as that between university students and shantytown housewives: on a continuum, the former two categories were closer to the center. Another category near the center was 46 uneducated wage-earning cleaners whom I interviewed at the University Teaching Hospital in Lusaka and the University of Zambia. Finally I interviewed the women whose lives form the basis of the present study: the modern young Zambian career women, who represent the educated end of the continuum of adaptation to urban life. Most of these women were office workers. A small number of qualified Zambian nurses were living and working at the teaching hospital at the time the interviews were being conducted, and I included them in the sample of 48 women working in the modern sector.

6

Altogether there were the family planning interviews, which included Dr. King's data, and full interviews of 153 women who were educated and 174 women who were uneducated. The questionnaires were, of course, fitted to the education/occupation categories identified for study. In the Mutendere and George/Matero surveys I used female interpreters whom the interviewees knew. The Mutendere interpreter was a local resident; the George/Matero interpreter had earlier worked with Dr. King. Three university women students helped with the interviews of student nurses, cleaners, and marketeers. Nearly all Zambian languages were used in the interviews, contrary to my expectation that Chinyanja alone would suffice. All other interviews I conducted alone and in English. The English came to be laden with Zambian turns of phrase, slang words, and expressions. I had to learn to use English the way Zambians do, and to understand their nuances and different shades of meaning with words we presumably used in common.

I felt that the survey was important as an initial technique and as an introduction to deeper fieldwork. Some of the data were instructive and useful: for example, comparing working women in the modern (formal) and survival (informal) economic sectors. However, even under the best of circumstances, people sometimes lie in surveys. When the interviewer comes from another culture, or even another subculture, she cannot quickly be aware of the particular subjects about which interviewees will lie. For example, Zambian university women tend to conceal casual dating, while American university women tend to exaggerate dating. For Zambians, casual dating connotes immorality; for Americans it connotes popularity. Working women of both cultures tend to inflate their incomes, but for different reasons. Americans derive prestige from high personal income from an occupation; Zambians derive prestige from the amount of money a "boyfriend" gives.

Some important data cannot be obtained in surveys, either because interviewees cannot or will not answer questions put by a stranger or because social interactions cannot be observed. Finally, one is at the mercy of verbal reports of behavior, which can be ideal rather than real. This was especially true in the images women presented of themselves. If I had relied exclusively on what women said about themselves, rather than what I observed, I would have written a book about angels.

Personal observations　In-depth participant-observation was accomplished very gradually over the survey period. By 1973–74 I was able to concentrate on a few individuals as case studies and to become deeply and personally involved in their lives and in those of their friends and families. The ethical, emotional, and intellectual difficulty of such involvement is proportional to the depth of the insight gained.

I felt that, as data, the gossip about other women and men in a

.7

woman's network was less important than what that woman confided about her own thoughts, fears, feelings, and experiences, as well as her observable responses to the gossip, and her behavior in public and in private. However, because Zambian society treasures secrecy and is more suspicious than trusting, I had to overcome a barrier of reserve in order to understand what was really happening in the women's lives and how they responded to people and events. This could only be accomplished by sharing confidences with women who became close friends. Friendship and fieldwork mixed and jelled in a not-always-easy balance. My own home was open to the women, and for periods varying from weeks to months, four women lived with me and my family. In addition, I lived in a subelite Zambian neighborhood from February 1971 to September 1974, and in an elite Zambian neighborhood from September 1975 to August 1976, and got to know some of my neighbors quite well. Such informal settings were great aids to my understanding.

I sometimes felt I was betraying my profession by rarely asking direct questions of informants. I accepted confidences but did not try to elicit them, and often found myself responding to informants' direct questions about my own life, my relationship with my husband, children and kin, my values and experiences: it made me wonder who the anthropologist was. At the same time, I felt I was betraying friends by analyzing their lives as I gradually came to understand them. Yet I never concealed my research interests or commitment to the study. Finally, I wondered if my deep personal involvement in an alien way of life was a betrayal of myself. Much of what I saw shocked and wounded my sensibilities. Yet these feelings are, perhaps, the essence of fieldwork.

I knew that I must repress many personal reactions so that informants would continue behaving freely with me, but sometimes I found it impossible. For example, an incident at a party for Zambia's tenth anniversary of independence in October 1974: I was at the Zambia High Commission in London, a private party following the formal celebration at the Commonwealth Institute. While gossiping with a woman I had known reasonably well in Lusaka, I learned that a mutual acquaintance in the room was planning to marry a Zambian woman whom he met in England. He left behind in Lusaka a girlfriend named Sarah, who had just borne his child and whom we all thought he was going to marry. I became angry. The man had been especially clever at "getting" Sarah by using what Zambians call "sweet talk"—and New Yorkers call "a line." (His "sweet talk" was well known to us, and it made him a much sought-after potential husband: he spoke out strongly in favor of women on the issue of women's rights.) I thought of how sick this news would make Sarah. The betrayal would grieve her for a long time to come, and the child would be a life-long reminder of her disappointment.

My anger was also generalized toward the country whose society shared responsibility for Sarah's plight. To my fellow gossiper I burst out, "Ah, your Zambia is crazy!" She readily agreed, but I nevertheless instantly felt ashamed of myself. An anthropologist is supposed to get behind the apparently strange outward behavior patterns of another culture to understand the logic therein. I felt inadequate because I had let my own culturally conditioned emotional reaction bias my work. I did not know if my fellow gossiper agreed with me to flatter me or because she really felt the same way I did at that moment. I just sometimes found it impossible not to express my personal reactions to close African friends, even though to do so might stop them from telling me things they knew would be upsetting. They sometimes laughed at gossip that would make me almost weep with anger and pain. When I was at my angriest I wondered how in the world I would manage to write objectively and contribute to the science of anthropology.

Later, I related the story about the engagement to an African male friend on the University of Sussex campus and said that I found this type of thing personally distressing. "It's good that you're angry with Zambia now," my friend said. "Now you'll just have to write the truth and not cover it up with false liberal pretensions. If you think Zambia is sick, just say it—and then try to figure out why." The task was to be objective about subjectivity, to bring the insight of art to the science of anthropology.

I left Zambia for the final time in August 1976 with the children. (I had spent an interim year in England, from September 1974 to September 1975.) My husband joined us in April 1977. On reflection, I realized that despite my culturally conditioned personal reactions to Zambian social life, I had repressed my own feelings a great deal: the rules by which Zambian women ordered their lives made sense to me. I, myself, had changed. Although I am now much more my old self, I doubt I shall ever perceive the world quite as I did before fieldwork in Zambia.

Fieldwork in a modern African city, much of it involving informants eager to read what I would write and already versed in anthropological literature on their own tribes, was a challenging, subtle, extended learning process. There were tremendous advantages to spending as long a period of time there as I did—I was able to observe the unfolding of people's lives over several years, and to see how values and attitudes expressed verbally at certain times were expressed behaviorally when the proper occasion arose. I could wait and see if early hypotheses were borne out. Over the years, my family involved themselves in my work and became excellent "research assistants," even while developing their own networks in Zambian society.

There were also disadvantages. People told me secrets and then feared me for my knowledge. I came to know too much for my own good, particularly about the private lives of elite men. My family and I missed the support of our own culture and society, and the affirmation that comes from really belonging to a community by right rather than adoption. It was time to come home.

To supplement survey and participant-observation techniques, I collected written material from a wide variety of sources. These included hundreds of letters, published and unpublished, written to the lovelorn columns of the two daily newspapers; letters, articles, and features about women in the national and student newspapers; essays on "Traditional Marriage in My Tribe" written by midwifery students for a social science course at the University Teaching Hospital; and copies of various representations made by participants in women's seminars and conferences.[3] Over the years I attended meetings of Zambian women's groups and held informal discussions about the problems of Lusaka's young women with African psychiatrists, physicians, lawyers, social workers, community development officers, nursing sisters, educators, journalists, colleagues on the academic and non-academic staff of the University of Zambia, and of course, my students, all but the nursing sisters including both sexes.

PLAN OF THE STUDY

This study examines the interplay between culture, society, and the individual. From the cultural standpoint, I ask: What are the beliefs about control of women, the danger of women in general, and of townswomen in particular? How are women affected by Zambian and western cultural beliefs about women? What are the women's culturally-based attitudes toward, and relationships with, males, and vice versa? What do the women think of Zambian traditions—what would they keep; what would they cast aside? What aspects of modern western life do they value? What are the problems that arise when their ideas are contrary to those of other members of their society—and when western and Zambian ideas clash?

In terms of society, this study explores some of the ways in which educated young women came to be socially differentiated from their uneducated counterparts in the very brief years since independence. It seemed to me that a few women underwent a radical change between October 1964 and February 1971 when I arrived, and I was drawn to try to figure out the process by which this change took place. I was interested in the position in which the educated young women of Zambia found themselves in contemporary society, and how they functioned in its midst. What were their life styles like now? Clearly, these women were hardly "beasts of burden"—their phrase for rural female horticulturists, whose lives were bound up with fertility of soil and womb. These were women living in the age of the jet plane—who, if they had not already done so, dreamed of flying to Nairobi, London, New York—and living in the age

10

of the birth control pill. They were well aware of what they called "the women's lib." How was society receiving this vanguard?

In terms of the individual, I was interested in the impact of society in molding self-images and how the self-image was projected. What were the young women's thoughts and hopes about the future, fears and problems, personal attitudes, values and experience? How did they adapt to becoming women of the city?

THE BOOK

Chapter 2 offers a brief history of Zambia, its evolution into an independent state, and the basis of the problems of modern Zambian women. Chapter 3 analyzes the process of socialization by family; Chapter 4 does the same for the school. Family and school prepared these young women for adulthood. In Chapters 5 through 8, I look at the lives of graduates of school and training programs now entering young adulthood as the first generation of Lusaka's modern African work force. The substance of these chapters is to describe and analyze various alternative life styles, conflicting and contradictory values, and the impact of these on individuals. Chapters 9 and 10 describe the intense ambivalence of the stereotypes and attitudes of the wider society. Images of women presented in the two daily newspapers are analyzed as an index of society's attitudes and as an example of how stereotypes are consciously and unconsciously manipulated.

A Historical Overview:
The Roots of the Problem

2

THE LAND AND ITS PEOPLE

Completely landlocked, mostly high plateau of between 3,500 and 4,500 feet elevation, the country of Zambia covers 290,586 square miles. Isolated mountain ridges rise to more than 6,000 feet above sea level, the occasional peak to more than 7,000 feet. But much of the land is flat savannah grassland broken only by small hills. Over half the country is covered by hardwood forest.

Although Zambia is in Africa's tropical zone, the high altitude makes the climate excellent: rarely is it uncomfortably hot or cold. In the wet season, from mid-November through April, rivers and streams swell and the bush comes to life. Toward the end of the rains it grows colder, and in June there is even occasional frost in some areas. Winter temperatures average 60 to 80 degrees Fahrenheit; morning and evening temperatures can reach as low as 40 to 50 degrees. The heat builds up slowly: by October the land is parched and the sun blazes. Maximum temperatures then range from 80 to 95, with daily variations of 30 to 35 degrees. Annual rainfall varies from 50 inches in the north to 30 inches in the south.

With its large land area—bigger than France, Switzerland, Belgium, and the Netherlands combined—its vast game parks covering thousands of square miles and harboring Africa's richest wildlife reserves, and its tiny population (4,056,995), Zambia appears to be a country largely without human inhabitants. Indeed, in 1969 the population density was only 13.9 to the square mile, according to the national census, and today fully 40 percent of the people are concentrated within 25 miles of the line-of-rail (the railroad that runs from Livingstone in the south to Chililabombwe in the north, through the mineral-rich corridor known as the Copperbelt).

Over 98 percent of the Zambian population is African. There are 43,390 Europeans, mainly families of temporary residents in which the household head works on contract to the government or in industry. The 10,783 Asians are mainly small-scale entrepreneurs. The African population is Bantu-speaking, split into no less than 72 distinct tribes, each with its own dialect and culture. Many of the languages are closely related and mutually intelligible.

There are five main tribal groupings: the Bemba and Lunda in the north, Lozi in the west, Tonga-Ila in the south, and Ngoni and Cewa in the east. Of all the groups, the Tonga are the longest settled in the region, having entered the land about 1,000 years ago. It is believed that they, and most other Zambian peoples, came from the Congo—and ultimately from West Africa—as part of a mass southwardly migration of Bantu-speakers. The Lozi arrived next, only 300 years ago, conquering the local people. Many northern Zambian groups derive from the expansion of the seventeenth and eighteenth century Lunda-Luba Empire of the Congo (now Zaire). By the end of the nineteenth century, the Bemba were masters of the area between Lakes Tanganyika, Bangweulu, Mweru, and Malawi. The Lunda closely followed, reaching the height of their empire between 1760 and 1860. The Ngoni of the east were the last to arrive, reversing older migration patterns by coming from the south. In about 1860 they reached their present home.

The problem of matriliny   The majority of Zambia's tribes have a tradition of matriliny, a rather unusual case in ethnography. Elsewhere in Africa, most tribes have a tradition of patriliny. In matrilineal systems, ego follows ascending and descending genealogical lines through females only. Inheritance passes from mother's brother to mother's brother's sister's son to his sister's son. In patrilineal systems, ego follows ascending and descending genealogical lines through males only; inheritance of property, rights, obligations, and so forth is directly from a father to his son to his son's son. Yet so strong is the matrilineal bias in Zambia that even some of the country's traditionally patrilineal peoples have absorbed some matrilineal tendencies. Some of the problems modern educated women face may derive from very deep roots in the structure of the matrilineal societies from which they come.

In Zambia's traditional matrilineal societies, the most important bond from a structural point of view exists between a brother and a sister.

13

A sister's son's inheritance comes from her brother. Thus a sister produces sons for her brother, not her husband, their father. In patrilineal societies, a son's inheritance comes from his father: woman, as incubator, produces sons for her husband and his lineage, and thus the important bond is of a woman to her husband and his lineage.

Many anthropologists working among matrilineal peoples have noted that, compared to patrilineal societies, divorce is relatively easy and marriage unstable. Fieldworkers also note violent sexual antagonisms and conflicts in several of the matrilineal tribes. Much theoretical work has been done, in fact, to try to figure out why this should be, and one of the reasons advanced is the importance of the brother-sister rather than the husband-wife bond.

Perhaps one of the roots of the problem of antagonistic and unstable relations between the sexes in contemporary Zambia derives from tribal times, when men required women's fertility to enhance their power and prestige, yet did not have personal sexual access to the women who gave them this power. For these women were, of course, their sisters. Frustration within the brother-sister bond could therefore have functioned in a way that undermined marriages. Sisters' and even men's own marriages could be treated lightly as fundamentally irrelevant to their personal power and the organization of their group.

Yet this explanation of the origin of the problem is only partial, and not entirely satisfying. Many of the same problems in relationships between the sexes are repeated in modern African towns elsewhere on the continent, where townspeople come from strongly patrilineal, patriarchal tribal societies. Certainly adultery was common in traditional patrilineal as well as matrilineal societies. An informant from a patrilineal tribe said:

> In traditional times, a widow could choose which of her husband's brothers would inherit her when he died. So naturally she had to taste them while her husband was still alive!

UNDER COLONIALISM

The first white people to enter the country came as missionaries and traders during the second half of the nineteenth century. In 1900, Lewanika, the Paramount Chief of the Lozi, accepted British protection in exchange for the assignment of mineral rights to the British South Africa Company. It seems to me that the greatest blow of all to enduring male-female relationships in Zambia was the experience the people endured under foreign rule, first under the British South Africa Company (which subsequently extended its domain to the other tribal areas), and then, after 1924, under the British crown. The colonial economic policy in this part of Africa was by its nature devastating to spousal relationships. The tensions and conflicts that were already part of tribal social life became exaggerated, while at the same time unprecedented new tensions and problems arose.

In the early 1900s, before white people discovered major copper ore deposits there, the territory of Northern Rhodesia (as Zambia was then known) served colonial economic interests primarily as a labor reserve. The British South Africa Company administered the territory as an area in which labor recruiting companies were free to round up healthy young men, often through trickery, to work on contract far from their home villages. Zambians thus migrated to Southern Rhodesia (now Rhodesia), Katanga (now Shaba, Zaire), Tanganyika (now Tanzania), and South Africa. As early as 1912 the Northern Rhodesia Labour Bureau had established a complete chain of agencies and labor depots throughout the colony. Conditions for transporting the men to the labor centers and for work within them were harsh. One recruiting poster I saw for the Eastern Province of Zambia offered the possibility of travel by truck as a special inducement to recruits. The poster explained that the men would not suffer sore feet from walking several hundred miles. So many of the men recruited to work in the gold mines of the South African Rand died that eventually the administration became concerned that "tropical natives" could not endure Rand working conditions. Other young men were permanently lost to their home villages not through death but through settlement and assimilation in other regions. Others became permanent transients and drifted from one wage labor center to another. Still others returned to their home villages to stay but a few years, become restless, and leave again.

For many young men, there was no choice except to leave their home villages and seek wage employment, for the colonial government had instituted a "head tax," a sum of money native men had to pay. If there was no way of making that money at home, the men had to migrate. It was a way of ensuring that European industries had a supply of labor. The justification for getting Africans into the labor market was to "uplift the native male out of his primitive somnolence," but the profit motive was, of course, unambiguous.

Despite the predominance of labor migration to surrounding territories, local development on a small scale was also taking place under the auspices of the British South Africa Company. Hundreds of African men were employed in the building of the railroad and the Broken Hill mine, as construction workers building the tiny European settlements, and as farmhands on the European farms.[1] Unfortunately, the records of this early period are written from the perspective of European development, in the form of Colonial Office Reports. We know little of the African response or of the change in African social and economic life that resulted. We do know that some African labor was short-term and casual. But cer-

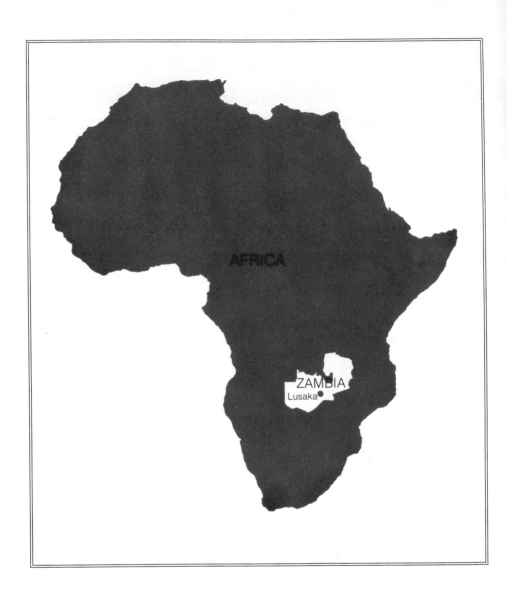

tainly not every man returned to his village with his proverbial blanket, bicycle, clothes, and shillings. We have no systematic study of the men who returned and the men who remained in wage labor; only tantalizing hints scattered in the literature and individual family histories of living Zambians. We know that as early as 1910 African shopkeepers were com-

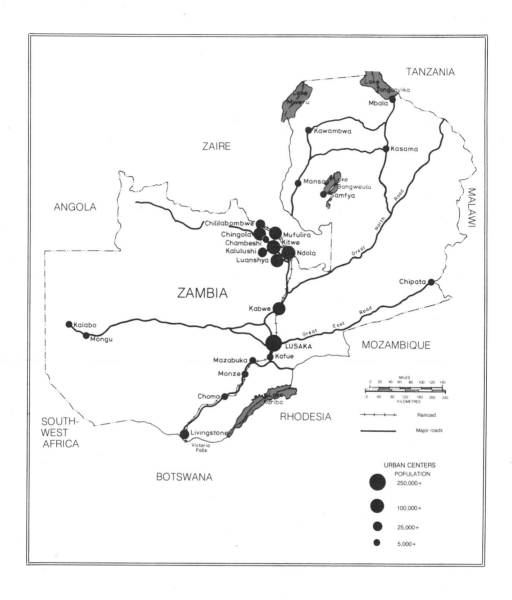

peting with European shopkeepers in Livingstone, the southernmost Zambian town and its earliest capital, and African farmers were competing with European farmers in Lusaka.

This very early history of social differentiation begs to be written. For example, one top elite man told me that his father and a friend walked from their Eastern Province village near the small town of Katete to Malawi so that they could go to school. People in their village laughed at them, for this was the 1920s, when such things simply were not done. About twenty years later, the same man, by then a school teacher in Lusaka, took another unprecedented step that was criticized by Lusaka neighbors who were his tribesmen. He educated his own rather than his sisters' sons. Hence the ultimate success of my informant and his brothers in the 1960s and 1970s, but not of their sisters and other relatives, who are either in low-status jobs in Lusaka or living in Eastern Province villages.

Migration and wage employment were features of social life for Africans from the very beginning of British colonial rule. When anthropologists visited the territory twenty, thirty, and forty years after this early phase, villages had already responded to change even though they appeared to maintain much of their traditional culture. Even before copper was mined on an industrial scale, Zambians had three decades of white overrule and economic policy. The elements by which a new national society were to be created had been introduced—the mass migrations, urbanization, social stratification, underdevelopment of some areas, and indigenous development in others.

Following World War I, the western industrialized nations faced a need to expand both their foreign markets for manufactured goods and their quest for raw materials. Dollar and copper shortages created during the war had increased Britain's interest in developing Commonwealth mineral sources, and a new, well-financed wave of prospecting began between 1925 and 1928. It was at this time that Zambia's rich copper deposits were discovered.

From the mid-1920s until the Great Depression in 1932–33, and from the end of that slump through today, copper mining has overshadowed all other economic activity in Zambia. The nation became one of the world's leading exporters of copper, and the development of the copper mining industry and the minimal infrastructure needed to export copper efficiently became the very *raison d'être* of British interest in their colony. Concessionary rights to exploit the rich copper deposits were awarded to the Anglo American Corporation and the Rhodesian (later Roan) Selection Trust. Even more than the colonial government itself, these two companies influenced the establishment of a new social order in the country.

Copper mining transformed the life of the Zambian people as well as the country's landscape. Mining made Zambia a major center of urban employment rather than an exporter of rural labor. By 1930 Zambia was still in a transitional period, the mines not yet fully developed. Yet of the 70,478 adult Zambian African males employed in the country that year,

30,000 were working on the Copperbelt. Wage labor was not the odd decision of an adventuresome young man, but was on the way to becoming institutionalized. Copper also made Zambia a center of enormous capital investment, not only for mining equipment but in the creation of towns around the mines. This was the origin of urban development, government townships growing alongside mine townships. No longer a neglected, impoverished backwater, Zambia became a place in which enormous profits were made by European investors—profits that were by and large sent out of the country, virtually never used for the social and economic development of the territory or its citizens.

The country became a nation of migrants, moving from various rural areas to the towns, between rural areas, and between towns. The degree of geographic mobility of African men from the 1930s onward cannot be exaggerated. Virtually all the provinces were drawn into it. Western Province peoples went to Livingstone, Central Province peoples went to Kabwe, and Eastern Province peoples went to Lusaka. While members of one of the large tribes from the Northern Province, the Bemba, became the largest group on the Copperbelt, all provinces are represented there.[2]

The colonial government was weak in power and influence compared to the mining companies. The colonies were supposed to be administered at minimal cost to Britain. Therefore, the development of social services and modern amenities had to be paid out of local taxes. Lack of funds to build schools, hospitals, and communication and transport services was a theme running through the Colonial Office Reports of the period. Tax monies were inadequate because African wages were very low, resulting in almost total lack of opportunity for African advancement. At the time of independence in 1964, there were only about 1,000 graduates of secondary school and a scant 100 university graduates among the African citizens of Zambia. The policies of the colonial administration were mostly *ad hoc* responses to social problems that became too acute to ignore. Africans expressed their grievances in strikes and riots, developed trade unions, and ultimately mobilized themselves politically to demand independence.

In the area of male-female relationships, government policy worked in collusion with the interests of private investors in Northern Rhodesia's industrialization. Profits for investors were maximized by keeping the wages of African male laborers at the minimum necessary for their personal physical survival. It was thus too costly for men to bring their wives to town.

Even were the cost not prohibitive, government policy regarding the migration of women made it extremely difficult for wives to join husbands in town. Labor laws made it impossible for them to work even if they did get there. As early as 1916 in Mumbwa District (Central Province), it was declared illegal for single women to migrate to town without the permission of the Native Commissioner. Although District Officers were instructed not to support this order, they sometimes did so anyway. Thus, in the 1930s and 1940s, all possible measures were undertaken to keep African men and women apart. The justification of such measures was that men were "really" tribesmen, not townsmen, and they were only temporarily in town. After a spell of urban employment, they were expected to return to their villages.

In the 1950s government thinking changed to a policy of "balanced stabilization" of population between the urban and rural areas. Impediments to female migration to towns were ended so that urban-based families could be formed. By the 1960s female migrants to towns outnumbered male migrants, and the imbalanced sex ratios characteristic of towns was corrected. But by then the harm had already been done. An urban social system had already grown up; behavioral expectations of town life had been formed.

The exploitation of African men under colonial economic conditions was obvious. The harm done to their women was more subtle and worse. The men had to face race prejudice and a color bar limiting economic opportunity. The women faced not only race prejudice but sex prejudice as well. Misogyny came at them from all sides. African men in the rural areas, including chiefs, sought to keep them "under control"—they did not want their women running off to town. African men in the towns also wanted to control the women. The British colonial authorities thus had the cooperation of African men in keeping the women down, in limiting their freedom of movement and socioeconomic mobility. Many townsmen were even opposed to their wives joining church-run homecraft classes.

The social pressures of the grind of poverty, men working on shifts, women with no possibility of legitimate employment and hence with little to occupy their time, and an imbalanced sex ratio, with men greatly outnumbering women, demoralized townsmen and townswomen alike. Under these conditions, few marriages contracted in town were even *intended* to endure. Men wishing to remain in town and wanting to be properly married sent word to their rural relatives or took a brief "home leave" themselves in order to find suitable brides. But even these arranged marriages had little chance of survival in town. The alternative was to leave a properly married wife back in the village while the new husband returned to town.

The influence of the Christian missions did little to redress the situation. Under colonial conditions, the European-financed Christian missions, divided among numerous sects, had the primary and often exclusive responsibility of providing such meager health and educational facilities as were possible. Most missionary activity was directed, naturally, to the religious conversion of pagans. They lacked the resources necessary to

20

develop schools and hospitals on a massive scale. The result is that contemporary Zambia is largely illiterate, but Christian.

Today's moral overseers of Zambian society continually bemoan the immorality rampant in the country, its deviance from Christian and traditional ideals of behavior. They pretend that Christian and traditional morality are the same, and that they share a common foundation in their understanding of male-female relationships. In doing so, they simply compound and confound the problem. Expressing a Christian value, for example, they call for a return to traditional morality, as if premarital adolescent chastity and marital fidelity were the traditional norm. They ignore the profoundly differing world views that make repression of sexuality through the inculcation of guilt feelings and consequent abstention "normal" for Christians, and indulgence in the expression of sexuality, albeit discreetly, so as not to be shamed, "normal" for traditionalists.

The moral chaos of contemporary Zambian society and the suffering such chaos brings on its people thus has a historical basis. Old tribal structures, an exploitative colonial economic system, instability of social life caused by large-scale migrations of healthy young men, demographically artificial conditions of rapid urbanization, lack of freedom to advance in education and employment for the men, almost total absence of any opportunities at all for women, all contributed to the present situation.

ZAMBIA AS AN INDEPENDENT STATE

Zambia gained its independence from Britain in October 1964. Initially it was a multi-party democracy with a President elected by universal suffrage. Nine years later, the government, under the ruling political party, U.N.I.P. (the United National Independence Party), declared a Second Republic and a "one-party participatory democracy," banning opposition.

Government priorities have undergone enormous changes since independence. Health and educational facilities have expanded. The economy has diversified. The labor force has been Zambianized. ("Zambianization," a key word in modern Zambian life, is the hiring, training, and promoting of Zambian citizens to formerly white-only jobs.) Priority has been given to the creation of national unity and identity. With national policies now designed to promote the upward social mobility of Zambian Africans, the social structure has changed. Whereas in colonial times the top elite and subelite populations were entirely white, now they are largely black.

Occupation and income, which depend on amount and timing of education, are the chief factors that differentiate classes in modern Zambian life. The *apamwamba*, or top elites, are nearly all a first generation of wealthy, educated men and women. They are very young, having been appointed to top positions immediately on the attainment of their basic educational qualifications. With one foot in Zambia and the other foot on a plane carrying them to western cities to conduct official business and to buy western luxuries, they set the trend for urban subelites to emulate.

Since independence, there have been explicit attempts to upgrade the position of women. The government has encouraged, directly or indirectly, opportunities either specifically for women or equally for both sexes. At the official level, government thinking is that women should be involved in national development and should form homecraft training centers, poultry cooperatives, and branches of the Women's Brigade of U.N.I.P. Girls must go to school, delay marriage until well after puberty, and aim to take training in the typically female occupations of nurse, teacher, air hostess, or office worker, or compete with male students at the university or in civil service. Because of the acute shortage of Zambian manpower, government leaders continually exhort women to take advantage of these new opportunities. Among the leaders of the top elite are women as well as men, all of whom follow this official line. At a non-leadership level, subelite women agitate for legal changes to further enhance the position of women.

As the overall social structure of contemporary Zambia is changing, the position of women is changing even more, shifting their status and their roles. These changes are felt more immediately in the urban areas and in the urban enclaves of the rural areas than in the traditional subsistence sector: towns are historically the centers of innovation and change. The men have long been involved in wage labor and in what little education the colonial government and local missions offered, but among the women, social change is dramatic and sudden.

One of the biggest changes for women is that their status is no longer determined solely, or even primarily, by traditional bonds to a patri- or matrilineage, to a husband, and sometimes to his group. As modern young women find socioeconomic niches for themselves in the new national context, their status is determined by personal achievements, abilities, and choices, as measured against those of their male peers.

The city of Lusaka   As the capital city, Lusaka is an important focus of change. It is the center of national and international political activity, the home of the top black Zambian elites who have naturally desegregated all public and most private facilities. As the headquarters for government, the home of new light industries, the university, and the new parastatal corporations,[3] all of which are in the process of "Zambianizing," Lusaka has become the country's innovative center.

In colonial times, the focus of change was the Copperbelt north of Lusaka—a group of towns that grew up around copper mines. Today's Copperbelt continues to throb with vibrant life. And though the mines are

22

still dominated at the upper levels by racist white personnel, young educated Zambians have begun taking over control not of the mines, but of the civil service and other commercial enterprises. Many of these are true children of the Copperbelt who know no other home, and they are creating a prosperous new subelite ambience. But they take their cue from Lusaka's top elites.

Although Lusaka has a population of about 400,000,[4] one must exert some effort of the imagination to regard it as a city. Evidences of the distinctive architecture and town planning, public transportation system, and variety of institutionalized forms of entertainment normally associated with urban living elsewhere are absent here. The drive from the airport to "downtown" on the four-lane Great East Road reveals only sprawling ranch houses set back on spacious lawns half hidden by trees and shrubs. One passes an area of dense settlement called Nine Miles Compound, but it is carefully hidden from the traveller's eye by a grass-backed fence of magenta bougainvillea, kept in splendid condition by municipal gardeners. Also tucked away from view are the shantytown Kalingalinga, the low-income homeowners ("site and service") scheme[5] of Kaunda Square, and the quasi-legal Mutendere. On the surface, Lusaka puts on a wealthy face.

Downtown there is a single street of "European" shops: the "first class trading area," which looks like a small American suburban shopping

The "second class" trading area. General stores, like these African or Indian owned shops, pocket the East and Central African urban landscape.

23

area complete with parking lots, multi-story office buildings, supermarkets, and small shops. Only the rows of flame trees and the island dividing the road are reminders that one might be in Africa, the island being lined with petty traders sitting on small stools or squatting on the ground next to their displays of Kenyan and Tanzanian wooden curios, Zambian malachite, and, now and then, drums and ivory. The first class trading area caters to Lusaka's black elite and subelite and all its white and Indian population.

Parallel to this street are two other shopping streets with small shops owned and run mainly by Zambia's Indian citizens. Between these two is the main bus station and the open-air vegetable market, with stalls run by Zambia's white, coloured,[6] and black citizens, many of whom are of South African or Rhodesian origin.

Small groceries in the African market sell imported manufactured wares; dried vegetables seen in the tin wash tub and in burlap are locally grown by commercial farmers.

24

Near the downtown area is the "second class trading area," which caters to a subelite and poor African trade and has a more African flavor. Gone are the supermarkets and the concrete and glass "skyscrapers" of six stories. The pastel Indian shops sell brightly colored, two-meter-length cotton cloths called *chitenge*, which the poor African women wear over their western-style dresses. Grocery shops stock the basics of African consumer storable items when they are available: soap, detergent, candles, canned soups, pilchards (a kind of sardine), margarine, matches, and cooking oil. The open-air market, which comprises a main portion of the informal economic sector, is large and bustling. Women sell a small variety of fresh seasonal vegetables, groundnuts, tiny dried fish, and dried caterpillars in season, and some run "restaurants." Both sexes sell charcoal and live chickens. Men sell fresh fish. Also on the scene are tinsmiths, furniture makers, tailors, bicycle repairers, herbalists, and grocers. Licensed vendors sell toys, mirrors, combs, and toothbrushes. Well-loved Zairese music blares from radios, and the Zambian flag waves on high.

Over the years two-story garden apartment houses, one multi-story apartment house, and a few row houses have been built in the elite "low density" areas of Lusaka near the government and shopping centers. Basically, however, Lusaka remains a city of one-family houses. Neighborhoods are clearly distinguished by income, as in colonial times they were distinguished by race.

The overwhelming majority of Lusaka's population is poor and lives in shantytowns relatively far from the town center. Shantytowns have grown with breathtaking rapidity. They have a distinct atmosphere: women squat outside tiny tin-roofed mud-brick houses cooking on small fires; goats, dogs, cats, and chickens roam freely; gangs of small children play; and vernacular broadcasts can be heard on radios. There are also several legal townships relatively far from the town center. These are tiny houses owned by the city and rented to workers ranging from poor to subelite.

Townships and shantytowns, called "high density" areas, are exclusively African. The "low density" areas of sprawling ranch houses on plots ranging from half an acre to fifteen acres or so are for elites of all races. They could be mistaken for the west except for the large number of servants working with hand tools in the elegant gardens. Hidden from public view, behind the back yard vegetable gardens of elite houses, are the servants' houses.

Downtown Lusaka is dead at night. The bars close by 10:30, the movie houses by about 11. There are no restaurants: the few snack shops that have recently been opened cater to a lunch trade. Two international hotels, located near the government center, have restaurants and dance bands and try to be "European." The bars and nightclubs that are a fea-

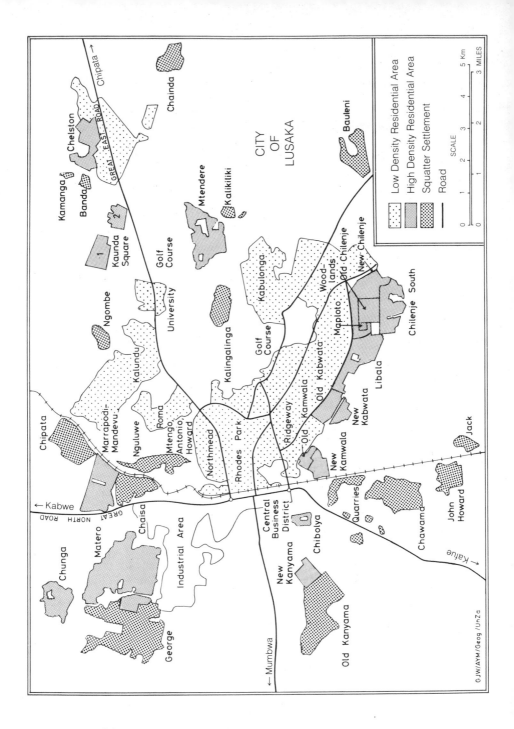

CITY OF LUSAKA

Low Density Residential Area
High Density Residential Area
Squatter Settlement
Road

SCALE

5 Km
3 MILES

Chipata

Chainda

Chelston

Kamanga

Banda

Kaunda Square

Mtendere

Kalikiliki

Bauleni

Golf Course

University

Ngombe

Kalundu

Kabulonga

Golf Course

Wood-lands

Old Chilenje

New Chilenje

Mapoloto

Chilenje South

Libala

Kalingalinga

Marrapodi-Mandevu

Nguluwe

Mtengo Antonio Howard

Roma

Northmead

Rhodes Park

Ridgeway

Old Kamwala

Old Kabwata

New Kabwata

New Kamwala

Quarries

Chawama

Jack

John Howard

← Kabwe

GREAT NORTH ROAD

Chipata

Chunga

Matero

Chaisa

Industrial Area

Central Business District

New Kanyama

Chibolya

George

Old Kanyama

← Mumbwa

Kafue →

GJW/AYM/Geog/UnZa

26

ture of African urban night life throughout black Africa are situated well away from the city. Hidden away in the farm areas outside Lusaka, unadvertised, one has to know where they are in order to find them.

SUMMARY

In this chapter, we have looked briefly at the forces at work in the dynamics of rural tribal life and at the impact of colonialism on male-female relations in towns and in villages in an attempt to understand something of the roots of the problem of male-female relations. The roots of the modern crisis have a long history, clearly predating Lusaka's emergence as a major Zambian town. Matrilineal institutions probably contributed in some way to the socially patterned defect of discord between men and women. Colonial economic policy, especially as reflected in education and employment conditions for Africans, exaggerated and exacerbated the situation.

National government policies toward education and employment changed dramatically after 1964, when Zambia became independent. The problem of male-female relations among today's modern urban elites and subelites has been exacerbated by this rapid social change. Western models, new prosperity, western education, individualism, and alienation have contributed a new style to the *expression* of problems between the sexes. New socioeconomic classes of elites and subelites have arisen, and the position of women has changed to a greater extent than the position of men. Suddenly women can achieve high status in society, whereas previously their status was ascribed. Yet the socially patterned defect of relations between the sexes persists. The capital city, Lusaka, is the best place in all of Zambia to study the new type of African woman because it has replaced the Copperbelt as the center of dynamic growth and change.

Childhood and Adolescence:
The Role of the Family

3

A miniskirted typist running for a bus in Tokyo bears a striking resemblance to her counterparts in London, Tel Aviv, New York, New Delhi—and Lusaka. She may well share the same taste in music and movies as well as in fashion. She appears a child of the twentieth century, the product of a shrinking, westernized world. Appearances can be deceiving, however. In some ways Japanese, British, Israeli, American, Indian, and Zambian typists are alike; in some ways they are different. Twentieth-century technology and mass urbanization have not erased deep-rooted cultural influences, but have simply masked them with a western veneer.

The family is a vital institution in all societies. Families play a major role in the socialization of children and in the development of their personalities. They "fit" a child into society. Older family members serve as role models for younger ones.

Family life in general, and child-rearing methods in particular, are often more conservative than values outside the concern and control of the domestic group. Early childhood and adolescent experiences of members of different cultures, enmeshed as they are in a framework of tradition, give us important clues to deeper cultural differences than appear on the surface.

When a society undergoes rapid social change, families must somehow adapt to new circumstances. No family can remain an island of tradition, uninfluenced by forces of change. Families are affected by new forms of social structure, new political and economic situations, and new ways of living. With the broadening of opportunity for female Zambians, there came to be new ways of relating as family members, and new kinds of problems for girls and their families. Girls were to be prepared for a new kind of life. The question was, how?

I could not, of course, observe Lusaka's young educated career women as children and adolescents. Yet I felt it was impossible to understand them as adults if I did not attempt to learn something about their early years, and about some of the forces at work molding their personalities and values. I asked the women whom I interviewed to describe their childhoods in detail. As I got to know some of them as friends, they were able to tell me more and more about their pasts, and I was able to observe their families at close range. Over the course of years, some of my informants themselves became mothers, and watching how they related to their own babies was most helpful. To obtain a fuller picture, I observed other families as well, where the children ranged in age from infant to adult.

THE PARENTAL GENERATION

The fathers   The generation that raised today's modern career women was a transitional one. They were between the worlds of traditional African and modern European society, having left the former but with no opportunity of entering the latter. They were neither isolated tribal village subsistence farmers nor highly educated, westernized, fully urbanized elites such as exist today. They attended Christian church services, and were active in the political struggle for national independence from British colonial rule. They were either townspeople or residents of urban enclaves in the rural areas. (An "urban enclave" is a self-contained western-type world: a Christian mission station with a hospital, a school, or both, or a British colonial government station, called a *boma*.) They worked with Europeans daily, seeing and appreciating their power and some of their customs and habits. But they were never admitted into European society. British racism, the unthinking arrogance of the colonial master, was an unbridgeable barrier to mutual understanding.

Many of the fathers (or father surrogates, such as an elder brother or mother's brother) of today's modern young women were the elites of their day—they worked for the Europeans. Nearly all of the young women had such a male relative. To be an elite African man in colonial times meant being a Christian preacher who could read the Bible in an African

29

Three generations: a visit "home" to the village.
A friend, her daughter by a white man, her
mother's sister.

tribal language, or a teacher in a lower primary school, not necessarily
literate in English, or a clerk, semi-literate in English. Such positions carried high status in the African community, but relative to white men, both
position and salary were very low. African salaries at this time were so
low that even if men knew about and appreciated certain aspects of a
European way of life, it was impossible for them to imitate it.

Other fathers or father surrogates of Lusaka's current elite and subelite women were in middle status positions in colonial times. Some were
self-employed retail shopkeepers or house builders. Others were skilled
laborers: medical orderlies, carpenters, some miners. Still others were
semi-skilled laborers, such as domestic servants. Fewer still were unskilled laborers, such as messengers in *bomas*, garbage collectors, cleaners, or municipal gardeners.

Few men had enough literacy in English or facility with arithmetic
to help their children with studies, check their homework or follow their
school progress closely and with understanding. Yet they understood very
well that their children should go to school. As the transitional generation,

they understood the changes that were unfolding in society and were anxious that their children should benefit from those changes. They were themselves successful in terms of the possibilities available to them in their time and place. For example, the father of one of my informants had been a cook in Johannesburg, South Africa, for many years before he returned to his home village in northern Zambia. Phoebe, my informant, was the first-born child of his new young Zambian wife. He provided Phoebe with enthusiastic emotional support for her schooling, and she eventually became a typist. But he could not help her with her schoolwork: she had to succeed on her own.

The mothers   The mothers or mother surrogates of today's young elite and sub-elite women had far less contact with white people than did the men in their lives. This was mainly because they had little possibility of employment. Men, not women, were the domestic servants, marketeers, and dressmakers. Given a particularly remarkable set of circumstances, a girl of this generation could go to primary school for a few years and become a teacher. (The wife of the President of Zambia, Betty Kaunda, was one such woman.) But by and large, women of the transitional generation were married at the onset of puberty and instructed by female elders in the proper role of a traditional African wife. It was later in life that they adapted to the new elite or subelite status of their husbands. They attended homecraft centers run by the wives of the white Christian missionaries, where they learned to crochet and embroider and perhaps to sew, bake cakes, and grow flowers. Some became devout Christians. Some became active in local level politics, joining the women's brigades of the new political parties that had developed in the movement for independence. They demonstrated, organized boycotts, and supported the activities of the men. Typical descriptions of the women of the transitional generation, from some of my informants, were:

> They were the ones just beginning to take an interest in fashion, but they can't stay without headdress and *chitenge*.

> They were "superstitious" and naturally obedient and respectful to the husband. Marriage was everything to them and they wanted many children. But still, they were breaking away from many traditional customs. They were violent when angry.

> They were concerned about keeping the family budget and they wanted their children to shine in society.

The families   Marriage and family life in colonial times were highly unstable. Many modern young women come from homes that were broken by divorce or the death of one of their biological parents. Hence there were many surrogate parents. Men and women were also highly mobile, moving between towns, between town and village, between rural areas. It is rare to find a young woman who lived all her life with her own parents and siblings in one place.

Despite the harsh conditions of life for these adult women in town, they sometimes provided the opportunity for their daughters to become educated. They found ways to earn cash incomes: like Mrs. Kaunda, a tiny number themselves were teachers; some learned to sew; most brewed beer. A few braved the criticism of their neighbors and became marketeers. One informant, a high school teacher, said of her mother:

> We would have starved if my mother did not sell in the market when my father stopped working because of illness. She hated it because market women were known as prostitutes. After my father died she stayed in the market. She feared going gome [i.e., returning to the village of her birth], for then we children would die through witchcraft. She bore the insults of other women because she dreamed we would complete secondary school.

Some mothers provided emotional rather than monetary support for their daughters. Another high school teacher said:

> My father's religion was the beer hall. It was my mother who wanted me to become educated so I would not suffer as she had.

There was another reason for people in the transitional generation to want an education for their daughters and other young female relatives. For them, education was an investment. An educated girl would later have no trouble finding lucrative employment. Thus employed, she would be able to help when those who had supported her grew too old to work. She would also be able to help those younger than she.

Even today, many poor adults prefer that their daughters stay in school and prepare for careers rather than get married. They say once their daughter marries, her husband may control her income and they may not get any help from her. Let her stay single and strive for an education unless the potential husband will pay a very high bride-price (the money paid by a groom to his bride's parents) to compensate for their investment. These days some parents demand a high bride-price even if they come from tribes that did not have the custom. They have invented tradition.

It is common for people in a transitional generation, marginal members of vastly different cultures, to experience inner conflict. Times of personal crisis bring out such conflicts. Nearly all the modern young women remember being treated for various illnesses by both white doctors at clinics and by African medicines. In cases of serious illness, some remember being treated by African witchdoctors. These same women often

32

describe their parents as "superstitious," scoffing at African belief in witchcraft and magic as an explanation of misfortune and as a means of dealing with it. Modern young mothers do not put protective charms on their babies as their mothers did to them. But while they scoff at magic and witchcraft, the modern generation is as uneasy about the treatment of illness as were their parents. The conflict is passed on and the results can be particularly disturbing:

> Dorothy is a university graduate, the child of a highly educated senior civil servant. Both Dorothy and her father pride themselves on how westernized they are; both have traveled extensively in the west.
>
> Dorothy is troubled every few months with illness so severe that she requires hospitalization. Her symptoms vary. Once her

A witchdoctor's "office" in Luburma, Lusaka's largest African market near town center. The woman in the foreground carries her baby in typical fashion. The office building under construction in the background is on the border of the first class trading area.

left side became paralyzed from the waist down. Another time she had severe abdominal pains.

To her white friends, Dorothy explains the psychosomatic nature of her illness, analyzing its recurrence in terms of a correlation with stressful situations: university examinations, the end of a romance, and so forth. Her American-trained African physician, thinking that I might be able to help her, told me she was a "typical hysteric" in the Freudian sense.

To her female African confidants, Dorothy reveals that she has been suffering from "spirits" since the age of four. When she had her first attack, her frantic father turned to several white doctors, who could not help. He then took her to an African witchdoctor, who prescribed an elaborate ceremony of exorcism. Horrified at the prospect, her father refused to have Dorothy "dance it out." He kept the African doctor's diagnosis secret from Dorothy. Instead, he became especially solicitous of her well-being and especially close to her.

Dorothy was secretly aware of the witchdoctor's diagnosis. She feels that her father was afraid to admit the true nature of her problem. She believes that she lives with the spirits, that they are in her body. But to face a curing ceremony at this point in her life, at the age of twenty-five, living with a white university professor and outwardly so worldly and sophisticated, is impossible, she feels.

When I told her physician about the spirits, he said: "Well, I thought she was neurotic. But I made the wrong diagnosis. She is psychotic."

Whatever the correct diagnosis of Dorothy's problem, the least we can conclude is that childhood impressions of Lusaka's young career women are deep and lasting: Dorothy could easily believe in two explanations of her illness, one fostered by her childhood experiences, the other supported by her knowledge gained later in life. This two-fold manner of thought is expressed in other ways by other women. For example:

Susan is a telex-typist and high school graduate. She often jokes about how "civilized" she is, not believing in "old superstitions." She gives the typical example of how she is not afraid to "put salt in the relish" when menstruating (an old taboo). But she faithfully washes the wooden spoon used for stirring *nshima* (the corn meal staple), although the cooking pots and serving dishes may stay unwashed for days.

She explains that if a girl neglects to wash the spoon she will not find a husband. She jokes about it, as she jokes about getting "love medicine." But she washes her spoon and travels to the Copperbelt to consult with a witchdoctor who has a good reputation for having strong love medicines. She does this, she says, "just in case."

Infancy and early childhood   Lusaka's young career women, born in the colonial period to members of a transitional generation, were reared in a largely traditional manner. For a westerner, perhaps the most striking characteristic of this child-rearing is the close physical relationship between a mother and her infant.

The mother uses a two-meter-length of brightly printed "African" cotton cloth (*chitenge*) to tie the infant to her back, where it stays nearly all day long. The infant goes everywhere the mother goes. Mother does not curtail her activities because of her child: the infant travels with her to meetings, demonstrations, bars, cinemas, on buses and to shops.

The infant is breast-fed freely and frequently. A mother's automatic response to an infant's distress is to offer the breast. Thus, comfort and security become associated with mother's breast and back. A distressed toddler will run to his mother and, if she is seated on the ground, go behind her and try to scamper up her back. She may give him a boost, then swing him around and offer her breast.

Mother and nursing baby sleep together. This and the traditional African belief that semen sours breast milk make sexual intercourse forbidden until the baby is weaned. As members of the transitional generation, the mothers of modern career women were probably not so strict in adhering to this tradition, and may have put their children to sleep alone and resumed sexual relations with their husbands before weaning took place. Women working in the modern economic sector return to their jobs when their infants are three months old. Poor, uneducated townswomen today resume sexual intercourse when their infants are three to six months old. A "good" husband practices *coitus interruptus*, but many husbands are not "good."

Weaning can be abrupt and sometimes harsh, with some mothers putting chili pepper on their nipples. But many mothers today ease the process by giving their babies supplementary bottles. Working mothers employ nannies to bottle feed their infants, and this can create problems: sometimes bottles are not sterilized or the milk is thinned with too much water, and infants have died of gastroenteritis and malnutrition.

The intimate bond that unites a mother and her baby is broken at weaning. The weaned toddler finds himself or herself suddenly an "independent" person, part of the wider community, something of a hanger-on and observer. The toddler (approximately 18 months to 2 years old) joins the older children, learning their games, dances and songs, and is looked after by an older girl, perhaps a sister. At this stage the mother may "give" the child to a relative. There are many reasons for "giving" a child to someone else, either at this or a later stage: someone else may "need" a child, having none herself; the child's mother or father might have died; the parents may have divorced; the father might have changed jobs and had to move to another part of the country and the mother might wish to join him but finds it too difficult to take the child with her; or the mother may have a new infant to look after.

The young child eats *nshima* and "relish" (the stewed meat or vegetable accompaniment to the boiled corn meal staple) with other children, sometimes with the mother or mother surrogate. Two large bowls are set on the ground, one with *nshima,* the other with relish. All those who are eating the meal take what they want—or can get—from the common bowls. The toddler must compete with the older people. Many babies die of malnutrition at this stage. One has to be aggressive to survive. The emotional distance that so marks family relationships later in life begins in these early childhood experiences: the sudden rejection by the mother at weaning, the competition for food.

As a female toddler grows into a little girl, she imitates adult females. The mother lines up for water around the common township water tap, puts the water in a drum, and balances it on her head. Her tiny daughter follows close behind, balancing a cup of water on her head. Mother puts her newborn infant on her back; her daughter puts a rock or Coca Cola bottle on her back, securing it with a rag as her mother secures the new baby with *chitenge.* Little girls at the age of four start washing plates and doing a bit of sweeping.

By the time a girl is seven or eight years old she is able to do most of the household chores that are required of an urban housewife with no western education. She can cook, sweep, wash plates, and launder clothes. She can do the daily food shopping and run errands for adults. She can be trusted to look after an infant. She will carry the baby, who is sometimes not much smaller than she, on her back while she plays with her friends.

A girl's domestic duties increase as she gets older, more competent, and physically stronger. Some of my interviewees who lived with various extended family members felt they were treated as servants, overworked, and left no means of redress. They were "wanted" and "needed" by the host family only to work. The woman they called "mother," in accordance with the genealogical rules of kinship reckoning, did no housework. Instead she waited for her "daughter" to come home from school. Giving the excuse that she was "training" her daughter, the mother sat on the ground and "supervised" the daughter's performance of the household chores. There was no redress for a girl who felt she was unfairly treated: by custom, a rebellious or spirited girl should be humbled. A shy, quiet, submissive girl is considered properly trained.

Nearly all the women I spoke to contrasted the "easy" life of boys in the family with their own "hard" life. Few women questioned the propriety of girls doing household chores while boys played, although they saw this as an outcome of urbanization—in villages, boys too had chores. Although some women felt they would want their own sons to share household chores with their daughters, most fully accepted the inevitability of "woman's work." But they did resent, sometimes bitterly, the greater freedom of movement and expression enjoyed by the boys of the household. All children were expected to obey their elders, but boys had greater freedom of expression: they could air their thoughts to a degree, go out evenings without accounting for their whereabouts, and buy beer with any money they obtained. Emotional distance in family relationships seemed to me to be greater in the case of women. This experience of repression may be a factor.

For boys and girls alike, "home" is everywhere there are kin, and yet nowhere. Few adults can recall, in the kind of meticulous detail that anthropologists like, all the places they lived as children and their genealogical relationships to the household heads where they had lived or had extended visits. Here again, the psychological results for girls seem to be harsher than for boys, who were less bound to the workings of the household.

Children are expected to start school when they are "big," size rather than age being the criterion. Most children start when they are seven or eight years of age. Normally children attend coeducational lower primary school and live at "home." This means they attend school for a few hours daily and live with relatives. Since schoolgirls are "big," they are expected to perform household chores. Few mothers believe that schoolwork should have priority over housework.

For many educated young Zambian women, these are the last years of home life, and the time of most intense learning of African culture and the role of the African woman. In these years, too, they experience and observe interactions and personal behavior patterns of adults. Apparently these experiences color later attitudes toward marriage. For example, I was particularly struck by how many women said they would never marry a man from their own tribe—indeed, their combined complaints added up to a long list of negative tribal stereotypes. I was puzzled by this data for a long time. Finally, one of my male Zambian colleagues at the university suggested that the women were remembering how their fathers treated their mothers.

All my informants agreed that the male household head—when one existed—was, in their experience, the final authority over the activities of the household members. The male household head decided if his wife should work and if the children should stay in school or drop out. He controlled the family finances and the household members' social activities. The relationship between the male household head and the girl was supposed to be characterized by distance, formality, and respect. Rules of etiquette governing their relationship were based on these qualities. By curtsying to him, casting her eyes downward, speaking only when asked a direct question, and answering in a low voice, a girl showed respect. After puberty, she showed respect by covering the lower parts of her body with *chitenge* so that the flesh of her thighs and knees was not exposed. She deferred to the male household head by rising to offer him her chair when he entered a room (an older man should never sit on the ground or a stool in a lower position than a girl). She served him and ran errands for him. Most of these demonstrations of respect were the same as the formal public demonstrations of respect expected of a wife, the difference being that there was a private relationship between spouses that did not exist between the male head of household and the girl.

Many interviewees felt that some of the traditional patterns of etiquette should be retained. For example, it would be unimaginable for them not to offer an older man their chair, or to refuse to serve him. They were fully prepared to serve younger men as well, but young "westernized" men made a point of using western etiquette, offering a woman a chair at a party. A host or hostess would sometimes say "ladies first" when offering food, and then remark that this was contrary to African custom.

Some modern male household heads tend to relax some of the respect rules governing the relationship between themselves and the young females who live with them. This relaxation is most obvious at the dinner table. Traditionally, the sexes dine separately, and this practice is retained among the urban poor. Men and women dining together is an elite innovation, copied by some subelites. When unself-consciously carried out by a nuclear family, it is considered a sign of westernization. Modern male household heads allow the girls to wear modified miniskirts, make eye contact, and talk with them directly about matters of mutual interest or conflict. For example, Dorothy and her father talked about politics, mutual acquaintances, their travels abroad, and alternative choices of graduate training abroad or a career in Lusaka when we dined at their family home. A camaraderie existed between them that was based on the fact that both had greater education and worldliness than the mother. On the other hand, Dorica, who lived with her parents until her company provided her with a flat, also had a father who was a top government official and an uneducated mother, but in this family the distance between father and daughter was retained.

The mother or mother surrogate is supposed to act as a go-between for the girl and her father or father surrogate. A girl is supposed to bring personal requests to her mother, who then discusses matters with the father. Dorica's mother constantly mediated between Dorica and her father. There is a great difference, however, between communicating personal requests with one's mother and sharing confidences with her. Girls are not expected to confide deeply personal matters to their mothers.

Traditionally, the person to whom a girl turns for discussion of personal problems, guidance, and advice is an elder female relative. In villages, this traditional practice is easy to follow and is moreover highly adaptive in *uxorilocal societies*, since it furthers the atmosphere of female solidarity by transcending the mother-daughter tie. In town, however, such a relationship rarely develops.

Extended families usually do not live close to each other in town, and female elders who live in other towns, or even in the villages, tend to see little of the young girls in their families. The girls themselves move around a great deal. For example, by the age of twenty, Florence had lived in more than a dozen different places in four different provinces of Zambia. She grew up in four different domestic groups. She liked one of her mother's sisters very much indeed and felt very free with her. This woman lived in a village, but her youth had been spent on the Copperbelt, where she had been a *kapenta* (one of those loose young women who painted their lips and frequented the dance halls). Even in the village she managed to retain an urban chic. When Florence and I showed up for an unannounced visit to the village, one of the first things she did was to put on a string of imitation pearls and matching earrings to greet us properly. But Florence had the opportunity of seeing this aunt only four or five times in fifteen years.

Even if older female relatives do not live far away, girls often feel emotionally distant from them. As members of the older generation, they are part of a different world, a different social and cultural reality. Having little or no experience of western education or western culture, female elders are felt to be too limited in experience and understanding of modern realities to give good advice to the girls. Dorica's experience is the exception that proves the rule. Dorica turns to her mother's mother to share her secrets. Dorica says this elderly woman, who lives near her in Lusaka, was among the first African women to earn money in Lusaka, where she has lived most of her life. Dorica can be "more frank" with her mother's mother than she can be with anyone else, even her girlfriends. But the camaraderie between them is as unusual as is Dorica's grandmother herself.

The experiences of educated women naturally broaden their minds. Uneducated women live in a much narrower world. Not only do the educated women feel a barrier of understanding between themselves and older uneducated women, they feel it between themselves and uneducated women their own age and even younger. Within the family, barriers to communication sometimes change from emotional distance to hostility when young women disapprove of each other's lifestyle. For example:

Phoebe, a daughter of the Johannesburg cook who wanted his children educated, went to school, married, and works as a typist.

All five of her younger sisters were expelled from school when they became pregnant. Phoebe, as the oldest and best educated, sent them back to the village, to which she now sends money occasionally. But she does not want her sisters to join her in Lusaka, nor does she want to put them in a training program. She thinks they are loose girls and cannot be trusted to stick to the program.

Salina is the youngest and best educated of her siblings. Her uneducated elder sister lives in Lusaka. When Salina became engaged, her fiance, following custom, approached her sister to begin negotiations for the bride-price. But Salina's sister hated the man's ethnic group and refused to have anything to do with the couple, not attending their wedding, and refusing to visit them even after Salina had a baby.

Many young women say they would like to have close relationships with their own daughters in the future, that the personal reserve between a mother and daughter is unfortunate. Yet they remain reluctant to confide in their own mothers, even when their mothers initiate personal conversations. For example, when Sarah's mother, exhausted from pregnancies, asked Sarah how young women these days manage to avoid pregnancies, Sarah, a university graduate in a top elite post, could not bring herself to tell her mother the "secret" of the birth control pill. One wonders if today's young women will be able to break the pattern of reserve with their own daughters.

The adolescent years: becoming "modern"   Most of today's young career women spent their adolescent years in boarding school. They left "home" at about thirteen years of age in order to attend upper primary school, and continued on as boarders in the same or a different school for their lower and upper secondary education. Sometimes these moves entailed going to different provinces of Zambia. School in Zambia is held throughout the year, except for three vacation breaks of a few weeks each. Only during these breaks do boarders go "home"—that is, to stay with relatives. They go by train, by bus, or they hitchhike, sometimes travelling hundreds of miles.

When they first start going to boarding school, they try to get back to relatives with whom they already have a close link: a parent in a distant rural area, an uncle or elder sibling not so far away. As they grow older, more experienced, and more sophisticated, what becomes important is to go to Lusaka or to the Copperbelt at holiday time. They seek out a relative who lives in town, no matter how genealogically distant, extending their networks far and wide. Their familiarity with Zambia's geographic regions becomes extensive, as does their acquaintance with different members of the extended family.

Extended family members, particularly if they are closely related, often feel a sense of obligation to support the adolescent students in their families. Although the government absorbs most of the expenses for education, the student must pay for uniforms and transportation to and from school, as well as boarding fees. When in a position to do so, biological parents provide the money and the holiday home. Biological parents who have not raised their own child until this age sometimes begin to become involved at this time. In other cases, wealthy urban relatives provide support.

The case of one of my informants, Loveness, illustrates matrilateral extended family support and the reasons why a girl may get support from her matrilateral kin rather than from her genealogically closer siblings. Since Loveness's mother's young brother Potiphar had been raised by her sister Clara (Loveness's aunt), he felt obliged to accede to Clara's request to undertake responsibility for Loveness. If Potiphar had been poorer than Loveness's own elder brothers, Loveness would have stayed in Lusaka with them.

> Loveness's alcoholic mother lived with her two sisters in a village in Eastern Province. Loveness's father had divorced her mother and Loveness never saw him. When Loveness showed evidence of academic ability in the new village school, Clara, her mother's eldest sister, who had raised their young brother Potiphar, notified Potiphar of Loveness's potential.
>
> Potiphar was married to a teacher and had a high-paying executive position on the Copperbelt. He had the financial security that came from a good job, and good qualifications for the time: he had passed his General Cambridge Examinations. Clara did not contact Loveness's elder siblings in Lusaka because they were relatively uneducated and hence had little job security.
>
> Loveness finished her primary schooling on the Copperbelt while living with Potiphar, his wife, and three small children. Later they all moved to Lusaka. Loveness remained with them for secondary school. Potiphar drove her daily from their home to school, a distance of fifteen miles each way.
>
> Loveness finished her secondary school examinations; it took six months for the results to be published. Before the results were out and she could apply for various training programs, there was nothing for her to do. Potiphar arranged for her to work temporarily in his company. Then they quarreled. He accused her of insolence, and she moved to the home of his brother. The brother had himself recently returned from overseas training. She remained with this brother until she was accepted into a training program.
>
> Despite her welcome in the brother's household, Loveness never regarded it as her "home." She felt herself an outsider, a guest in this household, as she did in Potiphar's household. She

does not, in fact, regard herself as having a "home" as such; that is, a place among kin where she feels comfortable and wants to stay. She would never return to live in the village. Staying with her own elder siblings is out of the question since they are poor and socially beneath her. Her greatest ambition is to have her own flat.

This case illustrates the obligation wealthy kin feel to look after the welfare of promising young female kin. Potiphar watched his sister's daughter closely, driving her to school daily, arranging a job for her, keeping her fed, housed, and clothed. He gave this support although Loveness had siblings in Lusaka. He also kept contact with Loveness's siblings, helping them in emergencies. He never felt they should keep Loveness. Loveness was required to do washing and ironing for the family, and some cooking and childcare. But there were servants as well; the amount of work she did in return for her upkeep was not unusual or excessive.

Sometimes elder siblings act as effective parent surrogates, the younger sister residing with them either while attending day school or, if at boarding school, for the weeks of holiday. They are also the ones to finance the girl's school career. Agnes is such a case:

> Following Agnes's mother's death when Agnes was five, her father, a truck driver, moved to another village to reside with another wife. Agnes never saw him again. Her eldest brother, the firstborn of her mother, was a teacher in another district of Luapula Province. Her two older sisters were married, one living in Luanshya and the other in Zaire, near the Luapula border.
> The brother, Robert, though recently married, sent for his youngest sibling. She lived with the couple until she was sent to boarding school for her upper primary education. Meanwhile the family moved to Ndola. At holiday time Agnes alternated between spending her time with her brother and her Luanshya sister. Her brother felt she should live with the sister, who had fewer children and could guard her chastity more closely than would his own wife; despite her sister's husband's objections, she began going there.
> She became pregnant during one of the holidays, and moved back to her brother's home while awaiting the baby. Some months after the birth she left her child, a daughter, with her brother, and was accepted for training as a typist with the mines. She began living on her own, and left the Copperbelt to "get away from all of them."
> Every few months she returns for a visit and gives her brother money for the child's maintenance. She visits her sister less often.

Girls who return home on school holidays often have tense relationships with their parents or surrogate parents. The conflicts are generally over "freedom." Parents or surrogates who see themselves as "good" and "responsible" will try to keep their daughters at home and restrict their social relationships. They will not permit their daughters to meet men and will insist on modest attire. The obedient daughter is thus naive and inexperienced. As such, she is easily victimized when she begins to live on her own.

The disobedient daughter, on the other hand, necessarily must deceive her parents or parent surrogates. Deception is necessary because the reserve that exists between parents and their daughters means they cannot engage in meaningful discussions on issues concerning male-female relationships. "Good" parents or parent surrogates merely prohibit such relationships from developing. Sometimes they are successful in this. More often, however, they simply drive their daughters underground. Agnes said:

> In the six years I was a boarder, I never had a boyfriend. At home
> my "father" did not allow me to move at night so I had none
> there either. But when I was doing my Form IV, I went home for
> holiday and met a sweet boy who was a neighbor. We went to
> afternoon film shows and I got pregnant. I did not know what was
> happening because my best friend in school used to move with
> many men and she never got caught.

The distance developed during adolescence remains, separating the daily lives of Agnes, Loveness, and most of the working women I interviewed from their families. The women make decisions independently of their kin, as they did during adolescence.

Agnes often describes herself as being "without family." When we attended Valeria's large wedding reception, Agnes wistfully remarked how she wished she had family to make that kind of wedding for her. What she meant by "having family" was having relatives in elite positions. In describing herself as "without family" and in telling people I was "like a big sister" to her, she implied her blood relatives were socially beneath her. She is envious of girls like Loveness who had elite relatives. She feels little obligation to help her family, as the following incident illustrates:

> Because I had a car and we happened to be in Luanshya, Agnes
> decided to visit her sister. Her sister is three years older than
> Agnes, and at the time of our visit was heavily pregnant with her
> sixth child.
>
> Agnes remarked how sad it was that she was pregnant again,
> since her other children were so young and her husband was
> cruel. I asked her why she didn't tell her sister about the birth
> control pill. I thought she might say she could not discuss sexual
> matters with an elder sister, but she assured me that it was just

too much trouble to do so. Instead, she gave her sister a few of her old clothes she no longer cared for. Our visit took less than ten minutes.

On another occasion we visited her home village. She then said that if she had any choice in the matter this would probably be the last time in her life she would ever go there. A year later she returned solely to get the documents required for a passport.

Adolescent pregnancy   Pregnancy is a most common threat to a girl's future. Although the statistics on schoolgirl pregnancies are a closely guarded government secret, the frequency is staggeringly high.[1] The government considers such pregnancies a serious national problem, since pregnant schoolgirls are expelled from school or training programs and hence considered to be wasting government funds and inhibiting economic development. The problem of schoolgirl pregnancies is one subject of vitriolic debate in Parliament.

Schoolgirls want neither children nor husbands. They say they want to be wives and mothers eventually, but in a hazy, distant future. They want first to find a responsible, reliable man they can love and want to marry. Yet they get pregnant. They will sometimes refuse to marry the father of their child even when he is willing, still waiting for that reliable man to come along.

In addition to assistance and support with a girl's schooling, parents or surrogates have a primary responsibility to prevent pregnancy. One of their important functions is the girl's moral education. They "educate" the girl by watching her conduct and preventing relationships with men. In most cases they resort to purely external means of control. Sometimes, though, adults attempt to develop values in the girl that she will internalize, leading to the exercise of self-control. Devout Christians convey religious reasons for remaining chaste, and if the girl attends a mission boarding school this is reinforced. Some recall, with amusement, sincerely praying to the Virgin Mary that they too should remain virgins.

Strong traditionalists still insist that their daughters undergo initiation (*chisungu*). Initiation is supposed to take place shortly after the onset of the first menses, but initiation of boarding school girls is postponed until a convenient holiday time, when they go to the place where their parents happen to be living. Compared with traditional ceremonies, in which a girl was secluded for months, modern initiations are brief, lasting a few days. Some women recall their initiations as enjoyable, but the effect varies with the type of ceremony. The *banachimbusa* (elder female instructors) of some tribes attempt to instill a fear of sex. Salina, a Namwanga, said:

> After the initiation I was frightened even to speak to a boy. My parents arranged that I should correspond with the man who was

44

to be my fiancé, and for all the years I was in boarding school I wrote him letters but refused to see him.

The relationship between Salina and her "boyfriend" ended when she left school, and she began having sexual relations with men about a year later.

The *banachimbusa* of other tribes warn girls not to have intercourse before marriage while at the same time providing the traditional instruction for pelvic movements during the sex act and sometimes breaking the hymen. Irene, a Lozi who experienced this initiation, said: "It made me sick, it was so disgusting. I used to cry thinking about it, and I never went with men."

For Salina and Irene, the effect of initiation was to make them disinterested in sex during their early adolescent years. The opposite effect was suggested by other women. Some informants who had not themselves been initiated said their mothers found their older sisters, who had been, became "too curious to play sex" following initiation, and so lost interest in school.

Fear of pregnancy is not a major deterrent to sexual involvement in many cases: the Salinas and Irenes are briefly frightened of sex itself, not of pregnancy. Even when the value of chastity is internalized so that a girl eschews casual sex, she cannot resist having intercourse once she thinks she is in love. Otherwise, the price of her chastity is the loss of her boyfriend. In many cases pregnancy is the result of a "love" affair, for at some point in their young lives most girls fall in "love." A friend of mine named Sam, a Ngoni from Chipata District, returned to Zambia after a six-year B.A./M.A. course abroad. Shortly after his return, he said he wanted to marry. Like Ngonis traditionally, he wanted a virgin. The response of our mutual female friend was hilarity:

He is back home in Zambia! There are no virgins here. He will be arrested if he takes a small child—it is against the law!

Anthropologists writing of the high illegitimacy rate in urban Africa point to the breakdown of tribal traditions, the difficulty parents have in controlling their daughters, and the absence in town of a real stigma attaching to it. While this is true of Lusaka, another reason is that most Zambians think that sex is so natural and inevitable that all normal human beings must have it. It is chastity that is unnatural, not sex. This is why externally imposed preventatives are so common. For example, a Copperbelt hospital employed a security guard at its nurses' hostel. He was instructed to lock the nursing students in and keep all visitors out. The students complained they were treated like prisoners, but hospital authorities defended the measure as the best way to cut down the pregnancy rate. There is an element of the self-fulfilling prophecy: girls who wish for chaste love feel there is something possibly wrong with them, and platonic relationships are all but non-existent.

45

From time to time adolescent girls write letters to "Josephine" and "Soul Sister," the "lovelorn" columnists of the local newspapers, wondering why they feel no physical need for sex. Their boyfriends insist on intercourse, they report, urging that there is something wrong with girls who don't "feel sex." The following letter to the "Soul Sister" column of the *Times of Zambia*, although unpublished, is typical:

> I am a girl of 19 and working in a company. The problem is this. Since I was matured I started having boyfriends demanding sex only. If you refuse he goes away from you and starts telling you that you don't know what love means.
> So now if you can just tell me what love and sex means I will be very happy. They think we young girls are here to satisfy boys every day. And after making that young lady pregnant they go away to another girl.
>
> Fearful Girl, Luanshya

Half laughing, half crying at the conflicts she faces, adolescent schoolgirl Esnat threw up her hands and sighed, "What can a poor girl do?"

Just the desire to have sexual intercourse does not explain the frequency of pregnancies. Ignorance plays a part. Some girls say they did not think it would happen from a single act of intercourse. This idea derives from traditional notions that a young couple should have intercourse several times each night, "working hard to make a pregnancy." Some women use birth control pills improperly, borrowing half a friend's supply, creating the chance that both women will become pregnant. After experiencing bad side effects of the pill, some girls fall back on traditional techniques: a magically treated string is used for stringing the beads sexually active women wear around their hips for use in love play. Some young women say it is effective, and some say it is useless. Luck obviously plays a part. Women's fertility is erratic and personal. Some are able to have relations with many different men over a period of years without becoming pregnant. Susan was such an individual. Over the course of eleven years of active sex with more men than she can remember she has become pregnant only four times. Agnes, in contrast, became pregnant in her first sexual encounter.

In Zambia, intrauterine devices and birth control pills are the only reliable contraceptive means available. Women wanting contraception therefore have a limited choice and must first consult physicians. Obtaining contraceptives is difficult, time-consuming, and often humiliating. Officially, a woman who uses the facilities of the University Teaching Hospital must have the written consent of her husband. Unofficially, single women, especially university students and student nurses, can use this facility after obtaining permission of the nursing sister at the university campus or the warden of the nurses. Some students are reluctant to use

46

the facility because young Zambian doctors and nurses, rather than honoring the western idea of doctor-patient privacy, gossip freely about unmarried female patients. A man who suspects his girlfriend is on the pill can easily check with doctors of his acquaintance who, as a favor, look up the girl's record and report its contents. Girls at the secondary level of schooling cannot use these government birth control clinics. Anyone can use a private doctor to obtain contraceptives, and most working women prefer visiting these doctors' surgeries. But schoolgirls are normally much too shy to do this and cannot in any case afford the fees, nor can they get money from their boyfriends.

Men generally oppose the use of birth control by their girlfriends. Some hope the girls will get pregnant in order to prove their own reproductive powers. Some oppose contraceptives because they think women who use them will certainly be unfaithful—and what is worse, while they are being unfaithful they will be protected, so that men will not have the "proof" they need to make the women "pay for their misdeeds." Many girls fear using contraceptives because they think their boyfriends will lose respect for them. Others use contraceptives, openly or secretly, when they are involved in a serious relationship, but stop when the relationship ends. Then they suddenly meet a new man, become sexually involved without protection, and get pregnant.

The discovery that one is pregnant is described by the girls as a crisis that leaves them in a state of shock and disbelief for months. Usually the girl's first reaction is to conceal it from everyone. A number said they did not even realize they were pregnant until five or six months had passed; a few managed to conceal the pregnancy until they gave birth. Older, more sophisticated career women or toughened worldly-wise women in the shantytowns often obtain legal or illegal abortions. But the younger, less sophisticated woman lives in silent misery, confiding her feelings of anxiety and shame to no one, yet at the same time the subject of derisive gossip among friends and neighbors. For such women it is a lonely time.

When the dependent schoolgirl finds herself pregnant, her relationship with kin shows the familiar pattern of dependency and emotional distance. She is not rejected, nor is the child.

The initial reaction is disappointment. The girl is chastised. She must name the father of her child, and her parents or surrogate parents decide whether or not to arrange for a marriage or alternatively for "damages" (a cash payment made by the father of the child to the father of the girl he impregnates). The prime consideration in the decision is the girl's wish, but the social status of the man relative to the girl's parents is also important. Schoolboys and unmarried teachers are easier and safer targets to sue for "damages" than are married top government ministers. Once the relationship between the girl and her lover is clarified, she is fully accepted by her kin. But her future depends on the economic status

of these kin. The girl has been expelled from school and will not be read-
mitted after the birth of the baby. If the girl has no relatives to sponsor
her for training privately, her pregnancy has truly doomed her to low status. She returns to the high-density township or the village from which
she came.

If the girl does have relatives who have the money to sponsor her
in training, her long-range future is not affected by premarital pregnancy.
Her relatives take care of the baby and send her for private training. They
may keep the baby for years. Quite a number of women with illegitimate
children are now among Lusaka's young elites and subelites—in fact, it
is rare to find a woman 25 years of age who has not had a child at some
point in her life.

The closest bond: female peers in the extended family   Educated women
are not emotionally distant from all members of their extended families.
A strong and important bond between family members is that of two
women who have about the same level of education, are both unmarried,
and share the same attitudes toward religion and sex. The women are not
only related by blood, but tied by a bond of friendship, and this bond is
the strongest in modern urban Zambian society. They rely on each other
for succor in times of adversity. They understand each other as no one
else does. They share the same interests and therefore the same leisure
activities. They exchange clothes, wigs, cosmetics, shoes, records, money.
They help each other take care of their illegitimate children. They get to
know each other's secrets, and give each other advice.

Susan and her cousins are an example of this close friendship of
female relatives in the same social position:

> Susan lived in Chilenje South, an old African city council housing
> area of Lusaka. Her street was made up of row houses that were
> tiny one-room dwellings with kitchens and bathrooms. These were
> called hostels, and were meant to be occupied by one person.
>
> Most of the hostels on Susan's street were occupied by
> working women, and three of these occupants were Susan's
> cousins, Rose, Salome, and Rebecca. They particularly enjoyed
> visiting each other in the evenings because they could speak their
> local dialect, which was not understood by their other girlfriends.
> They also acted as friends as well as cousins by sharing food,
> clothes, cosmetics, wigs, and beer, and occasionally going out
> together with men.
>
> Each of these women had family relationships of her own.
> Susan hosted her young sister visiting Lusaka from secondary
> school, and kept the young daughter of a married sister for a few
> months. Rose kept the son of her unmarried sister, a nursing
> student, as well as her own child. Salome lived with her
> boyfriend, but when he was out of town she slept with Susan or

48

Rebecca since she was afraid to stay alone. Susan and Rebecca had lived together for a while, since Susan had not wanted to stay in the flat alone after her boyfriend had deserted her, following the deaths of their two children.

The women tended to regard the four council houses as family property. Over the course of months, they would live together in various combinations depending on which of their other relatives or friends was visiting and how they were faring with lovers.

They distinguished their friendship among themselves from outside friendships, even though they shared the same activities with outsiders as they did with each other. Outsiders often remarked that when the four women were together in a larger group, their deliberate use of their own dialect would make others feel out of place. If an outsider complained, the women would switch to a more widely understood language (*Chibemba*), but within the space of a few minutes they would bring the conversation around to their own language.

Susan's relationship to her cousins as friends was obvious to an outsider. Other relationships are not so obvious. Agnes, who so often spoke of herself as being without family, in fact had a relationship approaching friendship with a cousin, Lillian. Their relationship only approached friendship because Agnes did not truly like Lillian, whom she considered smug. Nevertheless, Agnes and Lillian shared a flat the first time Lillian became pregnant, when she came to Agnes for aid. A year and a half later, reestablished in a large flat of her own, with her sister acting as nanny for her baby, Lillian offered to keep Agnes's child because she knew Agnes was dissatisfied with the conditions the child was living under in her brother's home. She implored Agnes to live with her as well; several weeks later both Agnes and her baby moved in and they all lived together for a year. As another instance, it was clear that as Loveness became financially independent she would establish similar relationships with Beatrice, her mother's brother's daughter, and with Mary, her mother's sister's daughter, one a radiographer and one an air hostess.

SUMMARY

Close, rich and warm family ties rarely develop in Zambia because the norms of the society inhibit their growth. The pattern of residential mobility is a further limiting factor. At the same time, it is the very availability and willingness of relatives of varying degrees of genealogical distance to support a girl that determines her success. Girls who become pregnant at a young age and who are expelled from school still have a chance to achieve precisely because a society that accepts emotional distance as a norm finds it acceptable and even desirable to separate mother and infant. The young mother will be sponsored in training by her relatives; at the same time these or other relatives will look after her child, sometimes for years on end. With such emotional distance and material support a part of nearly every girl's background, the defect is built into the structure and functioning of the social system.

Life at School

4

Years ago, the time for formal learning for a young girl in traditional Zambian village communities was signaled by the onset of her first menses. The girl was kept secluded in a special hut for several months. She was attended by a young girl who slept with her in her hut, brought her meals, and accompanied her when she left the hut to relieve herself. She was visited daily by the female village elders. She was instructed in the rules, rituals, and etiquette appropriate for adult women of her tribe. The conclusion of her isolation was marked by an elaborate initiation ceremony, after which she was considered ready for married life. She was not, however, expected to be a fully knowledgeable and competent adult. This came only with age and experience in life. After marriage, her training in adult roles and responsibilities continued. She remained under the supervision of her female elders, her husband's female elders, or her husband's senior wife. Her education was largely an informal family matter.

Industrial urban society, with its technological sophistication, has added the formal institution of schools as a means of educating and socializing its children and adolescents. Schools have taken over some of the major teaching functions that were formerly the province of family and community, and so have come to play a vital role in a young person's life.

Although Zambia's towns grew up around technologically sophisticated copper mines, British colonialists did not intend for African men to participate in that part of the modern economy that demanded a high level of training and skill; they did not even intend for women to live in the towns. Nevertheless, over the course of decades, a permanent urban African population developed and the position of adolescent African girls became a problem.

These girls were not living in a tribal village setting where there were familiar behavior patterns and expectations of marriage after the first menses. Yet there was almost no chance of participating, in any kind of productive sense, in the modern life of the towns. Schooling was made compulsory for Copperbelt children between the ages of 12 and 16. In the words of one teacher, this was done mainly to "keep them off the streets," and girls in particular were "almost unteachable" by that age. Most dropped out of school after a year or two. Education led nowhere: there were almost no jobs. In 1953, 195 girls were enrolled in various nursing programs, mainly at mission hospitals. This figure was for the whole country![1]

COLONIAL ATTITUDES AND EDUCATION

When family, community, and school share the same basic values, attitudes, and beliefs, the process of socialization in school works smoothly. But if these shared elements are lacking, the process is full of conflicts and contradictions. Today's modern Zambian woman went to school toward the end of the colonial period and in the years immediately following independence, before the staff and curricula of the schools became "Zambianized."[2] At that time, schools were deliberately designed by the colonial authorities to be agents of social change, meant to expose African children to western culture as a means of "uplifting" them. The *Phillips Report* was prepared for Malawi, a neighboring British colony of Zambia (then known as Nyasaland), but describes the same approach adopted in Zambia:

> The education of females should put them on an intellectual level with men, train them to think for themselves, and to express their thoughts. . . . Their education should aim at a sound training in the arts of living, the care of children, the fundamentals of health education and food values, all closely related to the home environment. . . . Among the other aims, the education of girls and women should prepare them for economic independence. Provision should be made so that girls who leave secondary schools can train and qualify as teachers, doctors, nurses, midwives, secretaries, typists, or other suitable occupations.[3]

52

Each of the aims listed in the *Phillips Report* presented a challenge to traditional African values, attitudes, and beliefs. Early childhood experiences the children brought to the school with them were undermined. The cultural heritage of Africa was held implicitly inferior and wrong— it had to be replaced by western culture or, more precisely, by what the colonial educationists imagined western culture to be. This report was typical of the colonial authority's way of thinking, and the brief quotation reveals not only the insensitivity to African attitudes, but the whites' idealization of and inconsistency toward themselves.

Some goals that were supposed to be instilled in African girls were unacceptable in European women. How many European men actually wanted their wives to be their intellectual equals, to think for themselves, and to express their thoughts? How many approved of their wives working and being economically independent?

In the early 1960s for her *Report on Home Economics in Africa*, Teresa Spens, now a Cambridge, England, anthropologist, toured Ghana, Uganda, Tanzania and Kenya. Even at that late date, with the "winds of change" sweeping over the continent, Spens warned that teachers and leaders:

> . . . have to be careful to avoid fostering a militantly feminist movement. This would do more harm than good, for so much of home economics teaching depends on men.[4]

Another goal to be instilled in African girls was to lead an adult life that copied a middle-class British housewife's. Margaret Read, a professor of education who wrote extensively on the Ngoni of Malawi, expressed this view in reference to African women whose husbands were studying in Britain:

> Ten years ago I sat . . . with two African women who were teaching at Achimota. They . . . burst out with "We must have African women leaders—ones who have had all the advantages that English women have, and who will show the rest of us where we can go."
>
> A year later some of us in London persuaded the British Council to give a scholarship to the wife of a leading African studying in London, herself a former teacher, in order that she might share his knowledge of English life and ways; feel at ease when entertaining Europeans in their homeland; and learn what English women were doing in public service of many kinds.[5]

In other words, African wives should learn to play the hostess at high tea, and to participate in charity work. There is no mention here of how the scholarship might help the wife develop a professional career.

There was another aspect to the self-deception. The colonial authorities also professed the aim that African girls should think for themselves as a result of their school experiences. Yet if this were really so, a way would have to be found to reconcile African and British cultural traditions. What the colonial authorities really meant by "thinking for themselves" was that their charges should echo back what the authorities wanted to hear. Success was measured in strictly western terms. Students had to learn enough information to pass examinations.

The sexist bias of European notions of "suitable occupations" was transplanted to Africa. This was admitted in an International Labor Organization Report, *The Employment and Conditions of West African Women*, which was quoted in the journal *African Women* (V, 2 (1963), 35): "Many kinds of vocational training were offered only to boys, simply because no one had thought of girls taking them up."

The emotional distance girls developed in response to their home lives came to be paralleled by an intellectual distance from their subjects at school. Inevitably, the very process of adjusting and adapting to the formal and informal aspects of life at school was a process of becoming alienated.

FORMAL ASPECTS OF SCHOOLING

In the days when modern Lusaka's educated young women went to primary school, the first few years were spent learning the basic skills of arithmetic, British songs, sports and games, history, geography, civics, and speaking, reading, and writing English. One of the schools even required children to memorize Scottish clan names! In writing of her experience as a schoolgirl in colonial Nigeria, a teacher said:

> I had learnt many useful things at home but not many of them were made use of when I got to school. . . . If my teacher had used my pre-knowledge to teach me, many things I found very hard to grasp would not have been so. . . . Some subjects had no relation with the home life.[6]

Even if texts were not imported directly from Britain, they were written by white people. Sometimes this material was not well understood by the poorly trained African teachers themselves, and they would lapse into an African language to interpret foreign ideas. The contrast between home and lower primary school was great but not overwhelming. The contrast between home and upper primary and secondary school, where teachers as well as curricula were foreign, was much more drastic.

There are four cut-off points in the Zambian school system: lower primary school (which used to be called Sub-A, Sub-B, Standard I and Standard II and are now called Grades 1 through 4), upper primary school (Standards III–VI; now called Grades 5–7; a year has been eliminated), lower secondary school (Forms I and II) and upper secondary school

54

(Forms III–V). After each cut-off point there are fewer schools, geographically more widely dispersed.

Social pressures   One of the problems of primary schools at the lower level was caused by their being coeducational. Almost every one of my informants who was academically successful remembers the hostility of young boys to girls whose academic performance was superior to theirs. Male classmates tried to make girls stop competing by ridiculing them in the classroom and beating them as they walked home from school. Teachers were severe and corporal punishment was used freely. Girls were under pressure from teachers to perform well, and under pressure from boys not to get higher marks. The women recalled responding with resolve: they wanted to shine, and they did. But these women are a select sample. There is no way of knowing how many girls responded to conflicting pressures by underachieving or dropping out. Coeducational primary schools and conflict between the sexes continue to be a feature of Zambian schools in the 1970s.

Another crisis area is the examination Standard VI children take (years ago it was marked in Britain, but this is now handled in Zambia). Passing this examination is an important event in a child's life, since it provides a selection process for further schooling, and is the ultimate focus for virtually all academic learning in primary school. Yet even after passing the examination and finding a sponsor, not all girls continue to Form I—the shortage of places, lack of money, and lingering attitude that higher education is wasted on girls work against them. Students fill out applications at the time of examination, indicating their first, second, and third choices of secondary school, and are assigned according to their examination results. Some continue in the schools they attended for their upper primary education.

At the end of Form III (formerly Form II) the students take another examination. Those who pass can stay on in their schools for upper secondary school. My informants often spoke of a "Form II crisis," when they would have to make up their minds whether to continue in school or to leave, either to take a job or to get married. Not all who passed the examination continued schooling.

There were no selection procedures for the next three years, so if girls were not expelled for misconduct, and if they had the money, they continued and at the end of Form V took examinations for the prized Cambridge School Certificate. Depending on the examination results and access to information about various training programs (more or less adequately described in her school), a girl was now launched into adulthood as a highly educated woman about to begin a career.[7] These conditions still prevail in the 1970s.

Training programs for women who had passed Forms II and V

mushroomed in the late 1960s and early 1970s. Programs in office work, nursing, and primary school teaching were offered. (Even girls who had passed only Standard VI sometimes got places in training programs, but normally were only able to do so through family contacts.) Training is subsidized by the government, participants receiving a monthly allowance and free tuition, books, and accommodation. Thus, after leaving school, a girl becomes financially independent of her kin.

Boarding school life In the 1960s, most of the children who remained with their kin throughout their primary school years left "home" to attend secondary boarding school. At that time, as in the present, the only strong reasons for leaving were illness, financial reverses, or adolescent pregnancy, any of which might compel a girl to drop out during her first two years. But most continued on through boarding school.

There are four types of secondary schools in Zambia: government day schools and boarding schools, and mission day schools and boarding schools. The government has expanded facilities by building new schools and subsidizing the expansion of older mission schools. Day schools are located in townships from which students are drawn. Boarding schools, more numerous, seem to have been located for maximum isolation from their surroundings, whether near towns or in rural areas.

Some mission schools, such as the fundamentalist Protestant Chikankata, are attached to hospital compounds and form a large community in the bush. In these instances the school for girls is only a small part of a wider society including a school for boys, European families of teachers, doctors, nurses, administrators, and technical maintenance crews, all living in close proximity. Other mission schools are not attached to any other institutions. These school compounds, with their gardens, dormitories, teachers' houses, and scattered academic and administrative buildings, are worlds of their own. The Roman Catholic Roma Secondary School for Girls of Lusaka is an example. When Roma was built, it was surrounded by hundreds of acres of barren grassland, approached by an unmarked rutted dirt road. This school is located within the boundaries of Greater Lusaka, but apart from its ready access to transport at holiday time (its boarders need only walk to the main road to get a ride), it might as well be in a rural area. Secular government schools, usually coeducational, are equally isolated and offer the same basic academic curricula.

The teachers in all the secondary schools are expected not only to teach their subjects but to supervise the students' morality. They censor mail and grant or deny visitation rights and permission to leave the school grounds. Living in small houses on the school grounds, they and their families are expected to be role models for their students. Most teachers in the Catholic schools are nuns. Some of the students convert to Roman Catholicism as a result of their school experiences; a few flirt with the

A University of Zambia
student on the campus.

idea of becoming nuns themselves, and some do. The Protestant mission
schools are staffed by devoutly Christian, young married white men and
women.

The atmosphere in the mission schools for girls tends to be restrictive for staff and students alike. Students liken their experience to prison.
The less devout staff sometimes chafe, however mildly, at restrictions. For
example, a teacher at Chikankata begged me to bring a bottle of sherry
and a pack of cigarettes to her when I visited the school. On my arrival
at her home, she closed the curtains before pouring herself a drink and
lighting a cigarette. She apologized for her "moral laxity" and assured
me that she did not often indulge in such forbidden activity, saying she
would be ashamed if she were caught.

The atmosphere in secular government schools is much freer than in mission schools. The same restrictive rules are supposed to apply, but supervision is less strict. For example, the new Kasama Girls School, located in the far north of the country, has the reputation of being a training ground for the fast life of sexual freedom and high fashion that its graduates later find in Lusaka and the Copperbelt.

Government schools at the time my informants attended were staffed largely by young Europeans recruited from the Commonwealth, mainly Britain and Australia. In order to staff the expanded school system, the Zambian government sponsored a program: recent university graduates were flown to Zambia, spent one year at the University of Zambia studying for a Post Graduate Certificate in Education, and were posted to the new schools, where they worked for two years, after which they were flown home. The program was discontinued when the University of Zambia began producing its own Zambian graduates with B.A. or B.S. degrees in education to staff the new schools.

The school year in Zambia begins in January. There are three holiday breaks of several weeks each: late March to early April, mid-August to mid-September, and in December. Children who take Standard VI, Form II, and the Cambridge examinations after Form V have a break of several months while waiting for their results to be published. Standard VI pupils are examined in early November, but publication of results normally takes longer; sometimes six months pass before a pupil knows the results and can apply for various programs. At these holiday times boarders leave the school grounds to stay with relatives. On very rare occasions a student obtains special permission to remain, and may work for the teachers during the holiday weeks.

Daily life in boarding schools is routinized and communal, almost prison-like. Girls live in large dormitory rooms, awaken, wash, dress, eat their meals, pray, study, and do chores together. In theory, they are supposed to go to sleep at the same time, after prayers and lights out. Years ago, they were supposed to speak English at all times. They attend classes and participate in clubs as individuals, but always in the company of others. All is done at assigned times, according to schedule. They are always watched. Following the British system, teachers are aided in surveillance by selected students, called "prefects." There are prefects and deputy prefects in classrooms and dormitories to ensure that school rules are obeyed at all times. The only legitimate escape from surveillance is to join a church off the school grounds: if one's religious affiliation differs from that of the mission, one is permitted to worship elsewhere on Sunday mornings. Visits from outsiders are not normally permitted, and visits of men claiming to be relatives are treated with special suspicion.

A variety of voluntary extra-curricular activities are available. The girls are encouraged to join clubs. There are Bible study groups, Young Farmers Clubs, debating teams, netball teams, and choirs. Movies, dances, and debates are sometimes arranged with neighboring boys' schools. In a few schools, students teach women in nearby villages the principles of nutrition they themselves learn. All non-academic activities are closely supervised. Time is tightly organized. Girls are expected to do something constructive all their waking hours.

Manual labor is required in most schools. The amount and type of labor varies from school to school, depending on the amenities that are already available. For example, the normally male task of slashing grass with a meter-length cutting tool (a "slasher") is sometimes required of the girls. At one of the newly built government schools, girls dug the ground for a swimming pool and built an open-air theater. At other schools girls perform more common women's tasks: making mud bricks, drawing water from streams, and gathering firewood. Almost everywhere they are required to wash dishes, clothes, and linens, and to sweep and wash dormitory and classroom floors. This is the extent of the "African" content of their school curriculum.

THE INFORMAL FRAMEWORK

Student-teacher relations   Teachers and students live in close proximity in boarding schools. Promising students often form close relationships with one or two of their teachers. Many informants told me they admired their female teachers, the first professional women they had known personally, and that particular teachers took special interest in them, encouraging them to succeed. Typical comments were:

> One nun especially pushed me to do well. She was very understanding and frank and I came to her with all my problems. School was nicer than home. I could forget my problems and get on with my work.

> My Senior Mistress in charge of discipline was so friendly and sociable. She used to take part in clubs and in dancing. She used always to talk about what to do in the world, have a career and work by liking to discipline yourself. I loved the school and was very happy.

> I was made deputy head girl although I was afraid because I was young. But my teacher and my headmistress insisted. I did not want to disappoint them so I worked very hard.

> I thought I was dull. My father wanted me to leave school. My mother and one teacher, an evangelist, talked to the Principal and got me to continue my studies. I got confidence and did very well after that.

> My mother wanted me to leave school after Form II because my

father died. My women teachers and headmistress told my mother I could help more if I continued in school and finally she let me stay.

For this first generation of educated Zambian women, teachers sometimes served as the role models they were intended to be. Teachers were personally involved in their students' lives, and the students, who served as babysitters, were reciprocally involved. At the same time, barriers between African students and European teachers necessarily existed and undercut the closeness of these relationships.

Student–teacher friendships were mostly efforts on the part of teachers to encourage their students to work hard and achieve academic success. The teachers did not confide personal problems to their students, although the reverse sometimes happened, nor did they reveal confidential information to students. Girls who got on well with teachers were, typically, the brighter ones who also showed evidence of mastering some of the western culture of teachers. But relationships were able to develop only when teachers themselves were basically sympathetic to, however ignorant of, the African culture of their students.

Ignorance of the subtleties of each other's culture was mutual. Students did not lose what little of their African cultural heritage they brought with them to school, but they did learn to conceal African ideas from European teachers. For example, African girls usually kept secret from their teachers their strong beliefs in magic and witchcraft (often their explanation for academic success or failure). Girls certainly kept secret from their teachers information about their love lives. For their part, teachers sometimes mistook the shyness and reticence of African girls for dullness, and their passive obedience for compliance or agreement.

As so often happens in cases of culture contact, misunderstandings arose without the individuals involved necessarily being aware of this happening. Young, enthusiastic European teachers, for example, were not aware of the impression they created by agreeing to dance several dances in succession with the same male student at a mixed inter-school social gathering. Students interpreted this as the public indication of a sexual relationship. It was the subject of scandalous gossip among the students in both boys' and girls' schools, the teachers unaware of it. The boys responded either by silently "falling in love" with the teachers or by publicly bragging about their conquests. The liberal teacher who acted innocently and in a spirit of friendship alienated the affection of her own female students, who saw her as a rival.

Student friendships   An important part of the process of socialization and adjustment to boarding school life is making friends among classmates. Although some girls enter schools where they already have a relative or a neighborhood friend, most begin their boarding school lives as strangers. Those who are unable to make friends are often the ones who leave school to marry. They are never able to overcome their initial sense of isolation, shock, and homesickness. Young boarders have good reason to be unhappy. Older girls bully them, the diet is poor, and the manual labor is unpleasant. Speaking English is difficult. Most of all, living among strangers produces a sense of unease.

Over the course of the first year or two, girls form friendships with each other that last into adulthood.[8] Girls feel freer to laugh, joke, and confide in their friends than their relatives. Despite rules prohibiting such activities, girlfriends share the same bed, hugging, kissing, and fondling each other. They gossip, share secrets, and affirm each other's developing values, attitudes, and beliefs. They are united by common interests in fashion, pop culture, the excitement of a new life almost but not quite within reach, and sometimes a common stand against the restrictive authority of family and school.

Friendships form between girls who share similar ideas about religion and sex. Tribal affiliation is not a criterion—girls learn each other's languages despite the ban on speaking African languages in school, and become familiar with at least verbal reports of each other's different tribal practices. They learn each other's tribal songs, dances, and initiation rites. Although there is sensitivity to socioeconomic differences in family backgrounds, these too are not necessarily a barrier to friendship. A poor girl is sometimes "adopted" by a wealthy girl. Salina, the daughter of a poor rural preacher, became friendly with Dorothy, the daughter of a senior civil servant. Salina began spending holidays with Dorothy's family in town. Over the course of a decade Dorothy's family, although of an unrelated tribe and a higher social class, became "like a second family" to Salina. School is an avenue of upward social mobility for students from poor backgrounds who work at gaining acceptance as social equals of girls from wealthy backgrounds.

Strong Christians form friendships with each other, often helping each other remain chaste while schooling. They live happily within the school environment for up to seven or eight years, venturing out only when required to do so, at holiday times or for prescribed events. In fact they may become so involved in school activities that they lose contact with values, attitudes, and beliefs learned at home. Sister Bertha, a nun, told me that her family would "never understand or forgive" her for taking her vows. They were Roman Catholics themselves, but they were also matrilineal Tongas and could not understand how she could consider herself "married to Christ" when she should be producing children for them.

In less extreme cases, good Christian girlfriends, imbued with the spirit of service learned from the missionaries, participate in extracurricular activities. Agnes and Salome enjoyed their volunteer work teaching village women the nutrition they learned in their classes. After leaving school Agnes joined a nutrition group on the Copperbelt to continue the same sort of volunteer activity. She found her motives questioned by her other girlfriends, her relatives, and especially the women she was trying to help—altruism is not appreciated or understood. The "good" girls who successfully adapt to mission teachings and reinforce each other throughout their years in school enter the harsh urban scene rather naive and innocent.

Despite the importance and enduring nature of friendships formed between female adolescents during their school days, there is a strong undercurrent of tension and mistrust. This derives partly from competition. Encouraged by the school authorities, girls compete for high marks and in sports. In addition, there are the girls' own personal rivalries, related to religious purity, clothes, and boyfriends. Although friendships do exist across social classes, wealthy girls tend to be snobs and poor girls tend to feel inferior. Girls from relatively poor backgrounds often say that rich girls are lazy because they know someone will take care of them if they fail at school. There is envy and frustration. Gossip undermines friendship.

Some girls adapt to school life by maximizing opportunities for illicit meetings with men. Secondary schools are considered excellent "poaching grounds," as they are called in Zambian–English slang. No secondary school is so completely isolated that it is totally inaccessible. Boys from paired secondary schools, civil servants at local *bomas*, and local politicians strut in competition for the attention of schoolgirls. Teachers too sometimes have affairs with their students. Schoolgirls are considered highly desirable girlfriends—in fact this is an index of their high personal status relative to uneducated women their own age.

Girls meet schoolboys at inter-school functions. A popular way to meet working men is at church services. Some girls deliberately identify themselves as adherents of religions with churches off the school grounds so they can make these contacts. Since it is against school rules to have boyfriends, girls escape from their dormitories at night after lights out to meet men at a prearranged spot. Without any apparent conflict of conscience, these girls lead the double life of schoolgirl by day and "dolly girl" by night. The usual evening activity is to accompany a boyfriend to a bar where the couple drink, dance, joke with their friends, and afterwards leave to "play sex."

Some students develop serious relationships with their boyfriends, and some of these develop into marriage (sometimes first resulting in divorce of the men's older wives). But many women who are seriously involved with their first lovers are disappointed when they learn the man only pretended to be serious. Still others are much more committed to future careers than to marriage, and approach affairs with an essentially casual attitude.

Ironically, the illicit activities of these adolescents are more adaptive to the urban situation they face after leaving school than the adaptation made by girls who operate entirely within the formal institutional framework. The rule-breakers learn the importance of deceit in social relationships. Having more experience with men gives them the advantage of learning how to judge men's characters, and what sort of "sweet talk" to expect. Loss of innocence and naiveté makes them less vulnerable in the world they will shortly enter.

WESTERNIZATION OF THE ADOLESCENT

Another effect of schooling is the superficial "westernization" of young men and women. They are able to speak English fluently and use slang; they develop an appetite for European material possessions, a competence in dealing with some aspects of western technology, and an ability to mix relatively unself-consciously with Europeans when required to do so. They also learn to mingle freely and easily with each other regardless of tribal affiliation.

Boarding school dormitories, perhaps more than any other institution, help create the beginnings of a kind of national "Zambian" culture, a synthesis of African and western. Students at boarding schools, spending much time with each other and having a shared common experience, develop a camaraderie and a level of understanding among themselves that is often greater than that which exists between themselves and their kin. They add western information to their tribal knowledge. Many from urban backgrounds have only superficial understanding of tribal culture; their western education, which excludes reference to their tribal cultures, is all they can believe in.

For the women, embroidered or crocheted antimacassars become a sign of elegance in home decor. They get the idea that "real" cookery means the ability to prepare European food, so that women who say they do not know how to cook mean they are unable to prepare European dishes or bake cakes. Both sexes learn European table manners, using a knife and fork the way British people use these utensils—they accept the idea that this is a "superior" way of eating. Both sexes believe in careers and in "love." Their literacy enables them to read love magazines from the west, and they are passionately fond of movies and western popular songs. They absorb western slang expressions and develop some of their own communication styles in Zambian–English. Both sexes struggle hard to master their subjects, since there is no alternative road to success. They feel stupid at not understanding certain references, but do not question the western curriculum itself. Sarah, a teacher, said:

> In a novel I was reading there was a "French window." I
> struggled to imagine what a "French window" was. I couldn't

imagine what it could be. I was ashamed of my ignorance and did not ask the teacher. One of the first things I wanted to see when I got to Britain was a "French window." It made me laugh! Now that I've been there, I can appreciate European novels more, but I prefer our own African novels which are coming out now.

Apart from reading and arithmetic skills and a facility in English, all of which serve a woman in a career, there is little in a young woman's formal learning that she can apply later in life. This is true not only with regard to purely academic subjects such as British history, geography, and literature, but to subjects that are modified to be directly appropriate for African girls. Cleaning, cooking, gardening, and childcare are taught, but the students will be achieving a social status that negates their engaging in these activities. Theirs is education for high status rather than education for the sake of the intellect.

Finally, conflicts between beliefs learned at home and those learned in boarding schools are rarely consciously expressed. Rather, they are internalized and often relegated to the subconscious. Children in boarding schools, who repress so much of their personalities, also repress this conflict and consciously accept and enjoy westernization. Yet the subconscious conflict keeps alive their early African learning at home, and may be the reason for the continued belief in magic and witchcraft by otherwise westernized students.

THE EMERGING ADULT

The academically unsuccessful girl returns to the womb of her family to live in a life style that has changed little since the 1930s. The successful girl does not perceive her own marginality as long as she is succored and protected by the school environment. She must, however, leave the school environment and face society at large as an independent, individualistic young woman, neither fully western nor fully African.

Boys, who experience the same school situation as girls, do not necessarily respond with the same sense of alienation. They have to change fewer personal habits and personality traits. They already have a measure of freedom of expression and movement at home, and so are not expected to put on a mask of reserve or develop emotional distance. The contrast between their conduct at home and at school is not as great as it is for girls, who are required to be reticent at home and to speak out in class. While boys are equally removed from their academic subjects and feel culturally inferior to European teachers, they are provided a measure of comfort by their feeling of superiority to African females.

Socialization is supposed to fit a person into a society. The

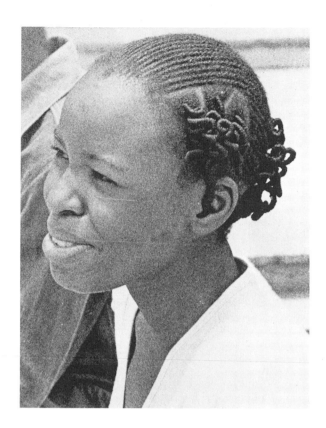

A University of Zambia student. Hair plaiting replaced Afro wigs as the "in" fashion in urban Zambia in 1974.

background of the young Zambian elites and subelites has done this unwittingly. They are prepared to accept an arbitrary, inconsistent, authoritarian society. Throughout their lives as youngsters, there have always been external agents of social control. Authority figures in home and school achieved conformity almost exclusively through the use of external sanctions. Social control was based on the shame of being caught. The young person socialized under this system follows rules of conduct only as necessary to avoid being caught.

The problem for young graduates facing the urban world is that outside the narrow worlds of home and school there are no efficient bureaucrats to oversee their behavior. Left on their own in unsheltered training programs, at university, or at jobs, the facade of independence, individualism, and self-confidence characteristic of the academically successful high school graduate is easily shattered. Unsupervised, young people all too often end up hurting themselves or others.

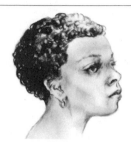

The Single State:
Women at Work

5

Success in school and in training programs has given young women confidence, pride, and a sense of their own worth. There is a solid basis for such high self-esteem, for such educated women enter the urban scene ready to achieve both financial independence and high social status. They feel they deserve the best their society has to offer, including fulfillment of their dreams. It is a time to enjoy independence, amassing personal possessions: an extensive wardrobe of clothes and accessories, a record player, refrigerator, electric hot plate, and furniture. Later, advanced training or a vacation may mean travel to Nairobi or, even better, to London. Still later, it will be time to find a handsome, wealthy, educated man and marry, then to go on to life in a big house, with the ideal four children, continued advancement in a career, and the chance to host relatives. These things constitute a happy life, and schoolgirls expect their education to ensure just such happiness.

But happiness and optimism are ephemeral. At 20, the typical sub-elite townswoman is starry-eyed, and with reason: she enters a communal society in which money, drink, and music flow freely, where her looks are appreciated, her achievements rewarded, and her presence on the lively urban scene celebrated. Yet nearing 30, she shows signs of the strain under which she has lived. Suspicious of relationships with both men and other women, she is deeply lonely despite the surface gaiety. She has learned to trust no one sufficiently to unburden herself of her problems, ideas, and experiences. She has learned to lie, to pretend, to conceal, to be constantly on guard, operating in social situations in which boyfriends, girlfriends, husbands, husbands' relatives, workmates, and even her own relatives cannot be fully trusted.

In short, the modern townswoman usually discovers that town life rarely brings the happiness and emancipation she expected. Her school-girl dreams turn out to be unrealistic products of a cloistered boarding school existence. Anxiety and stress cause physical ailments and she is liable to feel she has lost the legendary strength of the village woman. She will reject the old roles and relationships of village women and feel no nostalgia for village life—but she will also realize that town has many problems of its own.

JOBS AND ATTITUDES

To have a job in the formal sector of Zambia's modern economy is to have the magic ticket to a new life style. Because women earn high salaries, they can maintain a relatively high standard of living independent of male support and control. Researchers have already noted that prostitutes, beer-brewers, and marketeers throughout black Africa value their free-

A secretary at the University Library.

dom from dependency on particular, possibly abusive, men. But there is an enormous difference between the precarious marginal existence of these uneducated townswomen who struggle merely to survive, and the modern young women whose skills are in great demand, whose paychecks leave an enormous surplus, whose jobs are physically undemanding, and who can change jobs at whim. Yet although their lives are far more comfortable, the modern young women face new kinds of problems.

Government and private employers hold negative views of Zambian workers. Elite and subelite men in positions of authority frequently express the view in public that those beneath them are lazy, inefficient, unreliable, and unstable. And since men believe all women are naturally inferior to all men, all women are included among the guilty, even though they may be of the same educational and employment level as their accusers. This attitude is then used to justify discrimination in hiring and promotions. Female university graduates in government ministries may remain in the same job for years while many of their fellow male graduates catapult to top positions.

Job transiency   The widespread impression Zambians have of the instability of Zambian workers is supported by my data on the employment histories of 48 working women.[1] Almost none of the interviewees remained in the particular institution where they started for more than two or three years, including time spent training. Many stayed less than two years. A few left companies that sponsored their training almost immediately after completing the training program, without any apparent sign of guilt. Alice, who left a mining company only a few weeks after finishing company-sponsored secretarial training, said: "I just told them my mother died and I had to stay at home and look after the children. There was nothing they could do except release me."

Alternatively, even if a young woman did remain with the same company for several years she might still move around a great deal:

> Susan worked for the same mining company for five years, the longest of any interviewee. She spent six months of those five years training in Luanshya, two years in the Ndola office, and two and a half years in the Lusaka office. During this time she changed residence several times, had two "marriages," four children (two of whom died), and innumerable lovers.

This kind of transiency, moving from job to job, town to town, alternating between marriage and divorce, parenthood and childlessness, is a feature of the urban Zambian landscape from the lowest unskilled laborers to the very highest echelons.

Although employers complain about employee instability, it is clearly a feature built in to the structure of Zambian political and economic life. At the top level, President Kaunda's frequent reshuffles of management and political personnel are widely seen to be positive steps to prevent too great a consolidation of personal power by any one individual. But the job transiency of workers lower down the scale is condemned, and workers are called saboteurs of development. Of these workers, President Kaunda once said:

> It is lazy people who are hindering . . . development, and these are the same people who reduce our country to a laughing stock by the racists who savour anything that hinders our progress.[2]

Among the saboteurs of development are said to be women who get pregnant during their training, women who spend their time being lazy, inefficient gossips, and women who are obviously not serious about their work.[3] These reasons are given for not hiring a Zambian woman when one can legally employ either a Zambian man or an expatriate, and for not promoting women who are already employed. By the same rationale, employers conclude that the complaints of Zambian women do not have to be seriously considered.

Women leave particular jobs because of unsatisfactory conditions of service. These include disputes with employers, boredom, relatively low wages, and awkward working hours.

There are three common types of disputes with employers. One type is caused by the sexual advances of male co-workers and bosses. Some women, enjoying the prestige and hoping for career advancement, are prepared to "play sex" with their bosses. Others quietly quit their jobs, responding with silence and secret anger. Fearing ridicule, they rarely complain publicly. They have little choice.

In a press release in April 1972, the Attorney General said women should speak out so that their allegations could be proved or disproved. But what young typist could seriously think of bringing a case against the general manager of a large company? Most women treated the Attorney General's suggestion as a joke. They knew that rather than being believed, they would be reviled as "troublemakers." Clementina, a secretary, presented the following written complaint to her company:

> It all started two weeks after Rose had left, the girl I took over from. Mr. Chalwe called me into his office and asked for a cup of coffee, I made him a cup of coffee. Two days after, he walked into my office and jokingly accused me of poisoning him and went on to say he had never loved his secretary in his life, so I was the first one. I laughed it over and ignored him. At lunch time I was told to remain behind to type a letter which he wanted before 14.00 hours. I had my mother, sisters waiting for me at home, and I had to collect the child from the nursery school, but remained in the office.
>
> Mr. Chalwe walked near by, and started to touch my lower parts. I told him in a polite way that I was not interested, and

went back to my office, he followed me, to my table where he tried to kiss me, I closed my mouth, then he kissed me on top of my lips, by then his zip was undone, he pulled me into his office and locked the door and pressed me against his conference table. He managed to undress me half way but failed to undress the pant, so he pressed his thing in between my thighs, we started struggling but he managed to discharge on the floor, then he left for his lunch, by then it was 13.00 hours, and soon after he left, my mother came and she wanted to know why I could not take the child, then I gave her the lame excuse. Fifteen minutes later my boss came back with a big smile, and greeted my mother and sisters.

I thought of telling the Personnel Manager, but somehow I was put off, since they are good friends. It kept me worried and I discussed it with a friend, who advised me to resign.

So many things started to happen, we lost the working relationship. I told the Personnel Manager I was fed up with the behaviour of my boss. Later on, while I was on leave, I received a letter of transfer. The P.M. [Personnel Manager] had told girls that, this time even if you go wrong we won't be putting you right because you are blaming us loving you, and you are reporting us. I just wonder whether I have a right to complain.

The top boss of her company says Clementina has made the same complaint on two other occasions. He says she is ugly, does not get the promotions she wants, and is almost certainly imagining these sexual encounters.

The second type of dispute with employers arises over leave pay. It is considered legitimate to take time off work for family matters, such as to visit the sick and to attend funerals. Male and female employees abuse this privilege. Agnes said:

It's easy to get off when you want to go to the Copperbelt for a change. I telephone my friend there and she cables me that someone has died. I show the cable to my boss and he has to allow me to go. If I need to take the afternoon off or two days I can get a note from the private doctor. No problem!

Disputes between employers and employees arise when employers deduct wages for excessive absences.

The third type of dispute arises when employer and employee accuse each other of inefficiency. Employees want a predictable and balanced work load. They resent having days with nothing to do, and then suddenly being confronted with large assignments and a deadline. They feel such imbalances are due to bureaucratic inefficiency, so that they are alternatively overworked and bored. Employers claim workers are not interested in their jobs, and are, therefore, careless and slow. Employers rarely dismiss workers they feel are inefficient: more often, employees quit after a few quarrels with employers.

Women sometimes leave government jobs for work in the private sector because of the relatively higher wages. Awkward working hours, especially when late nights are involved as sometimes happens in government service, cause some women to leave particular jobs. Job changes also occur when government and private companies transfer their employees to branches in different parts of Zambia. But when in a position to do so (that is, when she is not involved in a serious relationship with a man), a woman is likely to accept transfer orders, however fearful she may be of the change. Friends of a top elite woman appointed to a post abroad recalled how she had a two-month long series of farewell parties, just to delay departure. Nearing thirty and still unmarried, having already spent many years studying abroad, she had hoped to remain at home and find a husband. Yet she accepted her assignment with grace. Other young women accept transfers with enthusiasm. Agnes said:

> I took the job with Maamba Collieries because I wanted to live in Lusaka to get away from the Copperbelt. It was nice. But then, the company moved headquarters to the mine (in rural Southern Province). I went there and stayed for a year. It was very interesting to see the Tonga people in the villages around there. They lived like chickens in their houses. Some of the women even knocked out their front teeth! We Luapula people are much more civilized.
>
> In the mine compound I got a white boyfriend who treated me nicely, not hiding me from his white friends like on the Copperbelt. We had dinners at his friends' houses and went to the company bar and the swimming pool every day. After one year he left Maamba. He asked me to go with him to Lusaka, so I did. He was a good man and I loved him.

Only a minority of women are in a position to accept transfer orders. Men order their wives to adjust or be gone, but women cannot be quite so cavalier in their personal lives. A husband will rarely move to comply with his wife's transfer.

Men also say women cannot be trusted to keep their jobs on a long-term basis because they get pregnant. However, none of the women I interviewed left employment because of pregnancy. Some, indeed many, had found it necessary to take maternity leave, but none wanted to remain at home indefinitely. In fact, most were anxious to get back to work. Over and over, mothers who were asked why they wanted to work said: "To make use of my training"; or "It is boring to sit at home." Finally, although most interviewees consider it shameful to admit that their "husbands" do not support them and they must work to feed their children and themselves, this motive is widely acknowledged. Male and female

Street scene: going home after work on Cairo Road.
Note the contrast between traditional chitenge and
modern dress styles.

politicians sometimes even push the view that women should work to support themselves and their children instead of "sponging," as they say, off the men.

Forced to leave jobs when the boss makes sexual advances or when not free to accept a transfer, women are unwilling participants in social forces beyond their control, but for which they are held responsible.

Career advancement   Women do not generally give lack of opportunity for career advancement as a reason for changing jobs. Yet with possibilities for upward social mobility so obvious in the towns, it is not surprising that women are as conscious of and eager to participate in advancing their careers as are men. The government requires most large companies to have advanced training programs for their Zambian staff.

Few people actively seek training on their own initiative, but they welcome it when the opportunity arises. As new recruits they do not feel free to inquire about training programs. They fear they will not be hired if they question personnel managers too closely about such programs, for then the managers will consider them poor prospects for staying on the jobs for which they have applied. Thus they have little choice except to wait passively until opportunities are presented. Career advancement therefore tends to be a long-range rather than a short-range goal.

The women tend to have realistic expectations for the type of advanced training they would like. Only a few dream of glamorous careers as models and entertainers; most are content with more modest ambitions. Registry clerks would like to study typing, typists would like to study stenography, nurses would like to study midwifery, vernacular broadcasters would like to do broadcasting in English, journalists aim for editorships, and civil servants aim to progress through the ranks.

Women want advanced training both to make more money and to have physically less demanding jobs so that they can continue to work when they grow old. Single or married, they do not anticipate a time in which they will not work, depending on men for their support. Yet, according to my interview data, more married women than single women take evening courses. The probable reason is that husbands transport wives to and from evening courses, but single women face the difficult problem of finding their own transport. Whether single or married, women are equally ambitious.

Tension at work Employers naturally want efficient, productive employees who take pride in their work. Yet employers set the work standard by their actions: they disappear for entire afternoons following heavy drinking bouts at executive lunches in posh hotels, go for fittings for their hand-tailored clothes, carry out hectic social and sexual activities, take frequent trips abroad combining business with shopping and pleasure, and, finally, give jobs to their relatives, tribesmen, friends, mistresses. From the employees' point of view, then, rewards rarely relate to performance and there is little incentive to do a job well. If their employers subordinate productive efficiency to social activities, why should they not? If they never see "the boss" decline an invitation to a cocktail party or a luncheon on the grounds of "pressure of work," why should they not "enjoy themselves"?

Women consequently feel that they have a right to consider certain office amenities as theirs to enjoy, perhaps even to a greater degree than their employers, who live in a world of luxury all the time. For the women, their life of struggle outside the office, in flimsy flats, fighting for transportation and short-supply consumer goods, contrasts sharply with the luxury of the new office buildings in which they work: the thick carpets, leather lounge suites, chrome-and-glass occasional tables, potted plants, oil paintings, indirect lighting, large mirrors in the ladies' toilets, and the messengers, tea servers, cleaners, and telephones. Women, therefore, are likely to spend part of the work-day before the bathroom mirrors, chatting with friends and lovers on the telephone, with men who visit the office, ordering messengers to buy groceries for them, or absenting themselves from the office on private business. Employers, when they are around to observe it, get annoyed.

An important function of the workplace is to give interested men and women opportunities for meeting new lovers. Men passing through offices on official business notice attractive, well-dressed, well-groomed young women and later stop by specifically to visit them. If a woman's co-worker is sexually interested in her, such visits from strangers can cause jealousy and tension. Although some top elite bosses and middle-rank employees treat female workers with distance, formality, and respect, deliberately avoiding sexual encounters or innuendos, many view their own and nearby workplaces as important places in which to meet potential new wives, mistresses, or casual lovers. Tension in the workplace arises when the sexual interest is not mutual, when men mistake flirtation for agreement to have sex, when women mistake "sweet talk" for genuine feeling and interest, or when one mistakenly regards the other as available for exploitation. Because men also have difficulty accepting women as their equals, tensions arise between male and female co-workers at the same grade in their jobs. It chafes the male ego to have to sit in the same office, day after day, with a woman doing the same job. The man may be driven to provoke the woman or she may provoke him, if only by treating him as an equal or less. She does this by making sure he knows that, although sexually active, she is not available to him but rather to men with better jobs and cars.

Between many women and the lowest ranking male employees—the cleaners, tea servers, messengers—there is a steady war of nerves. The women consider such men truly inferior. Here the usual roles are reversed: the men clean up after the women, the men serve the women tea, the men shop for women. As if this were not sufficient to gall the men, the women may remind the men of their position if a service is not properly performed. The men are quick to sense an insult to their dignity even if none is intended. The "war of nerves" can erupt in a shouting match, with insults traded vigorously.

Women are in a no-win situation with men at work. Rarely can a woman work for several years without experiencing an unpleasant confrontation. Men are convinced that women they desire should make themselves available to them and, when refused, accuse women of being "too proud." At the same time, a woman is not necessarily intimidated by a man whose position is higher. A decade may separate her and her boss in

74

age, giving him experience in business and in life. But he is not necessarily more highly educated, and if she is attractively dressed and socially out-going and at ease, she feels she is his match. She wants the right to accept or refuse him as a lover.

Sexual antagonism constantly lurks beneath the surface.

"At least go outside and greet him properly," Lucy told her cousin Lillian when her boss drove up to her flat and presented Lucy with a kilo of beef.

"He can just go away and not bother me when I am at home. He is the boss at work, not here. I didn't ask him for this meat," she said. "I don't have to thank him."

Lucy said, in response, "Ah, this girl is just too proud."

There are two ways in which a woman can avoid tension at work. One is to be very quiet and submissive, to make herself inconspicuous and unattractive. Some women are naturally this way. It is hardly a formula for career advancement, but at least they can keep their jobs and a steady routine. It is unrealistic, however, for women who are naturally ebullient to change, and it is contrary to urban values for them not to enjoy pro-vocative clothing, cosmetics, and hairstyles that announce their pride in their social position.

The second technique to avoid tension is to assume a maternal role. The media advocate this image of the career woman, and it is a favored role of women who have what they hope are stable marriages. Some single women try it, and are successful at it. Sooner or later, however, they be-come depressed by the image they have created, for they too would like lovers or husbands and find they are unable to meet new men precisely because they have acted as if they are what they call "off the market." It is almost impossible for them to play the role at the office, day after day, of one who is conservative, understanding, friendly, and respectful, and then change personalities the moment they leave the office. The switch seems to be too great.

DOMESTIC ARRANGEMENTS

Women's domestic arrangements reflect their anomalous social position. Their basic problem is simply being an independent, educated, unmarried woman alone in town. Where can such a woman live? How can she express her new-found status and yet protect herself? How does she allocate her resources to provide for her needs and pleasures?

Housing   For people of all income levels, the housing shortage in Lusaka is severe, and yet the goal of nearly all modern women is to rent a flat. Despite the housing shortage, their desire is a realistic response to social and sexual pressures, but limits their flexibility. Men have developed a number of ways to cope with the housing shortage, but women are not free to choose among the same variety of alternatives.

Instead of waiting for a flat to come on the market, men can build their own houses in shantytowns or "site-and-service schemes," rent a room, or live with relatives. In contrast, women in this category almost never build their own houses; they would still have to find accommodation for a year or more until the house was built, and women alone fear that they will be raped in these neighborhoods without male protection. Nor can women feel safe renting a room, even from a family they know, owing to the likelihood of unwanted sexual involvement with the male adults and visitors in the household.

Similarly, sexual fears or experiences of being exploited prevent many women from wanting to live with relatives, although every one of the 48 interviewees had some relatives in Lusaka. These fears have a definite basis. The husband of a female relative well might try to have intercourse with the guest: many schoolgirls, visiting on holidays, experience this type of situation, and schoolgirl pregnancies ("blow-ups") sometimes result when the girl submits. Married women recognize the problem, and for that reason some wives discourage young female relatives from moving in even for holidays. In such cases, the idea that an adult woman would be welcomed is unrealistic. The following cases illustrate the problems that can arise when women live with relatives:

> Ten months before he died of cancer, a senior civil servant impregnated both his wife and her niece whom the wife had asked to help in the house for three months while she was attending a course in another town.

> Olive went to live with her cousin, at his invitation, while his wife was on an extended trip abroad. She cared for his three children. During her stay she became pregnant. She named her cousin as the father. This was a grave charge as it was tantamount to incest. Her cousin denied the charge.

> As a child, Rebecca lived with her father's sister's daughter and the woman's husband on the Copperbelt while she attended school. Just after the onset of her first menses, the husband began making sexual advances. She was too terrified to say anything to her other relatives at first, but when she could no longer dodge him she confessed her problem to another relative, who took her away.

When sex is not the problem, exploitation is. If a woman lives with relatives, she must accept the right of the head of the household to control her movements and her associations, thereby going against her own notions of freedom and independence. A nurse said:

My cousin wanted me to move in after he divorced his wife. I did— and discovered he wanted me as a watch-dog. He never wanted me to leave the house and quarrelled with me when I did. But he went out, leaving me alone evenings and weekends. I should not have to be a watch-dog, and after failing to make him understand, I left.

For unmarried nurses, teachers, personal secretaries, and administrators, the solution to the accommodation problem is company housing, subject to availability. This may be a multiple-room apartment. The majority of single working women, however, are not eligible. Low ranking employees receive a sum of money called a "housing allowance" instead of accommodation. They must compete on the open market for housing, fully exploiting their kinship and friendship networks to obtain a hostel, flat, or small house of their own. This can take months or years, for vacancies are rare as people pass on their rooms to relatives or friends without informing the authorities.

Lusaka's city council hostels and high-rise "bed-sitters" (studio apartments) are always filled to capacity with unmarried working people. Most of my single interviewees lived in one or the other.

Council hostels are found in all of Lusaka's older townships. Tiny row houses, they are unfurnished and self-contained. Each has a main room, large enough to contain a bed, a small table, a few chairs, and a wardrobe. A closet-size room behind the main room contains a sink with hot and cold taps, shelves, and a counter. This is the kitchen. A doorway leads directly to the shower, which also has hot and cold taps, and there is a separate water closet (toilet). Because the hostels boast electricity, indoor kitchens, showers and toilets, hot water, and concrete and plaster construction, and because they are meant for only one person, they are well above the norm by national standards. Nevertheless, most women feel they are shabby and too small.

A "bed-sitter" is a small apartment in the new high-rise apartment house complex that is managed by the government parastatal INDECO and located between the High Court at Government Center and the posh Intercontinental Hotel. The bed-sitters are larger than the council houses. Each unit contains a full modern tiled bath to one side of the entry, and a small kitchen opposite. The entry leads to the main L-shaped room, which is divided by built-in shelves and a heavy curtain into the living room and bedroom. The bedroom area has a built-in closet. Like the hostels, the bed-sitters were designed for single occupancy, and by the

The Indeco high rise flats: home of modern young singles.

housing standards of Lusaka they are small but luxurious. Hostels and bed-sitters are supposed to contain only one occupant, but they rarely do. Overcrowding is a real problem.

Before finding personal accommodation, a woman is most likely to live happily with either an unmarried female relative in the same socio-economic educational status as herself or with a friend from school days. If her friend or relative lives in a flat or house with two or three bedrooms and the women share similar attitudes toward sex and leisure activities, the arrangement can last indefinitely and come to include their children and a young female relative or servant who acts as nanny.

Domestic harmony is shattered when one of the roommates decides she wants to go all out to marry a particular man. To accomplish her goal, she must cultivate a new image. She must no longer be the sophisticated dolly girl. Rather, she must appear to be sweet and mild-mannered, soft-spoken and slightly innocent. Her new image and the role she must play conflict with those of her roommate, and so the roommate must go. The situation is handled in an indirect manner; the sexual undercurrents implicit in the change are not confronted directly. If the woman with a man in mind is also the "owner," as Zambians say, of the house, hostel, or flat, she will tell her roommate that she requires the room for a relative. Officially, the story Susan and Agnes gave when Susan asked Agnes to leave was that Susan needed Agnes's room for her young sister. Unofficially, these friends since boarding school days said of each other:

Susan: That one was just too wild. Moving up and down,[4] every night out boozing and screwing useless boys. It was too much! Let me rest just now.

Agnes: What a dull girl! If not for me suggesting to go places in the evenings, she would just go to sleep. Without me she'll get very fat and ugly because she is too lazy. Last year her boyfriend left, he got so fed up.

What Susan kept secret from everyone was that she was aiming to get married. The domestic unit of two females, their children, and a nanny always ends when one of the women marries. Susan, for example, evidently thought her chances would be better without Agnes there, for Agnes was younger, prettier, livelier, and sexier.

Wanting to live on one's own in a singles flat in one's own name is not the same as wanting to live alone. The concept of, and the need for, privacy is not meaningful for men and women raised with none. A Kenyan married to a European said:

Of course, when we arrived home in Kenya there were literally dozens of my relatives coming day and night to see me and to meet my wife. I expected this and I tried to prepare her for it. For a while she took it all right. Then she began demanding more and more of what she called "privacy." She made the word sound as though "privacy" was something sacred. I have come to hate the whole idea of privacy, I'll tell you.[5]

Zambian women express their dislike of staying alone by saying, "It is too quiet." Their experiences in social life of the village community, the urban household with numerous siblings, relatives, and visitors, and the dormitory at boarding school mean that they have spent their lives surrounded by people. A favorite role, therefore, is that of hostess. These women do not enjoy hosting their elders. However, young female relatives on holiday from boarding school, relatives who are working women, girl-friends, and relatives who will serve as nannies for their children are all welcome. More rarely, women will host boyfriends who are between jobs or flats. Rarer still, and only in multi-room flats, school-age male relatives are accommodated. It is against the rules for women to accommodate relatives in the high-rise, but the main function of this rule seems to be to give women an excuse for keeping out relatives they dislike. The rule is openly flouted by anyone who wants to have someone live with her.

Those who live alone for any length of time leave their doors open and tend to turn the flats into a communal compound—a vertical steel-and-concrete one rather than a horizontal mud-and-thatch village community. The very old value of communal living has been retained by apparently alienated young women and has taken the form of accommodating same-age or younger females and keeping doors of their flats open to neighbors.

Allocation of resources   Among the working women I interviewed, salaries ranged from K80[6] to K290 per month for beginning clerks to stenographers respectively, exclusive of housing allowances, after tax and other deductions. This is much more money than the women require for personal survival in town. The surplus and the freedom to allocate it as they see fit is one of the major sources of women's sense of independence and high status.

Clothing is the major expense of single working women. It is difficult to exaggerate the hunger for a full wardrobe in the latest fashion trend from Britain or Italy. Women scorn clothes manufactured locally since they have low status. They are occasionally tempted by credit-offering peddlers who visit their dormitories, hostels, and entrances to their office buildings selling home-sewn frocks in imported fabrics and dress patterns. This is impulse buying. When a woman actually plans to get a new dress, she rarely buys fabric to take to a dressmaker, far preferring to buy an imported dress (at a wildly inflated price) from a "chic" boutique downtown.[7] It is not unusual for a woman to spend one-third of the month's salary on clothes, excluding the money she spends on shoes, cosmetics, accessories, hairdresser, and wigs. Furthermore, the hunger for many expensive clothes is matched by a passion for variety and change, so that women are quite prepared to give things away they have worn once or twice—or sometimes not worn at all.

Food and rent are proportionally small expenses, about 20 percent of the monthly income. Transportation cost is considerable, since most women depend on taxis. Cosmetics and phonograph records are regular monthly expenses for the majority. Those living with their children support them and support the relative or servant who cares for the children.

80

ZCBC: a favorite "first class" supermarket.

If relatives keep the woman's children in their homes, she sends them money now and again.

Women maintain savings accounts. Normally they or their companies deposit their full paychecks and then withdraw what they need every few days. Some months they use their entire pay, and if that happens before the next pay day they borrow money from office mates, friends, or relatives. They also lend these people money, so that reciprocity is maintained. Saving is irregular, and generally women do not save for a specific purpose. A personal savings account is an important source of independence because it gives a woman the freedom to leave a job before she has found another, and because it gives her the freedom to buy consumer goods of her choice. Except for buying dresses from street peddlers on credit, most women avoid time payments. When they have accumulated the necessary amount, they buy things on a cash basis. They rarely accumulate large debts, and this enhances the feeling of independence.

Women support female relatives, and enjoy being able to help those who helped them. However, it is only under exceptional circumstances that women are willing to help their fathers or other older male relatives, for they feel men should take care of themselves. Needy mothers, aunts, and grandmothers are supported fairly regularly, and fatherless siblings are supported for all schooling expenses. Younger male relatives are given occasional gifts of cash. As a general rule, the amount of money given to relatives tends to be proportional to their socioeconomic status: the higher the status of the recipient, the more cash gifts or high quality clothes he or she receives.

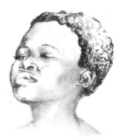

The Single State:
Women at Leisure

6

Although the work-day is not set apart from social life, leisure time, the non-working hours of evenings and weekends, has a special mystique. Society-at-large considers women very dangerous after dark.

Single women have the reputation of spending virtually all their free time "loitering around bars and hotels at night" tempting men to "lose their heads" and spend all their money on the women, leaving wives and children to starve. According to the stereotype, these callous girls live in "brothels," not hostels. They are hated and condemned for their immorality by married women, by elders of both sexes, by male and female politicians, and, most wounding of all, by many young bachelors. With the latter, a free trade exists in mutual insults, aggression, hostility. University women, for example, are said to "change boyfriends like shirts."[1] Many think they should know their place—"Women must be subordinate to men in a healthy society like Zambia."[2] The women answer aggression with aggression: "Girls should change boyfriends not like shirts but like tissue paper."[3] The stereotype is partly justified, as much socializing revolves around the hostels.

University women often point out that the bachelors who are most hostile are "monks"—that is, men who deliberately lead a monastic existence because they lack the self-confidence to approach a woman.

"Mojos"—bachelors who have girlfriends—tend to be less hostile when they are sexually satisfied. ("Monk" and "mojo" are slang words used by university students to label men according to their prowess with women.)

LEISURE AT HOME

In the hostels exists a world all its own, full of life, laughter, quarrels, and social activities of neighbors. Much the same atmosphere prevails in the hostels of the older townships in Matero, Chilenje South, Libala, Kamwala, and rebuilt Old Kabwata, in the flat complexes of new neighborhoods such as Emmasdale, in the formerly non-African neighborhoods of Northmead and Kabulonga, in the high-rise flats, and in the student dormitories of the university, the college, and the hospital. Impersonal building complexes have produced neither the isolation and alienation known in western mass housing projects nor a "lonely crowd" mentality.

The life is communal. Even the two essentially solitary activities in which women occasionally engage—sewing and reading—are done in the presence of others in an atmosphere of blaring music and the chatter of neighbors and visitors. When a woman decides to sew a dress for herself, her neighbors and friends, one of whom has lent her the sewing machine, will watch her cut the fabric, pin it, and stitch it. The "seamstress" will be as eager for the comments of others as they are eager to give them, and all will applaud the outcome. Reading is a casual pastime. Most women confine their reading to love stories in magazines or comic books. A very few read an occasional detective story, a few pages every few days over a period of several weeks. It is not uncommon to visit a hostel to find three or four women sitting around chatting while their hostess lies curled up in a corner of her bed reading. Even watching television is a communal rather than a solitary activity among the few single women who own or rent sets. It is an active participatory experience, not a passive observational one.

Neighbors are part of the home life of these women. In the absence of male visitors, neighbors spend evening hours after work visiting each other's rooms. Meals are usually spontaneously communal. If a woman on her way home from work passes someone who happens to be selling a favorite seasonal relish—mushrooms, okra, fish, caterpillars—she will buy some if she happens to have cash. During the course of the evening she will cook it. Someone else will cook the pot of *nshima* and three to five women will then share the feast. Neighbors who are included in communal food-sharing reciprocate, with equal spontaneity, as a matter of course. Since they do not plan this activity, rarely doing it when men are present, it is not a daily occurrence. Extra food can be stored; in a row of ten houses at least one or two women will have refrigerators. Most women in bed-sitters and flats own refrigerators. If two women spontaneously purchase enough ingredients for "relish" for the group, only one will cook and the other will put her purchases away for another day. Those who cook for themselves and visitors freely borrow ingredients from their neighbors.

Clothes are privately owned and communally shared. A favorite evening activity is to try on each other's clothes, wigs, and cosmetics. Among neighbors and friends, clothes and wigs are lent rather than given away. However, in addition to her neighbors, a woman has a network of friends and female relatives elsewhere in Lusaka with whom she also exchanges clothes and wigs. Clothes and wigs borrowed from friends are often passed on to other friends, returning not at all or months later, all worn out. In this case there is disappointment but not anger, since at one time or another most women have done the same. Reciprocity and, it would seem, mutual carelessness about another's possessions make spontaneous sharing succeed. There is a pool of shared wigs, cosmetics, clothes, novels, magazines, and phonograph records that seems to circulate in pockets throughout Lusaka. It has happened that a woman at a party will see a complete stranger wearing her new dress. Since she may be wearing the new dress of her friend, it does not seem to matter.

Apart from these exchanges, the women cooperate in plaiting each other's hair, cleaning and combing their wigs, and gossiping about mutual acquaintances or their own casual relationships with men of the moment: the equivalent of bawdy male locker room talk. Conversation is to entertain: the purpose of getting together is to laugh and have fun. Chatter easily breaks off to sing or to swing into a dance step in time with the ever-blaring music from the record player.

Theirs is an intimacy of the moment. In many ways, the women remain strangers to each other. It is not unusual for two women to spend months seeing each other daily without knowing where they work downtown, anything about their families, their past life, their possibly serious involvement with men in other towns. It is as if major aspects of personal life and thoughts are specifically *not* to be shared with neighbors.

The women also spend several hours each week in purely mundane activities such as washing and ironing their clothes and cleaning their rooms. They tend to do their own housework even if they employ nannies to look after their children. Finally, some thought is given over to decorating their apartments. Photographs of favorite singers and movie stars are cut out of magazines and taped onto walls, as are magazine photographs of women modeling high fashion clothes that the women would like to own themselves. If a phonograph record has been lost but the album cover remains, it too is taped onto the walls. A calendar and perhaps a photograph of herself and a boyfriend in a deliberately coy pose copied from Hollywood movies complete the wall decor. Covering the furniture in the apartment of a subelite woman who wants to show pride in her home, and her homecraft skill, are green, yellow, or white squares of cotton cloth which have been embroidered with flowers. Some women make these themselves; others buy them.

Even with friendly neighbors, streams of visitors, and household chores, the hostels remain frustratingly shabby and crowded and the women often feel bored. They want to spend some evenings away from their homes.

LEISURE AWAY FROM HOME

There are two major constraints to free movement around the city. The first is the inadequacy of public transport. The second is the vulnerability of women not accompanied by a man after dark to harrassment, assault, and sometimes arrest by the police as "unaccompanied women." Consequently, most women tend to go home after work. They are especially motivated to do so if they are seriously involved with a man, for he might stop by any time expecting the woman to be there, available to answer his need for food, drink, or sexual intercourse.

Some women like to spend time with friends or relatives who live within walking distance of their flats. However, they visit relatives who live farther away from their flats only when they have a specific reason to do so, for transportation is too much of a problem. Many months go by without visits to friends or relatives in other neighborhoods.

Other forms of leisure time activity, such as involvement in clubs or the numerous church organizations that are available in Lusaka, hold little interest for the women. Very few women attend church regularly or even occasionally, even if they were very religious in secondary school. Many clubs remain from the colonial period—the Lusaka Sports, Golf, Theater, Cinema, Flying, Garden, and Music clubs—as do a number of service organizations such as the Red Cross and the Y.W.C.A. A new club, the Zambia Women's Association, was organized in 1973 specifically for elite and subelite Zambian African women, modeled on the typical middle-class British women's service organizations. Club life holds no attraction for the overwhelming majority of Zambian career women, however. The older clubs continue as primarily white preserves with a few wealthy Zambian members. The Zambian Women's Association is still very small.

Foreigners and very wealthy Zambians frequent "European" places of entertainment: they go dining and dancing at the Ridgeway or the Intercontinental, two supposedly international standard hotels. Lusaka's young women consider an invitation to either of these hotels very prestigious, for only the wealthiest men can afford such evenings. In the early evening hours, however, some of the bolder young women hang out at the bars of these hotels or at the humbler, more accessible Lusaka Hotel, hoping to meet men.

For most of Lusaka's young women, leisure outside the home is associated with going to parties—the first choice of most people—and, for all but the few who profess to dislike the atmosphere, going to bars, nightclubs, discotheques, dances, and the army barracks. All of these places provide the opportunity to drink, chat with friends, and dance to live bands playing "hot" western-style rock music and Zairean rumba.

When two or three women sitting around one's flat decide they are bored, they may, in a spirit of adventure and daring (since they risk attack or arrest), hitchhike to a party, a disco, or the army barracks. (Hitchhiking is one way women get to meet men of the "right" socioeconomic class, and liaisons sometimes begin in this way.) Delivered to their destination, the women meet other men, old familiars or new faces with the "right" kind of cars, who spend the evening and perhaps the night with them. Or a group of men may visit the hostels and spontaneously invite a group of women out for a night on the town. Sometimes a group of men and women decide to make a night of it while sitting at a bar after work.

It is this night life that makes Lusaka come alive, in common with

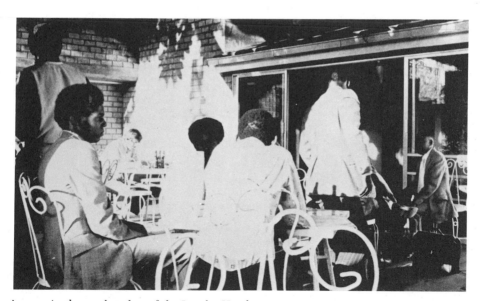

A scene in the outdoor bar of the Lusaka Hotel—a favorite subelite drinking place after work and on weekend afternoons.

87

African cities elsewhere which have few "European" amenities. Night life on weekdays begins some time after five in the afternoon at downtown bars; on weekends it begins Friday afternoon and continues almost uninterruptedly until four o'clock Monday morning. Downtown bars close by 10:30 at night, but one can drink beer every day until three or four in the morning by knowing the places to go. All that is needed is money, transportation, and a knowledge of the geography of Greater Lusaka. The nightclubs do not advertise or post signs, and are hidden on dirt roads miles from the center of town, accessible only by car.[4]

Night life is considered "rough" and "not quite respectable" by both those who partake of it and those who do not. It is uninhibited: gaiety and tension commingle. Men go first and foremost to get drunk. This involves waiting: pushing, shouting, smacking the lips, pounding the bar with *kwachas* (paper currency) grasped firmly in hand (there are pickpockets to guard against). Bartenders are considered by everyone to be maddeningly slow and inefficient, for they too drink and move to the rhythm of the music. Tempers get frayed waiting for beer to be served.

Soothed by the beer they finally do receive, men respond to the music and the ambience. The dance floor gets crowded: men dance with

A favorite night club on an unpaved road on the outskirts of Lusaka.

each other, men dance with women, and women dance with each other to attract men. Choice of dance steps, poses, and postures indicate socio-economic class and sexual interest. The shortage of women, however, creates tension. The sex ratio is always imbalanced since husbands rarely take their "respectable" wives to such places, prostitutes are few in number, and single women normally go with escorts. Men do not necessarily go to have intercourse with a woman, but, when drunk, sometimes become aroused. Then tempers run short and confrontations may develop: physical or verbal, between men over a woman, women over a man, or a man and a woman. These are isolated incidents, involving few people. Most who attend these evening entertainments escape personal involvement and, for the seasoned, these scenes provide additional entertainment and sources of commentary.

The subelite women who enjoy such leisure activity normally take care to know the men who escort them. "Knowing" a man means knowing where he works, whether the car he drives is his own or belongs to his company, and how he behaves when he is drunk. Women do not like to be "in for surprises," and feel if they have already seen a man drunk they know how to handle him. They rarely accept invitations for evenings out from men who are total strangers, unless it is patently obvious that the man is top elite and will give them money. The women feel they are under no obligation to have sexual intercourse with men to whom they are not physically attracted, regardless of the cost of the evening out or the service as escort, and this is why it is important for women to go out with men that they have seen drunk. To be able to refuse a man's demand for sexual intercourse takes courage, social skill, and some understanding of the man's character and personality to know how to phrase the refusal. A man does not consider it a woman's right to refuse to have sexual intercourse with him, especially if he has spent money on her or if she has, wittingly or unwittingly, aroused him. The men who find townswomen "rough" and condemn them most bitterly are often the ones who have been refused sex although they have paid for a woman's beer.

For the women, the joy of such evenings is to drink beer and to dance. For non-drinkers, the joy of participating in night life is simply to dance. The drinkers, however, can come to value these evenings equally with their work during the day, to the exclusion of other interests or responsibilities. I have heard repeated many times the remark of a Copperbelt "champion"—a loose woman in colonial times—recorded by Hortense Powdermaker in her book *Coppertown: Changing Africa* (1962, 163):

> I shall never stop dancing, even if I should have a child. While I am dancing, I will give the child to my husband to take care of. And the child I have by playing with ordinary darlings, I can give to anyone while I am dancing.

One of my key informants, who loved dancing and drinking more than anything in life, lost track of her new-to-Lusaka, five-year-old daughter by an "ordinary darling" for three days during one of her extended drinking bouts. The child, found wandering on a heavily trafficked road, was picked up by a man who first reported finding her to the police and then brought her to his wife to take care of.

THE MEN IN THEIR LIVES

The place of men looms large in women's lives. Women acknowledge that without men life would be sad and dull. But all but the very toughest take pains to conceal their involvement in casual social life from kin, people outside the neighborhood, and interviewers, because casual dating is not considered respectable. Yet my fieldwork in various neighborhood hostels showed that wherever there were residential areas with concentrations of single women's quarters, casual social life existed. For men the hostels were "hot, exciting—where the action is," party centers where "there's always something happening," or "supermarkets—where you can get anything."

Sexually available, single elite and subelite women are few in proportion to the number of "hungry" men, and making contact with men is easy for them. Married and single men of many different nationalities and nearly all of Zambia's tribes actively participate in casual social life. Every evening of the week, and all day and night on weekends, men cruise hostel neighborhoods in cars, alone, with a male friend, or in groups packed into a single car. The women identify men by the make and model of their cars; in a town where many have Mercedes Benzes, the women learn the license numbers and so know who is parked outside of whose house. The liveliness of these neighborhoods comes partly from the cruising of the "Benzes" of well-known Zambian politicians and businessmen and Nigerian diplomats; the Peugeots, Toyotas and Datsuns of Zambian, West African, and Rhodesian professionals; the Fiats of off-duty Zambian "soldier boys," subelite working men, and assorted Europeans—Yugoslavs, Italians, Greeks, and even the occasional British subject.

Any man who has the inclination and the requisite resources of money and transport is able to participate in the social life of these neighborhoods. Since Zambia women's kinship and friendship networks extend throughout the city, there is no lack of opportunity for making social contacts with men. Men freely drop in for brief visits on women to whom they have previously been introduced, and make the rounds of what one of my university colleagues jokingly referred to as "our constituency." When they find a woman interested in sharing the type of evening or afternoon festivities they have in mind on that particular occasion, they settle down for some hours. Sometimes they carry a few bottled beers with them, sometimes a bottle of whiskey, sometimes the offer of an evening of drinking and dancing out on the town. Such unplanned visits by a carload of men to a woman whose friends and neighbors are already gathered in her room quickly assume a party atmosphere when drink is available. The company laughs, chats about their drinking the day before, gossips about mutual acquaintances, drunkenly sings along with the music, and dances. When the beer or spirits run out, couples go to the girls' rooms for intercourse, or the men leave together, or they all go off to a bar, a disco, a nightclub, or a party. Some women make use of the discos, bars, nightclubs, and parties to make contact for future sexual liaisons while their escorts are buying beer, in the toilet, chatting with friends elsewhere in the room, or chatting with other women. Couples are always on the lookout, watching each other closely, ready to fight over a presumed sexual attraction to others.

Getting tough   In the hostel environment, an experienced and unattached woman maximizes her social, psychological, and economic advantages by maintaining contacts with numerous men. In 1976 two slang words became fashionable among Lusaka's subelite men and women: *toughu*, used to describe someone who is attractive, and *dis-as-ter-ous*, used to describe someone who is unattractive. Women who are *toughu* are threatening because they are capable of supporting themselves. Although they can always "go to the brothers" (i.e., prostitute themselves) for money if they want to be especially extravagant, they do not have to do so. *Toughu* women are admired; *dis-as-ter-ous* women are laughed at. The slang mirrors a deeper reality. *Toughu* women are indeed tough.

Women who defy society's public mores come to see men as men see them: playthings for their own pleasure. To the women, men are lying, predatory, and brutal. To accept this view of men and to still enjoy men's company—which they very much do—involves women in a psychological process of toughening up. Toughening up begins with the inexperienced, relatively innocent, naive schoolgirl and ends with the experienced woman of 25 to 30 years of age. The process is a product of acute suffering and mental disturbance caused by having succumbed emotionally to men who spoke falsely of love and marriage. After suffering shock and disappointment, depression and a feeling of "running mad," as they say, many end by protecting themselves from further hurt by refusing to take any man seriously:

> Why put all your eggs in one basket, especially since nearly all of them are rotten anyway?

They get themselves a number of boyfriends and an occasional mark—a man who, in his masculine arrogance and sense of social superiority, becomes vulnerable to mock-flattery and can be manipulated and exploited into parting with more money than he had intended.

> In the space of two months Lucy received a pair of shoes costing K25 from one mark. A potential boyfriend gave her a wig he had bought for her on a trip to Britain. Another mark gave her K20 "to help her out," he said.

Gifts are status symbols to the men, and hence marks and potential boyfriends have the reputation among the women of being particularly generous. Florence said:

> They like to tell all their friends that one is my girlfriend, did you see I gave her K20. That is what they really care about to prove they are big. The boyfriend knows he has you and he doesn't have to give you anything, so it is better to show you don't like them.

These gifts are treated as windfalls, used for buying more clothes and wigs or western luxuries.

Women who have not reached this degree of toughness recoil from the idea of having different boyfriends at the same time: how, they worry, would you know who the father of your child was? The tough, more experienced woman has overcome this reluctance and distaste either by using birth control pills or by naming one of her lovers as the father. Her choice is determined by personal advantage:

> Susan's first child died at about 18 months of age and the second died about six months of age.[5] Following these deaths, her "husband" left her—in fact with the corpse of the second child still to bury. Now aged 26, Susan vowed that the next long-term relationship would be a statutory marriage with a "soldier boy." She wanted the glamorous white wedding with the guard of honor crossing swords, a feature of military weddings at Lusaka's army barracks.
>
> Having made that decision, she resumed an old practice of drinking and dancing in the army barracks near her hostel and focused her attention on a young officer newly arrived from a rural province, who knew nothing of her past, as the other soldiers did.
>
> He did not get passes to leave the barracks often, so Susan was able to continue her relationships with other men during the course of the next year, but faithfully turned up to drink at the barracks at least twice a week. He was then sent away on a tour of duty in the north for several months.
>
> During this time Susan became pregnant. She did not like the man, but thought he would divorce his wife and marry her anyway. The man did not like her either and so refused. Susan then let it be known that the soldier was the father. After the baby's birth she managed to convince the soldier to marry her

when he returned, amazed, to see her with a baby. Her girlfriends kept straight faces as they served as bridesmaids in her lavish white wedding—with the guard of honor.

Brutalization is an almost essential ingredient to toughening. Nearly everyone can relate at least one shocking experience from some point in her life in which she has been abused. Nearly everyone has submitted to sexual relations out of fear of the consequences of refusing. Nearly everyone has been beaten by a man or at least threatened with a beating. Nearly everyone has been disappointed in "love."

Women who have not yet "toughened" are "transitionals." Transitionals cling to the hope that they can have a boyfriend with whom they can develop a satisfying relationship. This hope is nearly always ephemeral because relationships are so fragile. Rather than feeling relieved and secure in having a boyfriend, he is a source of worry, tears, and pain. Transitionals want to be sexually faithful. Unlike "toughs," they worry about gossip and their reputations, fearing being called "rolling stones," "hooligans," or "sex merchants," by other women and men. They worry about their chances of marrying their boyfriends. Although they may be at a neighbor's house when men drop by, and may participate in the spontaneous party that develops in her room, they do not have intercourse with the men. They are sexually faithful to their boyfriends and sometimes even refuse to believe their boyfriends are unfaithful to them:

> I thought my girlfriends were jealous of our love, spreading lies and gossip about him. I told them to go away. But I asked him and he said that they were jealous of our love because they knew he was going to see my relatives. [N.B., This is a sign of seriousness.] Soon after that I saw my lover with that girl together with my own eyes. I knew he was double-crossing me; he said it was his cousin but she was a relative of Salome next door and not his relative.

The sexually faithful woman with evidence that her boyfriend has "double-crossed" her risks a beating if she confronts him with the suggestion. For some women the beating is worth the risk if they can establish the "facts" of the case, but a man will rarely admit seeing other women whose status is equal to that of the girlfriend who is confronting him. Beating is a convenient and frequently used cover for men who wish to conceal their relationships with other women.

Sexually faithful women also risk the consequences of their boyfriends' jealousy since, in the atmosphere of the hostels, it is easy to decide they have been unfaithful. If a boyfriend keeps several girlfriends, thereby being unable to see each of them on a daily basis, he is convinced they are all unfaithful to him. If he hears gossip that a girlfriend has spent an evening in mixed company in his absence, he takes it as proof of her infidelity.

93

To show her his seriousness about their relationship and his attitude toward her "misbehavior" he argues with her or beats her.

Women respond ambivalently to husbands or boyfriends who beat them. On the one hand, they feel ashamed and try to conceal their injuries as best they can, because the conventional interpretation of a beating is that the woman deserves it. The man beats her out of love for her, to "correct" her conduct. When Lillian's boyfriend beat her one time, Agnes comforted her in this way:

> I told her my dear you must not cry like that. You know that he loves you too much and that is the reason he has beaten you. You will see soon he will forget about the whole thing after some few drinks if you just keep quiet.

On the other hand, many feel terrified of beatings, and deeply angry toward the man who beats them. Although they keep up an appearance of normality, as convention requires, they confide their anguish to a trusted woman friend. It is the friend rather than the battered woman who reacts with the expression of hatred they both feel. The confidant tells the victim, while dressing her wounds, that the man's behavior is wrong and cruel. She may bring a measure of emotional relief to the battered woman by describing a violent fantasy in which the man suffers injury at the hands of a woman.

Men use the accusation of infidelity as a weapon for ending relationships. If a girlfriend has been entirely subservient, a model of sexual availability and eagerness to cook, wash, and serve him, it is difficult to find a legitimate reason to leave her if she has also never complained about his infidelities, drunkenness, or lack of support (the typical complaints of women about men). Once she has been accused, there is no way a girlfriend can prove to her boyfriend that she has been faithful. She weeps, pleads, explains, and then may resort to magical means of keeping his interest. It cannot be, she feels, that he could reach this fantastic conclusion on his own accord, since it is so totally without foundation and he is so steadfast in his opinion. It surely must be the work of witchcraft. Some woman has gotten strong medicine from an old woman and stolen his heart. She must do the same:

> Victor discovered Lillian had aborted their second child from a Zambian doctor friend at the hospital who looked up her record as a favor to Victor.
> Lillian had decided on an abortion for the following reasons: Victor had promised to divorce his wife, go to Lillian's relatives to negotiate their marriage, and take her to London where he was posted. Faithful during the year of his absence, awaiting his return, Lillian became discouraged at his inaction and feared having a second child to look after so soon after their first.

94

Victor, who, in addition to his statutory wife and two children also had a second "wife" and child sharing his London flat, beat Lillian, told her she was obviously a whore, and used her abortion as proof of her infidelity. He could not, he said, have a wife who was a whore.

Lillian refused to believe her friends' tales about Victor's London "wife" until he actually divorced his first wife and married the woman. Lillian obtained strong medicines from an old Copperbelt woman.

From Lillian's point of view, the medicines have been at least partially successful. Now that Victor's contract in London has ended, he is back in Lusaka. He has forgiven her for obtaining the abortion, and is now visiting her again, although he does not yet take her out in public. She has accepted the status of second wife for the moment—although the new statutory wife is not yet aware of her status as co-wife. Lillian hopes that when her co-wife finds out about Lillian, she will leave Victor and then Lillian can have him for herself.

Women like Lillian can remain transitional for many years, constantly resisting the temptation to become tough. They continue to look upon tough women with society's damning eyes, refusing to admit the hopelessness of their own positions, continuing to be faithful to their boyfriends, living in the hope that they will be married to them ultimately. They are callous, of course, in their feelings toward the women their boyfriends have taken as wives, for they do not think of themselves as accepting polygyny. They direct their frustrations into socially accepted channels, surrounding themselves in a female world of girlfriends, young sisters, nannies, and their children. They get drunk as often and as quickly as possible. Some, in addition, try to harass the wife.

They fear cheating on their boyfriends, since they think they will get caught. They say, "Here in Zambia we are all one family"—meaning there are spies everywhere and gossip is rife. Since their relationships to their boyfriends are already so fragile, getting caught would be disastrous for them and they believe would end the connection altogether. To be sure a "special" girlfriend does not cheat, a man does in fact have kin and friends spy on her when he is not in a position to watch her because other women are keeping him busy. For example, Lillian and her relatives were convinced that Victor's friends and relatives spied on her.

While subelites usually gravitate to toughness, unmarried elite women tend to be transitionals in their relationships with men. They are very proud of their achievements but at the same time self-conscious about "pricing themselves off the market." They hope to counterbalance career success by acting servile, transforming a lover into a husband. Their servility is flattering for men, whose hatred, fear, and envy can then be hidden beneath a mask of condescension. At a small private dinner party of six, I observed the following interaction between a newly divorced handsome young top elite politician and the top elite single woman who was his mistress:

> She sat at the edge of her chair. He sank into his, putting his feet up on a footstool. He drank continuously. As soon as he came near to finishing a beer, she would immediately get up, walk over to his seat, take the bottle, rush to the kitchen, and get another. The hostess said she would take care of the drinks, as she did for her other guests. The woman told her please not to bother.
>
> She, rather than the hostess who was her close friend, served him dinner, although the hostess had served everyone else. The hostess let it be known that her girlfriend's mother had prepared one of the dishes, a favorite of Zambians, requiring much pounding. "We thought you wouldn't have had this for a long time," they told him.
>
> She listened to his conversation intently. She was the first to laugh at every humorous remark he made. At the same time, she kept her eyes downcast, maintained an air of cultivated modesty. He openly expressed amusement at her nervous willingness to serve him, with pleasure ordered her about, and teased the hostess who was well-known for her views on women's liberation: "You see, my dear, there is no problem with this women's lib for this girl; she knows how to take care of a man."

I was not surprised when he married one of several secretaries with whom he was having affairs. Neither was our hostess. But his mistress was crushed.

Acting tough   The women who emerge toughened from the transitional period become mirror images of the men who brutalized them. They share the same values: sex, drink, money, clothes, and status. They become capable of the same level of predation, lying, and exploitation. They play off one man against another. They are as contemptuous of men as men are of them.

Tough women enjoy taunting men for their lack of sexual power. Quiet, tender, and gentle men who themselves would like a genuine relationship with a woman are often thought to be "like a woman." Women come to expect men to be nasty. Among themselves, tough women describe with delight and satisfaction the fools they make of men. Eva described how, in return for a single act of sexual intercourse that took only a few minutes, she got nearly K100 worth of entertainment, goods, and cash:

> I knew the Prof wanted me when he asked my friend for an introduction. Such an ugly bald thing with that funny red hat! I

didn't want him, so she said no, I was with my boyfriend. It got him very excited.

The next time I told her he should get us at Il Bambino, (N.B., the most expensive restaurant in the downtown area, in the Lusaka Hotel), at lunch time, because I was going to be hungry. He told her of course my dear we'll all go together.

At Il Bambino he said, "Eat up, girls, anything you want, I know you are very hungry." He ordered steaks and champagne for us. So we ate and we laughed. With my friend I begged him for K50 for our rent. "Oh, Prof, we have no money for the rent! Please can you give us?" The poor man, what could he do? "It's all right, of course, of course, but let me go to the bank," he said.

I said to him, "Immediately I knock off work at 16.00 hours

Girl watching. The women cast their eyes downward to indicate modesty. The woman's headscarf is modern acetate; "traditional" women wear wool or cotton headscarves.

meet me outside the office, your car should be there." At 16.00 hours there he was and gave me K50 straight away. I said, "Oh, by the way, my dear, I am still thirsty, buy me some Cinzano," knowing that on the way to the bottle store we would pass some shoes I needed. So he bought me Cinzano and shoes costing K25. At last we went home after some few drinks. We screwed just once and the old fool went away.

To succeed with a mark like the Prof, a woman must discern the man's vulnerable point. If the Prof was made to part with as much cash as Eva claimed, it was because his public role was that of a "big man"— he invented the title "Chief" for himself before his promotion to a professorship—and self-described (to me) "playboy." A "big man" is supposed to throw money around casually: the more he is able to do so the higher is his prestige.

Agnes's mark was different: from a poor background, he painstakingly worked his way up to his present job as sales representative. He was long married to an illiterate woman and was the father of eight. His vulnerable point was simply his lust for the miniskirted young Agnes, whom he had met when doing his rounds of sales. His lust filled Agnes with contempt and she decided to "teach him a lesson."

Every day for a week I made him take me to the Andrews Motel for lunch [N.B., several miles out of Lusaka], where he had to spend K6 per day.

"But when can I come home?" he asked me. Finally I pressed myself against him and said, "Tonight, my dear, bring a crate [i.e., of beer] home and we shall see what is happening to ourselves."

I invited all my friends and we had a very nice time. We danced and we drank all his booze and I made him go for two more crates. Unfortunately the poor gentleman got drunk so we had to put him in the car with the keys on his little thing. The other gentlemen went away. I locked up my house and we went to sleep, because I am just a poor working girl, you know. I need my rest!

The next morning he came in the office as I was at my work. I do not like anybody interfering in my work, and this man started making noise and being very silly. I said, "Very well, I'll go and tell your wife how you have been trying to move with me. I am sure she will be very interested." He changed immediately and said "Oh, no, you must not do that you know I love you but my wife will make trouble for me." I told him to go away. He has not been pestering me recently.

The urban prestige system itself makes men vulnerable marks. Because of the shortage of subelite women it is prestigious for a man to be seen escorting a woman, and sometimes her girlfriend, out for a night on the town and to spend as much money as possible on drinks. The more he spends in this sort of public display the higher his prestige and the prestige of the woman he escorts. Women manipulate the prestige system and so gain the reputation of being expensive and demanding.

Men in public places, bars particularly, are highly vulnerable to manipulation. Women enjoy seeking "revenge" on men by making them pay for expensive drinks. A man in the mood to act "big" offers to buy drinks all around. His offer is the woman's weapon for expressing her feelings for him. If she likes him she orders beer, if she knows buying spirits would be a hardship for him. But if she dislikes him, with smiles of innocence and good humor, she will order an expensive mixed drink—brandy and ginger ale is a favorite—and will sweetly encourage her girlfriends to try the same. When the man informs the waiter of the ladies' order he must be casual, but the waiter and the women laugh as the man excuses himself for a moment and runs to a friend to borrow money to pay for the drinks. Marks are treated as contemptible human beings, easily dismissed from one's life, coming and going by chance.

Boyfriends are another category of person, posing a quite different set of problems from marks. Boyfriends are much more difficult to handle socially and emotionally. The boyfriends are men who, unlike marks, expect women to remain sexually faithful to them regardless of the casualness with which they themselves view the relationship, and despite their own infidelities. A woman cannot easily dismiss as a mark a man who decides she is his girlfriend. Yet women have a strong sense of reciprocity, and will not long tolerate a man who pretends to be a boyfriend but who is casual:

> If he double-crosses me, I double-cross him! Why not? The cheeky thing . . .

The problem for the woman is that she cannot openly express this view unless she does not care about society's condemnation of her immorality, or the possible beating she may receive from the man whose pride has been wounded.

Tough women who have a number of different boyfriends run a risk of being caught. Since visits to the hostels are unplanned, the woman, her roommates, and her neighbors must think fast when two or more boyfriends chance to call on her. A fight may ensue if two lovers of the same woman meet, so experienced women learn to handle the situation with diplomatic aplomb:

> I say, "This is my cousin from the Copperbelt." Or I start wailing, saying, "He has come to tell me the child of my sister is dying." I can say something behind the back of the other to make this one go away.

In the case of my friend I can say she is sick in bed or drunk or visiting a relative so the other boyfriend must just go away. Or I go out to the car and say no, she is angry and cannot see you, or I say she is just asleep.

THE TRAP OF BEING SINGLE

Socially, the typical subelite Zambian townswoman who lives on her own in the hostels is in another no-win situation. Socialized into requiring the company of others, she is incapable of a life of solitary isolation either by values or temperament and is inevitably drawn into the life of the hostels. It is a world that grants her freedom of movement and association in the sense of not having to obey a male guardian. But the very camaraderie and partying of the hostels damns her. A woman who is concerned with her reputation, with being labeled as morally loose, with being the subject of gossip, finds she must either become socially isolated or adapt to a life of trickery, danger, and chance.

Ideally, a woman must be wholesome, going home after work and staying there, visited only by girlfriends and by the man she hopes will marry her. However, the very fact that she lives in a hostel, where she is fair game for men, makes it impossible for her to live in that way. So there is no choice except to hope she won't get caught and to prepare a cover for herself if she is. The fact that she lives in a hostel means that no man will trust her, and that her relationships will almost inevitably be unstable. The hostel environment is, however, neither a necessary nor a sufficient cause of the no-win situation. As we saw in Chapter 2, the roots of the problem are far deeper than geographic residence.

Unmarried elite women face some of these same emotional problems, and socially their position is even worse. They cannot be seen in public dating different men. They must, rather, be models of decorum and dignity, which means non-sexual. The male politician is admired for being a "womanizer," but the unmarried top elite female politician must wear a carefully constructed mask. She is successful so long as she maintains either a non-sexual image or, appearing in public in the company of her male counterparts, that of a compliant and servile woman. She must reassure men she is not a woman's candidate but a people's candidate. Her image must mask the political ambitions that make her more truly the aggressive than the compliant woman. With a non-sexual and compliant mask she is not a threat to male or female voters. Knowing her ambitious side more closely, her male colleagues are more directly threatened by her as a competitor, and gossip viciously about her. The gossip is almost invariably sexual in content. For example, a woman appointed to the Central Committee of the ruling party from a non-political post in a rural area, who happened to be better educated than nearly all the men in the Central Committee, was rumored to have been appointed because she and President Kaunda were having an affair. Male politicians, like male university students, cannot believe that women can achieve greater success than they through merit; only through sleeping with some important man.

The tougher a woman gets, the more she goes against society's values. Ultimately she lives in a way that completely opposes society's image of women, enjoying sexual relationships with men, not wanting children, and valuing the same things men do. At that point she can serve as a scapegoat for all society's ills, for her life style defies the man's image of woman, the traditional woman's image of woman, and the modern married woman's image of woman.

THE COMPENSATION OF BEING SINGLE

Despite all their problems, modern single women consider themselves very lucky indeed when compared to their uneducated contemporaries and to the women of an older generation. They feel they have escaped the fate of village women who, although appearing to be independent, especially in matrilineal societies, are nevertheless tied to childbearing and to the soil. Women in rural Zambia are not simply part of the production process: they are the production process itself. It is their labor that sustains the community, their bodies that reproduce it.

Modern urban women reject the physically arduous role of sustainer that makes village women grow old quickly. They reject bearing an unlimited number of children and abstaining from sexual intercourse for a prolonged period after childbirth. They also are able to reject the life of an uneducated urban housewife, who gets pregnant even more often than her village counterpart, who lives a life of marginal survival, and is seen to be at the mercy of a selfish, brutal, drunken husband with whom she must fight for money for food. Educated women view village women and uneducated urban housewives who can earn no incomes of their own despite a desire to do so as "slaves," feeling a sense of alienation, contempt, and hostility. Zambian women are happy to be working at the professions that have opened to them. Their jobs are the heart of their independence and as long as they remain unmarried, the allocation of their incomes is a source of personal power:

> I wouldn't like to begin giving my salary to a man while my parents and family suffer. . . . I would not like to live under a hawk's eye every day . . . men are very jealous.[6]

SINGLE WOMEN: EMANCIPATED OR OPPRESSED?

Superficially, it is easy to conclude that the single townswoman of the 1970s has freely and courageously chosen a life of emancipation from traditional social controls, full of high fashion, gaiety, and sex. In *Urban Anthropology*, (1974, 108–09), Peter Gutkind wrote:

> If few women are resident in the town it is not unreasonable to suggest that they might be rather particular women, themselves young and unattached, who have recognized the unique position they occupy. They capitalize on this in two ways: either they circulate rather freely among men or they make unions of short duration. What we must not forget is that much of the great transformation which is taking place is clearly seen in the gradual emancipation of women.

Viewed in this way, the hedonistic and financially independent life of the women can be interpreted as a peculiarly urban African manifestation of the women's liberation movement in western countries.

The women have achieved independence of a sort, not being under the direct control of particular individuals. They have escaped from the kind of control usually exerted by male elders and are content to keep visits "home" to a minimum:

> I am like a stranger at home. It is good because at home, people watch you all the time. You are not free to move about as you would like. This is why I prefer Lusaka to the Copperbelt.

They are in a financial and social position to end a relationship with any man who bores or abuses them.

Yet the life of the single Lusaka townswoman does not bear characteristics of emancipation, but rather characteristics of what psychologists Kardiner and Ovesey call a "mark of oppression." The psychologists explain that mistrust and tension are part of what they call "the heavy adaptational load" carried by oppressed people who, because of their oppression, have lost the "capacity for positively toned affectivity" and therefore require "compensatory gratifications."[7]

We have now seen how the women are rootless, restless, and emotionally vulnerable in their young adult lives, as they were in adolescence: changing jobs, towns, clothes, boyfriends, and residences. They are continually frustrated because, despite their fashionable clothes, they have to go from luxurious offices to small, shabby accommodations, "fighting for transport," as they say, to do so. And women are forced to adapt themselves gradually to the attitudes toward male–female roles imposed by a male-dominated, male-oriented society. The typical townsman, married or single, regards modern women as existing for the purpose of serving his biological needs for food and sex, his social need for prestige, and society's demand for teachers, typists, and nurses. Although their services are necessary, the women are not respected.

As young adults, the women see no options leading to a happy and satisfying long-term relationship with a man. The choice is often seen to be between the low probability of a happy marriage and the life of the single, the plaything of men. The single women envy only the prestige, status, and comforts of married elite and subelite women. They do not envy the relationships their married women friends and acquaintances have with their husbands, and are in no hurry to rush into the same sort of nightmare. A case like Susan's shows that a mark is selected for marriage only when a hard-bitten, experienced woman has had enough of independence. And transitional women are mostly interested in men who are substantially better off than themselves. For example, for the year that she was faithful to Victor, Lillian kept up the hope that she would be rewarded by living in London as his statutory wife.

The subelite alternative to early marriage after secondary school is to be drawn into the social life of the hostels, where relationships with men are fraught with uncertainty, anxiety, tension, and suspicion. There is no shortage of men bearing compensatory gratifications: gifts, clothes, money, drinks. But to avoid being assaulted or exploited, the women have to learn how to manipulate men in return, pretending to be invulnerable, until they toughen up and lose the ability to experience love. Show that you love a man, they say, and he will suddenly turn abusive. The hostels resound with the noise of music and laughter, the joking of men and women enjoying a crate of "Castle" beer or a bottle of spirits. But beneath the surface party atmosphere is an unstable and anxious undercurrent born of the exploitation and brutality of the only male company available to the residents.

Young Marrieds' Households

7

Marriage is a three-ring circus:
First the engagement ring,
then the wedding ring . . .
then the suffering.[1]

    The life of an unmarried elite or subelite woman would be less tragic if marriage were seen as a viable alternative. To many of these women, however, the tough life of a single seems preferable to being the wife of a modern Zambian man. A single woman believes she is avoiding the loss of freedom, the loneliness, servitude, brutalization, and certainly the divorce that she has learned to expect of married life.

    Based on my study of married life among elite and subelite women, the apprehension of single women seems justified. We will examine the reasons in three basic and related aspects of the marriage relationship: *the domestic arrangement* of the couple as it appears in household composition, chores performed by husband and wife, allocation of economic resources, wife's employment, and use of leisure; *the issue of authority* within the relationship, whether husband or wife is responsible for decisions about household composition, allocation of resources, wife's employment, and so forth; and, in the next chapter, *the state of the relationship*, its durability, conflicts, tensions, and compensations.[2]

    It should be noted that, for the majority of Zambians, marriage remains a process rather than an event. Whereas in the west a single ceremony unites a man and a woman in wedlock, in traditional Zambian societies it can take a number of years and a number of ceremonies, including the birth of several children, before the union is recognized as a proper marriage by the community. Three broad types of unions are recognized in contemporary Zambia: consensual unions, involving nothing more than cohabitation; traditional marriage, involving marriage under customary laws of a couple's tribe or tribes; and, since independence, marriage under statutory law. The distinctive legal features of statutory marriage are that it is monogamous and that divorce must be obtained in High Court. Customary marriage is polygynous or potentially polygynous, and divorce may be obtained in Local Court. There is a wide behavioral range involving consensual and traditional unions. Because of the fluid and ambiguous nature of marriage as a process, it sometimes happens that one partner to a union considers them married and the other does not. This chapter focuses on women who consider themselves married and whose husbands agree.

STRUCTURE AND AUTHORITY

Decisions have to be reached by the young elite or subelite couple about household size, household chores, allocation of resources, the wife's employment, and leisure time. In Zambia, the elite or subelite husband likes to see himself unambiguously as the household head and the absolute and final authority in his home, even though he might spend few waking hours there.

The combination of a husband's socioeconomic status and his dominant role can completely determine housing and domestic arrangements. A wife can sometimes manipulate the relationship, or operate in secrecy, to gain her wishes. But, in theory, a husband's decision is final and a wife is powerless to impose her will.

Housing   The house in which the couple lives is determined by the nature and rank of the husband's employment. Typically, his house belongs either to the government or to a company, depending on his employer. The type of house is usually assigned according to occupational level, or, in competition for a given house, one's occupational level is one of the weighted factors. As a result, house and socioeconomic status are closely related. The overwhelming majority of middle and high income earning men are not private home owners, although this is a long-range goal for some.

Since housing is determined by husband's employment, it is denied to married women (thus creating difficulties for those who are separated

A new high density subelite area of Lusaka in Kabwata.

or wish to be). Housing for men at the subelite and elite level is spacious. The house itself typically consists of three bedrooms, living room, dining room, and kitchen. Internal construction is a status marker: subelites have concrete floors or tiles if they're lucky; elites have wood parquet. All houses are surrounded by spacious lawns and gardens, the landscaping of which is also a status marker. The maize grown by elites is hidden behind manicured lawns and flowering shrubs and vines; the maize grown by subelites is more obvious from the street. Neighborhoods too mark one's status. Top elites live in Sunningdale, middle elites live in Olympia Park, top subelites in Roma, middle subelites in Northmead.

Household size   While house construction, landscaping, and neighborhood are indices of a man's socioeconomic status, his personal prestige in the eyes of his countrymen—and his own eyes as well—is partly determined by the size of his household. Like the chiefs of another era, a man who can support a large household full of dependents is a proud success in modern urban Zambia. Elite and subelite men complain endlessly about "hangers-on," extended family members who occasionally come around asking for money, for temporary accommodation or for jobs. But in fact men exaggerate the problem and tend to be pleased that they are in a position to dispense or refuse favors. In none of the elite and subelite households I knew in Lusaka could visitors or permanent members be described as poor and uneducated rural-born hangers-on, "sponging off" their relatives while pretending to search for work. The hosting of rural migrants is, in fact, much more common among the urban poor.

Household composition   As soon as a man has a wife to look after the house, he welcomes his relatives on both a transient and more permanent basis. If he is satisfied with his wife, he allows her relatives to live with them also. But he expects her to retain her job to pay for the maintenance of her relatives out of her personal earnings (part of which, in this instance, he allows her to keep). Of twelve couples, five households included members of both the husband's and wife's kin group resident at the time of the interview. Apart from their various children, themselves and their employees, there were an average of 4.5 "other" kin living in a household. A newly married couple often ask their older siblings to give them some school-age children to fill up the empty bedrooms. The following situation evolved in the house next to mine in Northmead:

> Benson, a Tonga, married Godfrieda, a Lozi, at her home in Western Province. Following the traditional Lozi ceremony, they flew back to Lusaka. They took with them three of Godfrieda's nieces and nephews.
> Within a few weeks, Benson's parents arrived from Southern Province, the Tonga home area, to visit the newlyweds and to perform certain Tonga rituals. They brought with them three more school-age children.
> The elders remained for several months before returning to their village. The six children remained with the couple. Benson described them as "very happy" with the arrangements. Godfrieda explained: "It is not our custom to stay alone. There is no problem at all. The Tongas are learning Lozi and the Lozis are learning Tonga."

Young couples enjoy hosting their younger school-age siblings, nieces, and nephews who either live with them and attend a local primary or secondary school or visit for holidays.
    Also included in the newly established household may be the couple's other children by their previous lovers or spouses. Men do not hesitate to take their children away from their natural mothers despite the personal feelings of the people affected. If a man is politically powerful and wealthy, it seems that traditional custody rules are suspended, and women do not feel able to challenge their ex-husbands:

> After 25 years of marriage, a middle-aged top elite Bemba politician divorced his old Bemba wife, who had borne nine children, in order to marry a young educated woman.
> The old wife, by custom, should have had custody of the children. But the woman was uneducated and had no independent income. The man was wealthy and politically powerful, since he worked closely with President Kaunda.
> Over his old wife's objections, the man took their two youngest children to live in his lavish Sunningdale home. The new

wife took care of them. The old wife kept the older children, some of whom were nearly the age of the new wife. They lived in a low-income council house in Kabwata.

The man bought his old wife a grocery store and felt she had no grounds for complaint. She would not think of bringing the case to court because of their relative positions in society. All she could do was to hate and blame the young wife for causing her misery. The man had been unfaithful to her all their married life: this young woman must surely have bewitched the man to force him to marry her.

The "rule" is that the man's wishes are paramount. Regardless of their educational achievements, many women feel too powerless and too distant from their families, who could theoretically be supportive, to challenge the men. In the case of a young top Bemba politician:

The ex-wife was a non-Zambian African unable, for political reasons, to return to her homeland. The husband and his new young Zambian wife were not interested in keeping his two children by the first wife. The ex-wife wanted to give up the children, at least for a time until she could get established on her own.

The ex-wife lost her job when her ex-husband threatened her employer. When she tried to date other men, her ex-husband sent strongmen to beat up her dates. She became highly nervous and depressed.

She managed to obtain a council hostel and survived through prostitution. Following the death of her youngest child, the ex-husband began taking the remaining child to school every day and giving his ex-wife money for food.

The new wife sometimes prefers leaving her children by other men in the care of her own mother instead of bringing them into the new household. She fears her attractiveness to the new spouse might be diminished if he is daily made aware of the evidence of his wife's past liaisons. Sometimes too the new wife, desiring to make a fresh start, wants no reminders of previous men in her life:

The woman had two daughters aged eight and nine when the father of her year-old son proposed marriage. The woman, a typist, visits her daughters about once a month. They live with her mother in Libala, a middle-income African township in Lusaka.

She and her elite husband live in Sunningdale, in a big empty house. But she will not have her daughters live with her. She did not allow them roles in her lavish white wedding. She will fill up the house with this husband's children, she says. At the wedding the flower girls were her husband's young nieces.

No matter how westernized the couple thinks they are, many still "work hard to make a baby" as quickly as possible, and become worried and depressed if a pregnancy does not develop within the first few months of their sexual relationship. A successful union soon comes to include a new couple's children.

The depth of feeling that a good marriage should include a large household of dependents and closely spaced children of a new couple is most obvious in interracial marriages between Zambian women and white men. These marriages take on a distinct African flavor, as in the following case:

> On the marriage of Gyles and Salina, English and Namwanga administrative officers in the same company, their household included his daughter by a previous marriage, his temporarily unemployed male friend, her nephew, a school-age child from the Copperbelt, and an elderly couple from Salina's home area in the North, who had come for the wedding.
> The elderly couple and Gyles's friend left after a few months. Salina's girlfriend and her baby then moved in. Just under a year after the wedding Salina bore their first child. When the baby was 18 months old, Salina became pregnant again.

Age-mates of the husband or wife are frequent visitors to the household, and sometimes stay on for months. Although wives fear potential sexual involvement between their husbands and their friends or female relatives, they find it difficult to refuse a woman in trouble, so women who quarrel with their husbands take their small babies and stay with their friends or their kin. Children on school holiday, adolescents between jobs or training programs or for some other reason without personal accommodation, also join households. Husbands too bring in friends and relatives in similar situations. Households I knew contained age-mates of one or the other spouse but never of both. That would be asking for trouble because of resulting inevitable sexual tensions. Most of these age-mates are self-supporting. In special cases the household supports them temporarily.

Older relatives of both husband and wife must be welcomed regardless of personal feelings. If the elderly person is closely related there is a strong moral imperative, leaving no choice. Temporary accommodation is offered for those seeking hospital treatment in Lusaka, visiting other relatives in the hospital, or visiting to participate in a marriage or funeral ritual. Sometimes an old woman will arrive when her daughter (real or classificatory) is about to give birth. (A classificatory daughter is a female defined as a daughter according to a tribe's rules of classifying kin.) Of twelve households that were formally interviewed, only one had a permanent older member: the husband's mother. Another couple lived temporarily in a farm compound belonging to the husband's father while building their own home. It is rare to find households with permanent members older than the male head.

Household chores   Most household chores are performed by servants or young female relatives of the husband or wife. Any chores left over are supposed to be done by the wife. It is ironic that secondary education for women has come to mean that now they must do western-style housework like ironing and mending their husband's clothes. In colonial days, such work was done by the men in town. Western-style education, as we have seen, was to "uplift" African women so that they would learn western styles of homecraft. It has come to mean that if no servant is available wives get to do the chores that townsmen used to do for themselves. To reinforce the new trend, newspapers carry European-style women's features on childcare and recipes. Married career women, interviewed in newspapers as female pioneers in their professions, are often described in headlines as housewives. In this way, "progress" has come to mean that a woman takes full responsibility for running the household. Her husband is uninvolved except possibly as her driver to and from the supermarket.

There are rare instances in which a husband helps his wife with this "women's" work. He irons his clothes as men used to do in colonial times; he helps bathe a baby. Of the twelve households, one 23-year-old wife, recently married and the mother of twins, explained how her "elderly" husband, 36 years of age, helped her, when they both came home from work, with diapers and baths for their sons. A young Northmead couple, neighbors of mine, also shared tasks on the birth of their twins. A married female university student told me her husband was happy and eager for her to live in Lusaka for three years on a course while he stayed in Luanshya, a Copperbelt town, with their two small children. In her second year at the university, she was suspended indefinitely for her participation in student political activity, to her husband's annoyance. Yet two years later she was back again, quietly completing her course, avoiding student politics. She had used the interval to have another baby.

Husbands often allow their wives to leave the home to take courses in other towns. Long separations can indicate either complete role segregation and a shallow emotional relationship, so that the wife can be temporarily replaced by one or more other women, or it can indicate a deep understanding existing between a couple. When a woman feels the latter is the case, she expresses gratitude:

> My husband, who is deputy head of Munali Boys Secondary
> School, understands my passion for television. He is quite happy
> for me to go overseas for six months and leave him with the
> children.

He is wonderful and doesn't ever stand in my way. He always encourages me and I am grateful for that. . . .

I like him to watch my programmes so that he can give his opinion. He will always speak his mind without flattery. He doesn't spare me at all.

When I come home from studio, worn out from working, he makes me a cup of coffee and settles me down to rest. Most men wouldn't go out of their way to make a woman feel good like that.

I'm all for equal rights for women. . . . My job is just as demanding as my husband's and we share the burden of rearing the children.

Take the average family. The man expects his wife to work. But after work he also expects to sit down with the papers while she makes supper, bathes the children and does housework. . . . And it just isn't fair. . . .

Women are liberating themselves slowly. . . . They will shake off the yoke of the past.[3]

The companionship and equality described by this television personality in her marriage is obviously unusual. I personally have never observed anything even vaguely approaching it among other Zambian couples. It may exist in Zambia and elsewhere, but I myself have not seen it. It seems to me that it is precisely this type of true equality and sharing toward which some activists in the Women's Liberation Movement aim, but seldom achieve. In fact Cicewa, the Zambian television personality in the interview above, was in the process of divorcing her husband when I left Zambia in 1975.

WIFE'S EMPLOYMENT

Many Zambian women, old and young, rich and poor, uneducated or university trained, say they want to earn money for themselves. The poor, with no education, seldom find institutional support for earning legitimate incomes. In contrast, women with education are pushed out of the home by their domestic situations and pulled out by social forces in the wider society.

The push out of the home   The overriding motivation of married women in wanting employment is to combat the insecurity of marriage. Women feel they must depend on their own resources in the event of marital breakdown. And marital breakdown is likely, judging by Zambian statistics on divorce. A Lusaka lawyer quipped to me: "Why bother writing about marriage? Why not just write about divorce?"

Three additional forces help push women out of their homes and into the job market. The most compelling issue is boredom. At home, women rarely think of things to do. The housewife does no physical labor: she orders servants about instead. Male servants work in the house and rainy-season garden, and a young female takes care of the pre-school children. Most women own or wish to own a sewing machine, and they enjoy making dresses for themselves. But fabric is costly and women are limited in the amount of money they can spend on it, especially if they rely on their husbands for cash. They cannot sew enough to keep boredom at bay. I never met wives genuinely interested in expanding their knowledge of or skill in cooking, possibly because of the absence of enthusiasm from husbands more committed to drinking than eating. There is also little interest in decorating the home. Except for a vase of plastic flowers, embroidered cotton cloths covering furniture, and an old calendar or cross on the wall, most homes are bare of decor. The reading ability of most women is very limited and reading material is scarce, so this activity cannot occupy housewives. Nor are most women interested in joining existing charity-oriented voluntary associations. Finally, because Lusaka sprawls and has practically no public transportation, it is only with great difficulty that a housewife can visit her friends or relatives unless her husband drives her. The result is that after spending three months home on maternity leave, women are eager to return to their jobs.

Wives are also lonely because they spend most evenings alone, while their husbands are out drinking. To combat loneliness, some are able to obtain their husbands' permission to take night courses. Two or three evenings a week, a clerk will take typing lessons, a typist stenography. Husbands drive their wives to their courses and pick them up afterwards. In the interval the husbands drink with their friends. Wives often obtain permission to take courses by convincing their husbands of the advantages of increased earning power, appealing to the men's greed while plotting a means of escaping from them. Husbands are sympathetic to the idea that their wives will earn more money, and so will cost them less. Husbands are also agreeable because this way they are sure that their wives are not having illicit love affairs, at least during class hours.

The separation of childbearing from child-rearing is another factor making it easy for women to have careers outside the home. Women are not committed to personally raising the children they bear—despite the endless complaints that servants cannot be trusted, and the worry that their children are being neglected. Zambian mothers all come from cultures that emphasize the importance of extended family ties. One of the results of this emphasis is the lack of a moral or cultural imperative that a woman should raise her own children. Traditionally a woman's prestige comes from the sheer number of children she bears, although this is changing. Whether or not her children become successful in life is rarely seen as reflecting, even in part, the type of mothering she offers, even among educated Zambians. Women experience no conflict between career and mothercraft. Children grow up anyway. The attitude is that a child's future success depends on school performance, and parents do not believe they have anything to do with what happens to a child in school.

A woman who wants to stop work temporarily because she has a number of small children is more often motivated by a desire to rest than by any desire to raise them personally. Sometimes children come close upon each other, and there are three or four pregnancies in five to seven years. In between maternity leaves, the woman continues to work. Under these circumstances, she can become irritable and physically run down. In some such cases, she continues to work, only because she feels she has no choice.

The final push out of the home is the need for money. Marriages may begin cooperatively with the wife working to help purchase luxury items and even to pay toward the wedding costs. "Keeping up with the Bandas" is a conspicuous feature of life as educated Zambians look for cars, clothes, furniture, stereos, cameras, and appliances with which to impress their friends and co-workers.

The need for money becomes acute when the husband exercises his control over the allocation of income to deny his wife support for herself and the children. If he has allowed his wife to work, he feels that his obligations to her are fulfilled by allowing her to live in his home rent-free. Typical examples of the husband as non-provider to his wife were three young couples living in a row of company flats in my Northmead neighborhood: Davis and Esnat, Goodfellow and Lucy, and Henry and Kathryn. The men were white-collar workers for the national airline. Two of the wives were typists, the third a nurse. All three husbands were "men about town." Davis "played" randomly, but Goodfellow and Henry had regular girlfriends, Agnes and Eufrazia. Henry promised to marry newly divorced Eufrazia as soon as he got "rid of" Kathryn and the baby. These men derive prestige from personal public display rather than buying luxury goods for the home. The fashionable Goodfellow, for example, bought himself two gold rings and a watch on his trip to London. He also bought a wig and two dresses for Agnes. But his home was devoid of personal effects; the flat was furnished by the airline. A subelite on a salary of K200 per month can spend K25 for a night on the town and go home to a shabbily clad, sad wife and children to whom he has not given even a small coin (*ngwee*) for food. In a letter to "Soul Sister Says," the lovelorn column of the *Times of Zambia*, "Worried Housewife, Chingola" expresses a common thought of wives caught in this situation:

> Does this apply to my fellow married women who are working? Does their husbands not buy them clothes because they are also working? What can I do? What would happen if I was not

working? Was I going to eat? I don't know. What can I do with
this unreasonable husband?

To this wife, the husband seems callous. But he may feel a moral responsibility to support, more or less regularly and more or less willingly, his
kin. In her letter to "Soul Sister Says," "Worried Housewife, Chingola"
reports the following conversation:

> *She:* Why do you not want to buy me some clothes or shoes?
>
> *He:* You are also working, don't trouble me. Above all you
> are not my relative. I am supposed to look after my fam-
> ily and not you.
>
> *She:* I didn't know that my fellow women are married to their
> relatives. If I knew before, I would also have been mar-
> ried to my brother.

The Chingola housewife then writes that the conversation is followed by
a beating from her husband. She continues:

> He can't one day realize that I am the one troubled by cooking for
> him every day but his relatives come just to collect money but
> they don't cook him food. . . . The whole of my salary is spent on
> food.
>
> I haven't banked any money, but my husband has a lot of
> money in the bank. What can I do?
>
> He can't realize that when he feels sex he doesn't go to his
> relatives but he comes to me. He can't realize that I'm the one
> looking after him. He regards me as his wife the time we make
> love but not buying me clothes.
>
> He can't realize that he is to think of his new family, but he
> always receives advice from his unthinkable relatives who are
> leading him in a bad way.

Failure to support an economically dependent wife and children at
a level commensurate with income is commonplace in all levels of society.
A common response to an increase in income is not to improve the standard of living of one's wife and children—as the wife would expect—but
to become promiscuously involved with other women, fathering children
as a non-essential byproduct.

The problem of emotional and financial neglect has its roots primarily in the developments of the colonial period, not in the older societal
traditions. It does not really derive from a conflict between a man's loy-
alty to his matrikin and his wife: today he is not loyal to his wife, so there
is no conflict. His matrilineage is not a property-holding group, so there
is no conflict there. Nor is neglect due to an assertion of the old idea of
polygyny, because men are not regularly, responsibly, and reliably sup-

porting several women. Similarly, mode of descent and inheritance reckoning is not a critical factor: West African Efik, Ibo, and Ewe husbands in Lusaka, all patrilineal peoples, are also neglectful of their wives.

What is more, neglect is not necessarily a sign of the imminent breakdown of a marriage. Some marriages go on in this way for years. Informants who said they were suffering terribly from neglect by their husbands did not plan to initiate divorce proceedings—yet. The general consensus seemed to be that a woman waits until she can no longer bear the abuse—while gradually advancing in her career. Unless her husband divorces her first, she stays married until she can maintain a relatively high standard of living on her own. There are, of course, cases in which a neglected wife becomes the lover of a married man who in turn neglects his wife, who takes a lover. After years of intrigue, lovers may marry each other. These cases arise at all income levels and are the subject of much humorous gossip.

Pull of the wider society   Factors outside the marriage also contribute to a wife's desire for employment. In this regard, four factors seem to be important. The first is the ease with which qualified Zambians can obtain and hold onto jobs in an era of Zambianization.

The second factor is the surplus of women. There are more adult women in Zambia than men, more divorced or separated women than men, more widows than widowers. Statistically, women marry young and spend part of their lives single: neither remarriage nor polygyny is a general pattern. The feeling that marriage is insecure is clearly demonstrated by census figures. Women know that the chances of remarriage are not favorable. Thus, even after she is married, a woman knows that her personal security is more genuinely obtained through employment than through marriage. The women are very practical. Today they speak of "wasting" their education by not working, in the same way that women years ago felt they were "wasting" their fertility if men were not available to impregnate them.

Third, educated women are expected to support dependent relatives. Although such support normally amounts to only a small percentage of their earnings, in some cases it can come to much more. With pride, some women told me they built homes for their widowed or divorced mothers. They give their mothers pocket money to pay men to clear their village gardens. Schoolgoing relatives get pocket money, clothes, transport, and boarding costs paid. One interviewee was the sole support of her mother and sisters. The sisters had all been expelled from secondary school after becoming pregnant by men who refused to marry them.

Fourth, a housewife is completely helpless if her husband dies suddenly. If a woman works, at least she can continue to feed and clothe herself and her children, whom she may want or have to keep (rather than giving them to her husband's relatives). She can also buy things her late husband's relatives have stripped her of. All too frequently, young husbands are killed in car accidents. Owning neither land nor a house, they have never seen any point in making a will. Their movable assets are the only consumer items they and their wives have bought, and the relatives take all these away. The shock of their husband's death and their horror at the avarice of his relatives at this time make the majority of women too numb to prevent the loss of property even when they have jointly contributed toward its purchase. Women's own relatives rarely become involved in fighting on their behalf. Women's jobs thus become the key to survival with a measure of dignity.

> Karen's breast milk dried up, endangering her month-old baby's life; she grew thin, wan and listless, totally unresponsive, which was a great personality change, following the death of her husband in a car accident.
> Her husband's relatives accused her of bewitching him, thereby causing the accident. They took all his assets, their older children, and even her clothes which she had bought with her own earnings as a secretary. Five months after the accident, however, she moved to a new town, got a new job, and appeared more her old self.

Husbands' attitudes Husbands are either for or against allowing their wives to work. The leitmotif of a man's attitude is control. A man who is "for" has confidence that he can control his wife. He is also able to control his own sexual fears and jealousy. The man "against" is convinced his wife will not be able to resist sexual involvement with men she meets on the job. He cannot imagine his wife refusing a richer, more handsome or younger man than he, or his equal or inferior who can perhaps give her greater sexual satisfaction than he is capable of.[4]

The sexual fear has a basis. The sexual advances on women by employers and work colleagues, described in Chapter 5, occur without regard for a woman's marital status or her reaction, and it is a rare married woman who has not been subjected to sexual advances on the job. Also, the husband is fully aware of what goes on at workplaces since the chances are that he has played the male role of being sexually demanding and aggressive to his female workmates. While it is true that some men are by nature shy and some women aggressive, the personalities of particular individuals do not seem an effective counterbalance to fears based on stereotyped images of role playing.

Female gossip plays on men's fears. Female friends love to gossip about possible infidelities of their married workmates. In one office, a new bride who often took two-and-a-half-hour lunch breaks was assumed to be meeting a lover. The story went around that her husband's sterility caused the break-up of his first marriage, since his relatives thought his wife was barren. In order to ensure the support of the man's relatives for her marriage, the new bride wanted to become pregnant and secured a lover, whom she met at lunch hour, for the purpose. When in fact she became pregnant, the husband, theory went, was trapped by his need to sustain his image and pretended the situation was normal.

Events sometimes confirm gossip. In another office a pretty young woman's workmates thought she was unmarried, since a handsome young man she introduced as her boyfriend picked her up at lunch time every day. One day she did not come to work. Late in the morning a distraught-looking elderly man came into the office looking for her. Told she hadn't come in for the day, he broke down and wept. He was her husband, he said. She had run away the night before, following a quarrel. But first she dismissed their servants and left him alone with their three children. It was now evident to the workmates that she planned an elopement with her boyfriend.

Sometimes, it would seem, opposition to a wife's desire to work reveals the vulnerability of the relationship and the fragility of a man's ego. The case of Eddie and Lillian suggests such an interpretation:

> Five years ago, on finishing Form V, Lillian agreed to live with Eddie. Eddie was ten years her senior and therefore not a "small boy." He had a good job with Zambia Railways. They now have two children.
>
> Eddie describes Lillian as a "wonderful girl." He says he loves her very much, because she has great patience with him and never complains either about his drinking or about his other girlfriends. Nevertheless, she is still "on trial" and he cannot marry her. A problem has arisen. Now that their second child is weaned, Lillian wants to take a job.
>
> The couple lives in Kafue, a rapidly developing line-of-rail industrial town thirty miles south of Lusaka. A number of women commute from Kafue to Lusaka daily to work in offices, for as yet there are few job opportunities for women in Kafue.
>
> Eddie feels that if Lillian commutes, she will inevitably meet men and have sexual affairs. "I am Governor of the house, mate, and if Lillian wants to keep up with me she can't work in Lusaka. She has to choose: me or the job. She can't have both. Finito."

It is tempting to speculate that cool, fashionable Eddie feared that Lillian would seek revenge on him for his extramarital affairs. He happily described, for example, how "beautifully behaved" Lillian was when one of his girlfriends stopped her on the street and insulted her and later came to their house threatening to beat Lillian up. Her calm in the face of the other woman's attack was, he said, one of the reasons he loved her so. What kind of love is this, however? Can a woman who must commute sixty miles to work daily, work on an 8-to-5 schedule (8 to 1 on Saturdays), and care for her home and children, actually have *time* for an affair? Is Eddie so weak underneath the bravado that he fears the lunch hour— when many working wives who do not go home for lunch go shopping after eating a quick snack?

ALLOCATION OF RESOURCES AND AUTHORITY

"Easy, baby, to write about how husbands and wives use the money. He takes everything and drinks it up." So says a young Lusaka divorcee, a telex typist.

A secretary complains: "We live very poorly. We can't afford much." Yet this woman and her husband have a combined income of K825 a month.

Another typist, wife of a building contractor, says:

Sometimes I am able to keep some money. But if he takes it I can't refuse. If I complain, it's just looking for trouble. I just obey.

The statements of these women give some clues to how the resources of a married couple in Lusaka are allocated, and by whom.

In 1972, the combined incomes of husbands and wives ranged from about K200 per month for the lowest marginal subelites to something in the neighborhood of K1500 (of legally declared income) for top elites. A few earned much more, and the masses much less. The urban poverty line was supposed to be around K50 per month, but most unskilled workers earned about K28. The average combined income of my sample of twelve married couples was K541 per month.

The life style of elites in particular, and to a lesser extent subelites, was heavily subsidized by the government. The higher a man's occupational level, the greater the number of perquisites. Rent, for example, was heavily subsidized by the employer and therefore consumed only 12 percent of the income. On the open market rent would have consumed most of a subelite couple's income. Government and company cars were privately used as a matter of course, whether for driving children to school or going to out-of-town bars. Of benefit to all Zambians, particularly in town, were free schooling and medical services and government subsidies for urban food staples: maize meal, milk, break, and sugar. Taxes, rent, and sometimes insurance were deducted from monthly salaries, the remainder of which were sent by the payroll office to one's bank account. Water, electricity, and installment bills were the main items of household maintenance that consumers had to pay on their own.

After meeting basic expenses, there was a large surplus of cash. For example, in one fairly typical case of a subelite couple interviewed, the combined monthly income was K618. Their basic monthly expenses totalled K288 by the wife's accounting. Table I considers the recurrent expenses of this typical subelite couple with three small children.

Because the surplus was great, income management became an important issue. The greater the surplus the greater the number of decisions to be made, with more scope for conflict of interest and expression of a wide range of preferences.

Tribal affiliation does not seem to influence control over allocation of income. That is, women from matrilineal societies do not have separate accounts from their husbands unless their husbands specifically tell them they should. Seven of the twelve wives in the sample were from matrilineal societies and five of these kept joint bank accounts with their husbands. Of the three remaining women from patrilineal societies, two kept joint accounts and one kept separate accounts. Thus, of twelve couples, wives kept separate accounts in only three cases and in all these the husband had suggested it.

Whether a husband chooses to control the management of the income alone or in consultation with his wife, whether or not she feels free to spend her own earnings without asking him or keep money in defiance of his wishes, seems to depend on personality factors rather than cultural norms for conjugal responsibilities.

Tonga local court members gave a range of opinions that covered virtually all possibilities for the allocation of a wife's earnings:[5]

1. Husband and wife should share a wife's earnings including savings accounts even on the dissolution of marriage.

2. During marriage the wife should apply a portion of her earnings to her own maintenance, but on dissolution of the marriage she should be entitled to any accumulated savings without sharing with her husband.

3. Husband should control all earnings of his wife as head of the house.

4. Wife should control all her own earnings.

In another instance, a wealthy Bemba mother advised her newly married daughter to secretly bank a portion of the housekeeping money given to her by her elite husband. But a young Bemba typist told me she counted herself lucky to get any money at all from her spouse for herself and their three children.

Sometimes when a husband does not allow his wife to work and must, therefore, provide food in addition to shelter, he provides only in the most minimal way. In extreme cases, a man does not trust his wife with any money at all, but instead brings her food. A young uneducated housewife I interviewed in a study of poor women asked me how she could get birth control pills. After explaining the procedure I said it cost K1.00.

Table I

Recurrent Expenses of
A Typical Subelite Couple, Lusaka, 1972

Item	Kwacha per month	Comments
House rent	20	
Electricity	15–20	
Water	20	high because wife grows own vegetables
Servants:		
Nanny	8	
Cook	25	
Assistant Cook	12	
Food:		
Groceries (staples)*	50	seems grossly underestimated
Meat	28	
Market produce: chicken, fish, vegetables	20	
Savings	30	wife says couple involved in "special friendship" with Yugoslav expatriates involving currency exchange
Support of relatives	30	
Transport (private car)	30	
TOTAL**	K288	

*This includes maize meal, bread, sugar, milk, eggs, salt, and tea. Subelites buy few "European" foods, and consequently keep food costs down. The budget does not include beer.

**Items missing in this budget are entertainment, use of private doctors (which most subelites prefer), clothes, and other "luxury" elements. The expenses and income of the couple were probably higher than the wife was aware. The "special friendship" was with a building contractor whom the wife said "buys us beautiful things from Europe" and was eventually to build the couple's permanent home.

120

She had been sure she could forge a letter from her husband granting her permission to get the pills (a requirement at the University Teaching Hospital Clinic). But after hearing it would cost K1.00 she despaired. Her husband, she said, literally never gave her money. If he was planning to stay away from her for more than three days, he would give her exactly the amount she would need to buy greens and tomatoes for relish: "Five *ngwee* five *ngwee* five *ngwee*," she said. Another uneducated housewife whose husband would not let her work asked if I could give her a loan of twenty *ngwee*. With this money she planned to walk downtown, some eight miles away, and buy white crochet cotton, with which she would secretly make *madoilies* (antimacassars) and start a "business" without her husband knowing. Sufficiently desperate for cash, such women are obviously tempted to prostitute themselves when their husbands are away.

Typically, couples feel they never have enough money. A husband has either saved long months or gone heavily into debt to marry in the most up-to-date manner. He and his wife share expenses and the hunger for consumer items. The wife, as anxious as he to "keep up with the Bandas," defers to her husband's wishes in regard to making major purchases, whether or not she has kept her job. The husband decides if she is to retain her earnings or bank them jointly with him, and what her earnings are to pay for if he allows her to keep them.

Wives differ in the degree to which they submit to their husband's authority. No wife admitted she would buy things against her husband's wishes, openly or even secretly. At most, the wives would insist that their husbands should act "reasonably" and not refuse permission to buy something the wife wanted without giving a sound reason. A few said they felt free to buy small things, like underwear, on their own. Others emphasized that if their husbands drank heavily, they would not have agreed to keep joint accounts. Although not all women are as submissive as it might seem on the surface (just as not all men are as dictatorial as it would outwardly appear), it is clear that the Zambian situation is quite unlike that which apparently exists in West Africa. Zambian women have not yet achieved the level of self-confidence or the degree of sophisticated duplicity that enables so many West African women, who came from long traditions of independent female entrepreneurship, to keep separate accounts and to lead double lives.

In cases in which wives kept separate accounts, they obeyed husbands who "directed" them to use their earnings for certain recurrent household expenses. The Zambian wife was most often expected to provide food, money for servants, and clothing for herself and the children. Some wives, like some girlfriends the "playboys" call "sugar mammies," said they enjoyed buying their husbands' clothing from their salaries. This was meant as a sign of devoted love.

121

No wife worked exclusively for her own pocket money, and none kept a savings account with the idea of investing toward buying either property or a business of her own. Because their salaries were normally much less than their husbands' and they had to contribute toward the home and the support of relatives, the women found they were not able to save much of their personal income. A tiny number of elite Zambian women, mainly wives of diplomats who have lived abroad, began returning home in the mid 1970s to start businesses of their own. This may ultimately start a trend.

LEISURE

Leisure activities after work and at weekends are normally sexually segregated. Ordinarily, husbands spend several evenings a week, and sometimes whole weekends, drinking at bars, parties, or receptions around town. At such times they expect their wives to stay at home, awaiting their return. On the few weekday evenings when the husband is home, he tends to drink and watch television.

Top elite couples are sometimes required to attend formal government or business receptions together. In 1972–73 it had not yet become fashionable for a man to escort a girlfriend rather than a wife on these occasions, nor were prostitutes provided, as happens, for example, in Lagos, Nigeria, or Kinshasa, Zaire. Undoubtedly, President Kaunda's strong Christian morality acts as a brake on this development. Nightclubs, bars, and lesser formal and informal social functions are normally attended by men alone. Usually only a small number of women are present at public gatherings. Men go to gossip and drink, although they are not averse to an unexpected sexual adventure, should the opportunity arise. At most gatherings, women have no place except to be "decorative and make drinking interesting," according to one "man about town."

Some elite couples maintain open house on weekend afternoons. The husband's or wife's friends and relatives visit. Served by servants, children, or the wife, in that order of preference, they drink and gossip about people and politics.

Few subelite men would normally consider either spending evenings at home or taking wives out on an evening. Like the elites, these men have no personal interests, chores, or hobbies that would keep them at home. "Drinking is my hobby," they say. Husbands and wives rarely have mutual friends and they rarely go out together to movies, restaurants, sports events, or even to visit relatives or friends. Very few belong to the same religious denomination and still fewer attend church together. In the courtship stage, many men teach their fiancees to drive a car. Thus, skill

122

acquired in a companionate activity of courtship serves as one means of positive assertion of independence after marriage.

In defense of their predilection for segregated leisure, men often note that their wives prefer staying at home to attending public functions with their husbands. On a certain level this is quite true. When wives accompany husbands to parties, they tend to sit quietly for hours, sipping soft drinks, and then, apparently bored, ask their husbands to take them home two or three hours before the end of the party. Their excuse is usually fear for their children. Quarrels sometimes erupt between couples because the husband wants to remain.

Since wives do not normally attend nightclubs, their reluctance to attend parties and their boredom at the few they do attend might be surprising. But their behavior becomes understandable in the context of the extreme limitations on them in their rare public appearances. A wife can accept a dance from a man other than her husband only at the risk of being accused of planning an infidelity. If the party is western and all the music and dancing is western, a wife must sit and wait until her husband or a man he approves of—possibly her brother—decides to get her to dance.

The suspicion and jealousy of a husband can be irrational. For example, a painfully thin, sickly, 33-year-old remarried divorcee, who managed a house of nine children, held an office job, and suffered from a recurrent kidney infection, was only permitted by her husband to dance with her brother and himself.

Given these restrictions, while their husbands chat with men, dance with single women, and drink beer after beer, wives tend not to enjoy themselves. Therefore they put a damper on evenings out. The bind for a woman is that if she rejects the wallflower role, she is labeled as loose and is an embarrassment to her husband. There will in fact be men who become very aroused by the fact that she has accepted a dance and they will press against her body in an effort to arouse her. Knowing this, her husband will be very angry if he sees her dancing with another man. Yet he will also be angry with her for getting bored when he is having a good time. Gossip is her only outlet.

Women dislike their husbands going out alone, for they know that men are always ready for a chance sexual encounter. Hence wives who do not accompany their husbands also live in a state of perpetual jealousy, worry, and suspicion. Sometimes this gets transformed into nagging and hostility, which, when unfounded, angers the husband and results in a beating and further alienation.

A number of writers have noted that the uneducated, unemployed wife migrating to town from an African village had relatively little housework to do compared with her rural life of toil. Many wives used their long leisure hours for sexual adventures when their husbands were away at work. This was certainly the case in the poor areas of Lusaka in which I did fieldwork. It was supposed to be secret, but there was playful gossip among watchful neighbors.

The modern professional woman works at a career by day. Although she has servants, there are still things she must do herself in running the house. She has less leisure time than the uneducated townswoman. Arriving at home from work in the evening, she tends to the housekeeping and childcare chores she deems necessary, prepares food for herself and her husband, and leaves it for him since he is out drinking. Late in the evening she may sew, knit, glance at a love or fashion magazine, watch television, and then go to sleep, for she must be at work by eight the next morning. Her husband comes home and wakes her up to serve him food and have sex.

Unless a woman happens to be hosting a girlfriend or adult relative of whom she is fond, her life is socially isolated. Unlike wives in high-density areas who have intensive contact with neighbors living only a few yards away, wives in low-density neighborhoods do not have such interactions. Their homes are separated from those of their neighbors by extensive lawns and gardens surrounded by high chicken-wire fences and locked gates. There is no street lighting in residential neighborhoods; the dark of the night is formidable and people do not venture out of their homes for a walk or to visit next door. The German shepherd guard dogs that most elites and higher subelites keep to patrol their gardens are an additional deterrent.

The wives do not have to be inspired by the Women's Liberation Movement or have romantic or extreme notions of companionate marriage to feel painfully lonely, neglected, and desperate. The following letter to "Soul Sister Says" is typical of a type sent by wives:

> I am a married lady with four children my problem is my husband is too movious he never takes me out not even a day, he always comes very late in the morning hours. You try to ask him the answer is why should you ask me where I go it has no use to you. When I try to continue asking him you will here [sic] you can just go if you want.
>
> I am every [sic] lonely as a single lady no time to chat with my husband he is every busy chating [sic] with other ladies not the wife.
>
> I just support myself and children from my poor pay. He never clothes children all my problems are in my hands, and whenever I get my pay he wants me to take all of it to him, but I don't do that I just support myself and my children from it.
>
> Tell me sister what to do I am ever lonely I am never happy with all this, all what I do is to wait for him when he comes and

open for him at the late hours in the morning. I am very much worried because I am pregnant I don't know how I will entertain myself tell me please before I run mad.

Worried Mother, Lusaka

With almost no social life at home, with a job, a program of studies, and a husband who would neither notice nor appreciate efforts made in homecraft, the center of activity for some wives comes to be as completely outside the home as their husbands'. In contrast to the liveliness and bustle of the hostels, the homes of many elite and subelite married couples are somber and bleak, despite the presence of many children.

The children are left very much on their own. They are raised largely by servants whom they do not respect and who dare not discipline them. Primary school teachers often complained to me that the greatest learning and discipline problems they encountered were among children of elite parents. A West African psychologist whose son flung his toys at visitors remarked at how "naughty" town children are compared to village children. A British pediatrician, practicing six years in Zambia, said on the basis of her experience that malnutrition and infant mortality rates are at least as high or higher among elites and subelites as among the urban poor.

State of the Marriage Relationship

8

The fear of marriage expressed by the single women seems entirely justified. Marriages typically are a nightmare. They have almost no chance of survival. The situation seems pathological, not only to an outsider but to the people themselves. African politicans, lawyers, doctors, psychiatrists, journalists all have their theories about what they call the "social crisis" of Zambian male-female relationships, and they freely analyze the causes of marital discord and the resulting side effects of unstable marriages. Endless articles and broadcast talk shows discuss the causes of instability. Social and psychological problems are attributed to marital discord; for example, suicide and mental breakdowns requiring hospitalization are both said to be increasing along with divorce rates.[1] The non-intellectuals simply despair. "But why do they crack?" an unmarried typist cried to me as a couple took their vows at a wedding we attended.

One is struck not only by the fragility of marriage but by the women's desperation, anxiety, and insecurity. "If you are going to write about marriage, you *must* write about how Zambian women are suffering these days," a married typist told me. Such emotions might seem surprising in a situation that is so predictable. But one feels that perhaps the women's sense of urgency is not misplaced in a country where an educated elite man beat his educated elite wife, a mother of nine, to death in a

Copperbelt farmhouse and the reaction of another elite man was to joke "She was naughty."

After interviewing many women, it became easy to spot not only anguish, but fear. Some women were deeply afraid of their husbands. They feared losing them and they feared staying with them. In their lives, male violence always lurked just beneath the surface. A man could kill his wife and incur less of a jail sentence than if he stole a goat.[2] Marriage was for these women a trap from which, sometimes fed up, they carefully plotted their escape, were divorced by their husbands, or, alternatively, sought safe compensations.

THE ORIGINS OF CONFLICT IN DOMESTIC LIFE

The fact that there is divorce in Zambia means only that society permits this channel for the expression of marital disharmony. Other societies prohibit divorce or make it difficult or expensive, so that marital strife gets channeled into other aggressive patterns of interaction. Of interest in the case of Zambian elites and subelites are the issues around which strife develops, whether or not the discord leads to divorce.

The views of Zambians   Almost invariably, Zambians look to forces outside the relationship itself to explain marital conflict. Given the lack of companionship, it is not surprising that the relationship itself is de-emphasized. One is struck, however, by the enormous ill-will that people assume exists between members of the society. Thus, in the Zambian view, men are tempted away from their wives by the malevolence of other women. Other women are either young single career women or elderly female kin.

Unmarried women "cause" men to neglect their wives. A man is viewed as being helpless in trying to resist an attractive young woman who indicates sexual availability. A man loses control of himself and then neglects his wife because he is smitten by the young woman. Fights and beatings result from a wife confronting her husband over his neglect. The relationship between a husband who drinks and "womanizes" and his wife can reach a status quo: his behavior remains, she complains and cries, they fight, and he beats her. After some years she may come to feel he is "no better than an animal" and will pity rather than blame his new young girlfriends. Toward him she feels a dull hate, and toward her he feels boredom. Alternatively, rather than taking years, the positive relationship can end very quickly. The woman who was avidly courted before marriage, escorted to dances, parties, and nightclubs, and treated to words of love copied from movies and romance magazines, finds her status changed instantly after marriage. She has suddenly become a respectable wife. This means that while her husband continues his night life, she must stay home and wait. Stunned by this turn of events, she finds she can do nothing to change the pattern. "The wife who does not complain," said an older woman, "is happy with a lover herself."

The wife can end the relationship when confident she can manage financially on her own. Alternatively, the husband can end the marriage when he falls in love with a young woman who proves difficult to conquer and hence breaks through his bored and blasé facade. The second alternative is the more common.

"Seventy-five percent of divorces are caused by the man's relatives," declares a divorced typist. Her statistic reflects a personal view but also reveals a pattern. Kin remain unimpressed by a church wedding, a marriage certificate, the payment of *lobola* (bride-price), and the birth of children. Those relatives with reservations about the choice of spouse made by a son or daughter do not hesitate to attempt to undermine the relationship, and continue doing so for as long as the marriage continues. Dislike is often not personal, but based on the tribe of the spouse.

There is a variegated pattern of tribal stereotyping. For example, a Bemba said: "Bembas and Nyanjas are cousins, so intermarriages succeed." Another Bemba reported conflict between herself and her Nsenga (Nyanja-speaking) spouse. A Bemba and Tonga couple divorced, the wife said, because despite their "great love" his mother hated her tribe. Another Bemba/Tonga couple apparently got along. A Xhosa (from South Africa) married to a Ngoni says tribalism "can never be a problem" between them. A Lenje married to a fellow Lenje, however, foresees problems because her husband's family is steeped in tribal tradition and her family, devoutly Christian, ignores tribal tradition.

To undermine a marriage, a man's elderly female relatives may introduce him to another woman of his own tribe. They may gossip and complain about his wife, sometimes taking her clothes and the food she has bought to another relative of theirs living in Lusaka. They may criticize her for not following their customs. A couple may try to ignore the pressure, but people are not invulnerable and some just give up. A Mambwe wife of eleven years standing, with five children, said she had just returned to her Bemba husband after an absence of three months when he assured her of his support before his mother, who lived with them. She said her husband's sister, resident in Lusaka for 20 years, has never lost her anti-Mambwe prejudice, and has never visited their home and welcomed her.

Elderly relatives "advise" a couple, and most couples want to please the old people—at least when they are around to observe the young ones. But tribal differences rarely indicate culture clash insofar as the personal relationship of a couple is concerned, for most young people are so alienated from their tribal traditions that they are irrelevant. Inherently there is no reason for tension to develop as a result of cultural differences, given sufficient good-will and tolerance by everyone concerned. But it is precisely these that are so often lacking. A young couple is caught in the middle between their relatives, who agree only in that they all wish the young people would end their relationship.

Some young couples, experiencing what they regard as endless interference with their marriages by their relatives, want to get away from them, just as do single women. The advice of old people can be ignored only if a couple lives apart from them. There is still a strong moral imperative to obey elders, or at least to pretend to. The Xhosa/Ngoni couple, for example, was living on a farm with his parents in a village near Lusaka. Because of this intensive contact, they hoped his company would transfer him to the Copperbelt.

Elders were useful to a young couple in the past. A couple experiencing difficulties turned to elders for advice. Elders supervised the adjustment of a young couple and taught them the tribe's customs, rituals, and taboos. But modern young couples accept far less advice, viewing some old traditions as meaningless or insulting superstitions—for example, special taboos involving menstruating women—and others as simply horrifying—killing the baby whose top teeth appear before the bottom teeth, and ritual sexual intercourse to cleanse a widowed spouse. In their view the elders' advice on many subjects is best ignored. The problems they face, they say, cannot really be solved by reference to the traditional beliefs of elders. Even advice on what constitutes properly wifely behavior has been rendered irrelevant by modern technology: cow's milk, birth control pills, and a hot water tap in the bathroom change the wife's role. Gone is the mother who nursed an infant for two, three, or more years, abstaining from sex, going into the forest for firewood and to the river for water to prepare a proper bath for her husband. The basis for respect has shifted from wise elder to successful modern careerist. Now the wisdom of old age is seen as ignorance, and good-will is replaced by greed.

Moral overseers of Zambian society blame the young wives, at least in part, for the high divorce rate. Mrs. Mary Mwango, a Lusaka City Councillor, said:

> Women are to blame too, particularly our working girls who also want to be bosses in the home. What these girls should realize is that every woman was made to be under the control of their husband, however rich, poor, small, big, handsome or ugly he may be.[3]

Older couples in their second or third marriages face the additional problem of mixed households of children from previous marriages. Since the domestic unit is highly unstable, each spouse must see to it that the interests of his or her own children are protected. Wives contend they must be detached from their husbands' children because in the event of the death of the husband or another divorce, the children will go to his family and will not look after their stepmother in her old age. Because of the detachment, such wives find it difficult to impose discipline. Similarly, few husbands are willing to look after their wives' children—hardly surprising since they do not always feel they should be responsible for their own. Here again one is struck by the absence of good-will that seems to doom relationships from the outset.

Marital conflict and social change: the anthropologist's view Anthropologists disagree about how best to characterize the effects of rapid social change on society and individuals. One school of thought emphasizes the disorganization and breakdown of old institutions and the disorienting effects of change on individuals. Implicit in this perspective is an equilibrium model of society: sooner or later, things will get back to normal. The second school of thought argues that even in rapidly changing situations, the fabric of society may be preserved as it is transforming. Individuals are less inconsistent than would appear on the surface—they are, instead, selecting behavior patterns appropriate for particular situations: life goes on as normal.

Neither approach is *fully* satisfactory when applied to the problem of the relationships between husbands and wives in modern urban Zambia. It is difficult to escape the conclusion that *something is pathological* in this instance. Educated wives who beg for help the moment their husbands are out of earshot, describe extreme privation, beatings, fear, and above all, a continuing feeling of helplessness, vulnerability, and anxiety, reflect a society that is neither normal nor healthy.

The problem of marriage is not caused simply by people becoming alienated from their rural tribal cultural traditions as a result of living in town. On the contrary, relationships in towns retain many features that were, and still are, known in the rural areas, so that some of the problems of urban marriages have their roots in rural cultural traditions. Marriage is now fragile in town, but it never was secure. Women complain that they have no deep personal relationship with their husbands, but this was never a feature of married life. Men are now capable of complete dominance, but they always retained this privilege. Women are beaten by their husbands, but wife-beating has been a traditional method of punishment. Like rural wives, town women expect to spend leisure hours alone while their husbands drink with their friends or visit girlfriends. And everywhere women had their lovers as well.

Preoccupation with sexual activity in contemporary urban Zambian society is not new either. In fact, in a pioneering ethnographic report of a Zambian tribe first published in 1920, the authors say:[4]

> To write of the Ila and omit all reference to sex would be like writing of the sky and leaving out the sun. . . .

The situation has not changed substantially in contemporary villages. In villages, people are still scantily clad; for most of the year it is hot; life is slow and easy. There is little to do for a good part of the year after the rainy season hoeing. Under the circumstances sex is a major activity and preoccupation. Except where prohibited by incest taboos, the world view of villagers is that sexual intercourse is the only normal form of personal interaction between physically mature individuals, and that a great deal of sexual exploration—"play"—is natural among the physically immature.

Suspicion is always rife among village husbands and wives. They make up excuses to be in the bush where they can meet lovers in safety. An informant who grew up in a village says:

> You wait until your husband is going off to sleep and sweetly tell him you must go to the bush to relieve yourself. He tells you to go ahead and you go out to meet your lover somewhere in the bush.

The persistence of this attitude toward sex is obvious in town today. The University of Zambia student newspaper published the following opinion of platonic relationships:

> What's the use of carrying a defective torch [i.e., flashlight] without a bulb and batteries?[5]

While there was traditionally and still is a great amount of sexual activity in rural village life, a framework of custom also exists that results in unceasing opposition and conflict between men and women: girls are taught their primary responsibilities are to get pregnant and to satisfy their husbands sexually and are thus under pressure to please men; men are under pressure to have multiple orgasms to ensure that their wives get pregnant. This tension is clearly retained in town. A recurrent theme of letters from modern young husbands to "Soul Sister Says" and "Dear Josephine" (the latter being the lovelorn column of the *Zambia Daily Mail*) was concern over the loss of sexual power. The young men time themselves for frequency and latency of orgasm. One explained:

> When I first married, it took ten seconds to reach my orgasm. I repeated seven times per night. Now I require one minute and repeat only three times per night. Am I losing my potence [sic]?

Societal rules in town are derived from a variety of traditional village cultures and a superficial western culture, creating inevitable conflicts in the total urban sociocultural system. People choose freely among these rules, depending on the circumstances. They are often put into stress situations as a result of conflicting roles within inherently incompatible sub-systems.

Social and sexual relationships that might possibly have worked in the rural areas have ceased to be effective in towns. The external shame controls of village life acted as a brake on unlimited irresponsibility, adultery, and cruelty. But the comparative anonymity of town, and the alienation from tradition and from kin, have decreased the effectiveness of this sanction.

While weak compared to village life, shame controls are still somewhat operative in town, however. The fear of getting caught is a worry. Unfaithful wives risk much if caught, sometimes even their lives. A few husbands feel they must maintain a respectable image—whether the sense of responsibility derives from Christian or western bourgeois values. All they risk, however, is temporary marital discord, strife in their private lives, and being the subjects of juicy gossip. Most men are neither strong Christians nor bourgeois, and have nothing to lose. On the contrary, the pattern of poor marital relationships due to husbands' "misbehavior" is enhanced precisely because it is shared so widely. It is a socially patterned defect in Eric Fromm's sense.

In town, a man retains the dominant position he had in the village, and is reinforced by the actions and attitudes of most of his male companions. He can come and go as he pleases and need never offer an explanation. He no longer fears the control of others and yet has not internalized the alternative value of self-restraint. He can give free reign to his lusts without the slightest feeling of guilt. And town life has always been known for offering many temptations.

Women in town no longer have the same relationships with husbands and kin that they did in the village. They are far more dependent on their husbands for a high standard of living and are less likely to remarry after divorce. Emotionally distant from kin, and no longer psychologically able to accept the control of male kin should they divorce, they are more isolated and vulnerable.

Once married, a townswoman's options are often reduced to two: remaining in the unhappy marriage or adopting the often permanent status of divorcee. Since most women think they will marry at some point in their lives, and since divorce follows most marriages, it seems that the majority will be destined to be divorcees. The same may, of course, be true in the villages, but there the route to divorce seems quite different.

Among the features of rural marriage that seem especially magnified in town are a primary interest in maximizing personal rather than mutual gain and the almost total absence of mutual goodwill. These factors seem to underlie all quarrels and act to magnify disputes until compromise becomes impossible. Men and women act and react on the basis of personal convenience, and justify their actions by whatever existing norms are appropriate for the occasion. When a wife evokes tradition to exploit a husband, (or, much more common, a husband evokes tradition to exploit a wife), it is really selfishness or lack of good-will at issue. The same can be said when either invokes "westernization." But what is true of husbands and wives is also true of their relatives, their friends, indeed almost everyone else. One woman said the best way to ensure the break-up of an engagement is to have a big party and invite all your friends, who will then gossip about the other relationships you and your fiance have had so each one's suspicions will be activated. Another recalled a friend's wedding to which the bride, condemned by her brother for her immorality, invited the brother's wife, his secret mistress, and his children by both women.

The pattern of exploitation, self-interest, and lack of trust exists from the first moment a couple decides to marry, when they must decide what type of wedding to have. A bride-to-be yearns to have a wedding that is a precise copy of a "European" church wedding, with long white gown, flowers, flower-girls, bridesmaids, ushers, music, reception, and so on. She will struggle to eliminate all forms of tradition on her wedding

A wedding party arriving at reception hall after a white wedding on the Copperbelt. Cars have been decorated with hard-to-obtain streamers, balloons, and tin cans.

day. Yet, claiming adherence to traditional values, she will take it for granted and indeed insist that the groom must pay for everything since it is all part of *lobola* (bride-price), and his willingness to pay is a sign of respect. Those women who are inclined to contribute to some of the wedding expenses are advised against it by relatives. Some do help their fiancés, but secretly.

Modern elite and subelite men want statutory marriages and white weddings for the same reason that more conservative men, or men who married in the late 1960s and early 1970s, wanted customary marriages: to keep their wives under control. The modern men value the prestige of a white wedding and add they are willing to invest in it so that "the wife won't run away." Although willing to pay the cost, these men are often unwilling to accept the legal restrictions of ordinance marriage, particularly the one that prescribes monogamy for life for both husband and wife. This, they say, is too contrary to traditional African values. The conservative men, who prefer customary marriages, say they can keep wives under control more easily since it is easy to get rid of them if they misbehave or complain. "The other way around is too complicated and expensive," they say, "since divorce is in High Court." It is also a matter of convenience for them that a customary wife has no legal grounds for complaint against an adulterous husband.

Traditionalists expect their wives to work in the modern economy while at the same time behaving "traditionally." Yet a wife's traditional behavior is no guarantee of marital harmony. An unpublished letter to "Soul Sister Says" from a 23-year-old mother of three illustrates this point graphically:

> I JUST DO NOT KNOW HOW TO PLEASE HIM. I try to do all I can to please him. I read a lot about making my family happy and follow the instructions given. More to this, ours was a traditional wedding and so I follow my grandma's instructions on housekeeping. I wake up very early in the morning, not later than 0530 hours to warm his water, I make sure he has at least three clean shirts from which to pick which one he wants to put on, I make sure all his underwears are always clean. But all this is nothing to my husband.
>
> He goes angry for misplacing a teaspoon, just a slight mistake and I am in trouble. Sometimes he refuses to eat *nshima* because there are a few lumps in it or the meat is a bit overfried, or because the vegetables are a bit overcooked. He goes out fuming over things you wouldn't expect him to be angry.
>
> In addition to this, I have been insulted, Dear Soul Sister, sometimes for things I am unaware of or have no knowledge of. But I never answer back for it is our custom not to answer back our husbands.
>
> Heartbroken Mother, Lusaka

Townswomen sometimes say, "We are not as strong as village women." They think of themselves as more prone to illness. The anxiety and stress resulting from the abuses to which they are subjected certainly seem to cause physical ailments:

> One wife went into shock and miscarried at six months on hearing that her husband's girlfriend died in a car accident for which he was responsible. She was convinced the girlfriend's family bewitched her and killed her baby in revenge. She had not known, before the accident, that he had this girlfriend, however.

A wife's compensations   When an unhappy marriage is permitted to continue, the woman develops a variety of alternative compensations. One alternative is to defy what modern Zambians consider chic—having a small family of four children—and to bear children regularly and frequently. Many women told me they planned at first to have just three or four children, but when the last reached the age of three or four, they felt "too lonely—he began growing away from me." So they had more children. This is not an overdeveloped maternal instinct, but a physical need for tenderness, for contact with another human being. For an African

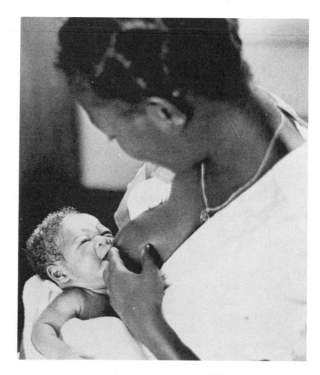

Portrait of motherhood. The mother named a sugar daddy as the father of her week-old daughter.

woman, there is no legitimate means of expressing this need apart from nursing an infant and carrying it on her back. Women happily carry children on their backs for many years, gently chiding them for not walking. Even a child of five might be carried on the back if the child is not too heavy or large. Women are aware that it looks slightly ridiculous to be carrying a big child on their backs and become embarrassed if caught in the act. The embarrassment is indicative of the sensual delight they derive from this bodily contact. It is why they so often put toddlers to sleep on their backs.

Another compensation is to deaden emotionally but maintain a proud facade. The woman married to a public figure well known for his "womanizing" is, in public, the perfect companion to her husband. This elegant young couple, in their rare public appearances together, appear all chic, charming, smiling, devoted. To her friends and close family, the wife admits she has "just given up" on her husband. She no longer cares about him, no longer is interested in him, no longer fights with him or attempts to maintain a personal relationship. She dares not have regular lovers, and either she finds men who are attracted to her as offensive as her husband, or they are frightened for their careers at the consequences of getting caught. So she concentrates on her clothes and her children's clothes and she keeps busy.

A final compensation is heavy drinking, to which many women resort.

DIVORCEES: THE TOUGHEST OF THEM ALL

We have seen in Chapter 6 how some single women toughened up after several disappointments with boyfriends. But older women who have been through divorce seem to be "the toughest of them all." They were forthright, honest and direct in their interviews, describing not what was considered "proper" in their society, but what they actually thought, felt, and experienced. In this respect they were quite different from the reticent women who had never married and were much more inclined to report society's values and attitudes about their personal relationships. The toughness of divorcees is the result of a number of shocks that they undergo in learning to live with their new status.

The loss of personal status that comes with divorce is numbing, especially in the case of elites. Being the ex-wife of a man of high status carries no particular afterglow, just as it affords no financial advantage. The idea of alimony for divorcees who were married under statutory law is still quite new, the amazing exception rather than the rule. Most women have never heard the word. For those married under customary law, no alimony is expected, but a "good" wealthy husband divorcing his wife to marry a younger woman will sometimes continue to look after her, albeit at a much lower standard.

The sudden drop in the divorcees' standard of living can be a major shock. As wives, they lived in their husbands' houses in low-density neighborhoods. Most of them must now compete for housing on the open market, which means they must use influence to get a council house or flat in a high-density neighborhood. The need for influential contacts brings with it the harsh realization that they need their very possibly previously neglected kin.

Influential kin help in a variety of ways, depending on their status and the divorcee's needs. They can come to her aid by sponsoring her in a training program, temporarily keeping her small children, and helping her find housing. This help is not inevitable and invariable, however, if relatives perceive themselves as struggling to maintain an elite or subelite standard of living. While kin cannot openly refuse aid, they can circumvent it by not keeping promises, by constant complaining, or, as hosts, by permitting her so little freedom of movement and association that her stay becomes intolerably confining.

Sometimes a woman is left very much on her own and comes to depend on women friends and the men who pass through her life. In such a case, her job and the contacts she makes at work are the key to her survival in town with a measure of security and dignity.

Child custody is another painful issue. Young children normally stay with their mother for a time even if ultimately they must go to their father. The idea is that the mother can best care for the little ones. Some divorcees have a very hard time keeping up their jobs, living in poor quarters, and paying nannies to care for young children. It is ironic that when the children grow big and childcare becomes easier, their father claims them.

Men who intend ultimately to claim the children give their ex-wives money toward the children's upkeep. When wives get custody of the children it is the exceptional ex-husband who sustains a constant interest in the children. Some women fear accepting an ex-husband's child support even though the man may offer, because they do not want the man to later claim the children. When a father has custody of his children, their mother may feel he is not doing enough for them. A Lozi divorcee, for example, paid for her sons to attend boarding school because their father considered boarding unnecessary and the sons and their mother thought boarding best. Their father, she said, was a drunkard and they would be maltreated if they remained in his home. He would never permit the sons to live with his ex-wife, however.

Relationships with men   A number of divorcees I interviewed had remarried, but all of them had been divorced when still in their teens.

Women divorced between twenty-five and thirty years of age, who had already borne four or five children, were not seriously considering remarriage: a realistic adaptation to statistical probability. Over time, selective involvement for financial gain comes to predominate. At the end of the process, the divorcee renounces dependency on men for anything except sexual gratification on a casual basis. In this case, a gradual adjustment to their status as divorcees has to take place. For many older divorcees I knew in Lusaka, adjustment begins with indiscriminate hedonism.

Just after divorcing, the woman in a position to do so embarks on an orgiastic binge in which her goal is to get drunk as much as possible and to have sexual relations with as many men as possible. While she appears to be acting self-destructively, the new divorcee takes care to maintain a sense of responsibility toward her job. She may be drunk at 4 a.m., but by 8 she appears at her office. Her main concern at this point in the process is that the men she is sleeping with should not chance to meet at her residence, so that jealous scenes are avoided.

Over a period of months or years, a woman tires of hedonism. Her involvements begin to narrow to men whom she can exploit financially. After being divorced, she has lost most of her material possessions except clothes. Council houses are unfurnished and a woman over the initial adjustment stage begins to want properly furnished accommodation. But buying herself furniture and appliances on the open market is costly: as high as K1000. She wants a car: for this she needs cash for a down payment because women do not qualify for car loans as easily as men, who are more highly placed. Her own earnings are sufficient for most items of personal expenditure, but major purchases remain a problem if she is unable to save. Installment buying is available but not commonly used. So at this point in the process, a woman turns to men as the most promising alternative. There is no lack of "sugar daddies" for an experienced woman willing to endure overweight and overbearing men.

As a woman advances in her career, establishes a home that satisfies her, and has produced all the children she cares to, she changes yet again. She no longer requires men for her financial stability and security, and is no longer interested in them apart from their role as occasional amusing sexual partners. A thrice-divorced Lusaka businesswoman named Esther, interviewed by a newspaper because of her financial success, said:

> By now I had enough from men and so I decided to divorce him and stay divorced. I realized that with a man I could not really make it.[6]

The lover of a woman in this stage of adjustment may be considerably younger than she, of a lower socioeconomic status, and possessed of little education. For an especially pleasing lover she may be "sugar mammy."

More commonly, however, she is simply not interested in the men who ask her for sex, and ridicules them to women friends. The mark called The Prof was also called "Jump Gate" by the older divorcee, whose locked gate he jumped over one night when he wanted (and was refused) sex. With mirth she recalled to her friends how this "distinguished" elderly man so compromised himself. She also found it revolting.

As we saw in Esther's case, women who feel in a position to do so divorce their husbands. It sometimes happens that a woman's personal ambitions and success outstrip those of her husband; eventually she becomes dissatisfied with the relationship and leaves him for a lover of higher social status. This seems to be unusual, however: of 48 women interviewed, only one case followed this pattern. Most often women divorce men whose abuses they can no longer bear.

CONCLUSION

In the first chapter, I quoted a passage from Eric Fromm's book *The Sane Society*, in which he suggested that a society can be sick. It seems clear that Zambia is a deeply disturbed, troubled society. Nearly every foreigner who has lived there and in several other countries in the first, second, and third worlds has noticed how coldly suspicious the people of Zambia are, how quick to take offense, how irresponsible, how prone to drink: all indices, perhaps, of this societal malaise.

Perhaps one of the strongest indices, however, is the state of the institution of marriage and family. Here, instead of harmonious cooperation, complementary role playing, constructive sharing and mutual fulfillment, there is deep hostility, antagonism, and violence. At some point in their lives, people in Zambia want to get married. Sooner or later, most of them do. Once married, people want to stay married. Yet they do not seem to be able to do so. One or the other or both behave in ways that destroy the marriage. The destructiveness is not random or unique to particular cases. It is patterned behavior. The institution of marriage in Zambia is itself defective, and claims individuals as victims.

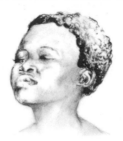

Ambivalence in the Media:
Women as Folk Devils

9

These next two chapters focus on information about townswomen in Zambia's two daily newspapers. National communications media conform to and reflect some of urban industrial Zambian society's most important norms, values, attitudes and beliefs. By studying how townswomen are portrayed in the media, we are able to gain insight into how society-at-large feels about the new type of Zambian woman in its midst.

The Zambian press presents news about townswomen in two directly opposite ways. This dichotomy conforms to intensely ambivalent attitudes of the wider society toward its townswomen. On the one hand, the women are stereotyped as "folk devils." Sociologist Stanley Cohen, in his book *Folk Devils and Moral Panics*, defines folk devils as "a group of persons. . . defined as a threat to societal values and interests. . . visible reminders of what we should not be."[1] On the other hand, the women are also stereotyped as "folk heroes." A folk hero is a social type that serves as a role model for members of a society. By treating the women as both devils and heroes in their news columns, the newspapers of Zambia are defining, reflecting, amplifying, and sanctioning these same attitudes in society-at-large. Indeed, the newspapers play an important role in making scapegoats of the women.

Zambia's women's liberationists are astutely aware of how the press amplifies the negative image of women. The first column published in a series called "Women's Forum," written by Zambian feminists in the *Times of Zambia*,[2] said:

> The Press reports that one sees on the position of women in this country are disheartening, to say the least. More often than not, they are hardly representative, and yet the influence of the Press on prevailing attitudes and valuations in relation to women should not be underestimated. . . .

The feminists claim that the press is not representative, but what they explain is that it is not representative of their views. Once weekly for six months they wrote a column they said would be "corrective." Then, when they stopped writing, the series was discontinued.

THE MEDIA IN ZAMBIA

The media occupy an important place in modern urban Zambian society. City people watch television (in 1972 there were about 30,000 sets), listen to the radio, and buy newspapers. "Modern romance" type magazines and comic books published in Britain and South Africa are read by the over-whelming majority of young literate women I interviewed. Many subelites are devoted to the cinema. The number of cinemas in Lusaka alone increased from three to seven between 1971 and 1975. Increased prosperity since independence and increased literacy have resulted in a proportional growth in the importance of the media. Even rural villagers listen to the radio.

All the media offer a mixture of western and Zambian content. The proportions of western versus Zambian content, and the type of western themes considered acceptable for Zambian audiences, are subjects of heated debate by leaders and by the public.

Although all the media present themes relevant to an analysis of modern urban women in Zambia, I chose to concentrate on newspaper coverage rather than television or radio broadcasts because data from newspapers are subject to verification. The file is permanent, the evidence accessible and tangible. From May 1971 to August 1974 I collected news articles, feature columns, and interviews by, for, and about Zambian women from the two daily newspapers. Clippings were sent to me until February 1975. On my return to Zambia in October 1975, I noted that many themes were repeated. Almost every day in which I was able to purchase the newspapers, there was at least one relevant item, so that hundreds of items were collected.

The two daily English-language newspapers are the *Times of Zambia* and the *Zambia Daily Mail*. The *Mail* is government-owned, and had a circulation of 30,000 in 1974. The *Times* was then privately owned by the Lonrho Corporation; it was nationalized in 1975, but even before nationalization its editor was appointed by the Zambian government. The *Times'* daily circulation in 1975 was 52,000; in 1975 it jumped to 72,000 with a Sunday circulation of 56,000. The *Mail* is not published on Sundays.

Most of the newspapers are distributed in Lusaka and the Copperbelt towns. In February 1975 the *Mail's* circulation increased to 39,000. At that time, 15,000 copies went to the Copperbelt, 12,000 to Lusaka, 6,000 to Livingstone (the southernmost line-of-rail town), and the remainder, 6,000 copies, were distributed "elsewhere." Since the last category includes the provincial capitals, we can see that the reading public is overwhelmingly concentrated in towns.

The editor of the *Mail* is of Rhodesian origin. The editor of the *Times* is Zambian. The staffs of both newspapers are mostly young Zambians. Most of the young reporters were trained in a two-year technical course in journalism at Lusaka's Evelyn Hone College (an institution roughly equivalent to an American community college), following the completion of Form V of secondary school. The bylines of both men and women regularly appear on special features of social commentary. Editors, reporters, and the majority of contributors are western-oriented. This orientation derives from their western-style education and training. The format of both newspapers and the style of journalism they employ are the inheritance of a colonial newspaper tradition, and both the *Times* and the *Mail* continue to model themselves on the western press.

In the years I studied the newspapers, there was very little independent investigative reporting by the newspaper staff. The government-owned news agency, ZANA (Zambia News Agency), to which both newspapers subscribed, did most of what little investigative reporting was done, so that the two newspapers normally contained identical news articles and varied only in minor ways, such as layout, typeface, choice of feature articles, and headlines. Although the *Times* never disagreed with government policy, the *Mail* tended to be more sycophantic in its support of government, as well as rather more sensational. International news was supplied by Reuters. Neither newspaper was free to criticize national policies or politics, but apart from this limitation, both were relatively free to present the news as they saw fit—or as it reached them—subject only to self-censorship. In fact it was the newspapers' support of the government that gave them an official aura. Although not seen as the direct mouthpiece of government, their management of the news appeared to have official approval.

The formats of both newspapers were similar during the time of my study. The *Mail* was eight pages; the *Times* was ten pages. The two extra *Times* pages were taken up by classified advertisements lacking in the

Mail. The first page of both newspapers contained national and international news stories. The last page of each was devoted to local and sometimes international sports. Inside were separate pages devoted to foreign and home news. Both newspapers had regular features from 1971 to 1975: lovelorn columns; women's columns providing advice on childcare, recipes, and fashion, and music, sports, and business columns. Most of these features were discontinued in 1976, following activation of the State of Emergency. The *Times* still publishes a widely read and often quoted column of social criticism and satire, not infrequently misogynist in tone, by a writer using the pseudonym "Kapelwa Musonda." In the early years, formal interviews of prominent and less well-known personalities were reported from time to time. The persons interviewed were often women and the stories usually appeared on the women's page but sometimes made the general news pages.

There was a great hunger for news copy. The editors of both the *Times* and the *Mail* willingly published almost anything handed to them, either as an anonymous contribution under the byline "Special Correspondent" or a signed feature column, quite apart from the "Letters to the Editor" section. Therefore, men and women could write almost anything they liked about each other and see it get into print. Failure to represent an opinion was due more to a lack of motivation than a lack of opportunity. The "Women's Forum," for example, was ended after six months because the contributors themselves stopped sending in articles. The result of the free play of opinion, however, was a lively confrontation between the sexes in which a great range of Zambian values, attitudes, and beliefs were presented.

This confrontation was due not only to occasional contributions from the public, but the views of the young reporters themselves. As young subelite urbanites, they represented the views of their contemporaries. They either wrote directly from personal experience or based their social commentary on interviews of their contemporaries, whom they identified as typical men and women on the street after the fashion of the western roving reporter. The reporters therefore had an open forum for publicizing their own ideas, opinions, and values.

Over the years, a style of fashion, attitudes, slang expressions, musical taste, and so forth emerged that was in part a product of the national media and in part a report on what existed in society itself. Expressions like "dolly girl," (a fashionable young single working woman), "playboy," "man about town" (an elite or subelite man who enjoys the company of dolly girls), "Mr. Right" (the ideal husband), and "Zamfoot" (people who do not own cars; pedestrians) originated in elite and subelite bars in Lusaka and the Copperbelt. The expressions got picked up by the reporters who were part of that world and used in news articles and features. The usage spread by this means to become part of the vocabulary of young literates elsewhere in the country, as evidenced by letters to the advice and music columns from rural secondary schools.

Similarly, when young reporters bemoaned the high cost of weddings and engagements, they were articulating a common concern among their contemporaries. When they wrote that white weddings were becoming fashionable, their impression was consistent with the statistics on the increase in church and civil marriages in the African population. Zambian newspapers were thus a forum for the exchange of ideas and opinions on the subjects of social change and social problems, particularly about relationships between the sexes. Although loaded emotionally, these were politically safe subjects, and given the hunger for newspaper copy, they were used to cover up the dearth of investigative reporting on socioeconomic and political issues and events.

Under the State of Emergency activated by President Kaunda in early 1976, features on male-female relationships were informally banned. Social problems came to be discussed only rarely, and the popular lovelorn columns were eliminated. In May 1976 the women's branch of the ruling political party, the UNIP Women's Brigade, announced the banning of beauty contests. At the time, Zambia was surrounded by countries at war and leaders claimed Zambia itself was in some sort of unspecific danger from foreign enemies bent on destroying the country. Moreover Zambia was faced with a grave internal economic crisis which was triggered by falling copper prices on the world market and the close of an important export route, and aggravated by economic mismanagement. There was massive unrest in the country. Perhaps President Kaunda and his political party felt themselves more secure when the publicity surrounding at least one form of danger and tension was controlled, leading to the quiet but firm ban of the male-female confrontation from the newspapers.

NEWSPAPER IMAGES AND STEREOTYPES

Newspapers operate according to their own internal dynamics. The need to create news is institutionalized: *something* has to fill up space on quiet days. The newsmaking process is itself selective and inferential. Not everything that happens gets reported; not everything that gets reported is told in full. The Zambian press responds to these dynamics in its treatment of townswomen. Whether stories about townswomen serve as filler or are protracted campaigns of a single theme, facts are selected, exaggerated, and distorted, and much of what is reported is erroneous. Sometimes reports are based on unconfirmed rumor. Headlines often mislead. The result is a portrayal of the townswoman as the folk devil of modern independent Zambia.

The stereotype of the townswoman as a dangerous, evil temptress is familiar in many parts of the western and nonwestern world. City woman is sexy, immoral, tough, unsentimental, materialistic, expensive. By means of her artificial good looks, guile and cunning, she manipulates marks and leaves them impoverished, sometimes having tricked them out of money without the compensating benefit of sexual contact, at other times having afflicted them with venereal disease. The young women of Lusaka and the Copperbelt came to be seen as a threat to traditional societal values and interests, a symbol of the loss of control of values and culture by the older generation, the men, and the less well educated. What dangers are said to be posed by these women of the city, and what is to be done?

Women who move at night are the cause of deaths.[3]

An undercover squad has mounted a campaign to keep erring husbands at home with their wives at night.
    Their secret weapon: a yellow circular, posted to suspect husbands, warning them against the deadly peril of Zambia's good time girls. . . .[4]

In the first article cited above, a man told the reporter he had stopped his car to pick up two well-dressed girl hitchhikers. When he opened the car door, thugs emerged from the bush and attacked him. The substance of the news story therefore involved only one incident, and the statement that well-dressed female hitchhikers were causing "deaths" was not supported by the story. The second article, in which single women were said to constitute a "deadly peril," was similarly exaggerated. This story was one of many involving the protests of married women whose husbands date single women, in which the single women are invariably blamed.

Prostitution in the press   The image of woman as devil is portrayed in a variety of other ways. One of the most salient and powerful is to present articles and features about Zambia's "prostitutes" and about "prostitution." "Prostitute" is used loosely, to label all women who have had sexual relations outside marriage.

The press uses "prostitute," "whore," and "call girl" interchangeably with "hip" terms not used in ordinary conversation: "pleasure girl," "fun girl," "late night girl," and "gay girl." Press reports also brand "good time girls," "flirts," "lone women," and "unaccompanied women" as prostitutes. Since in Zambian–English slang these terms do not normally imply prostitution, the press *extends* the use of the word "prostitute" to include a variety of sexual and social relationships and activities. When a "hip" reporter writing a feature on prostitution describes a schoolgirl as a "chick" and her clothes as "gear," a pimp as "playing the daddy game," a male client as a "sex maniac" and an "experienced seducer," the message is that he writes from personal experience. A reporter's distortions, exaggerations, and falsifications are insidious, generalizations from personal experience being confused with objective reporting and independent verification of events. Not only do politicians and ministers of religion indiscriminately brand all single women as prostitutes, the "hip" reporter does so as well:

> "Pleasure girls" are always smartly dressed and have a taste for the latest fashions. They do simple jobs like typing, factory work, and shopkeeping. Some may be school drop-outs who do not work at all. Most of these girls have a Grade VII standard of education, and, as a result of their low education, they do not receive enough money. They only receive between K40 and K80. From this, they want to buy expensive clothes. Because of their small earnings, the "pleasure girls" go about soliciting for men in order to supplement their incomes.
> In most cases they look for men with a lot of money, men who move in long beautiful cars. . . . Usually they demand anything between K20 and K30 per night. They will demand this from every man who flirts with them. No wonder these girls are invited to every function which takes place in town. . . .[5]

Subelite male reporters obviously envy elite men "who move in long beautiful cars" while they themselves drive Volkswagen Beetles belonging to their newspapers. They also envy the women, who, they imagine, are able to buy expensive clothes with the money they obtain from elite men, for they could not both clothe themselves expensively and give women money for clothes. They envy what they imagine to be women's advantage in income-earning and the "high life" this supposed advantage affords. In a special feature article headlined "Will prostitution ever be erased from our society?" one reporter writes:

> Hard-boiled prostitutes are business executives just like any other company director. As such, they either have to be equipped with exclusive commercial tactics or their accounts books will go red. . . . Some of these inventions have paid off handsomely to a majority of our local prostitutes some of whom even own beautiful Ford Capris and flourishing shops now. . . .[6]

A mixture of fact and fantasy shows up in inconsistencies even within single articles. For example, after describing the lavish life style of "hard-boiled prostitutes," the reporter who wrote the above paragraph goes on to say:

> Some Zambian prostitutes were even shy to ask for money especially when they have been going along with a man for some time because they end up becoming intimate mistresses. . . .

146

Despite the alarming increase of prostitutes in the country, many Zambians still believe that never will there come a time when we shall be having completely businessminded prostitutes like the Zairean ndumbas and the Soho call girls in London. . . . Apart from the few imported prostitutes we have around, most of the Zambian fun girls one meets in bars and pleasure resorts will hardly approach a man for accompaniment unless he was a lonesome stranger or foreigner. . . . The majority of our pleasure girls have that I-can-do-without-you mentality which no genuine prostitute can afford to have.

The newspapers play up an association of sexually uncontrolled townswomen with violence and danger by frequent use of headlines expressing a "war" theme:

It's full scale war on prostitute hotels[7]

War on whores[8]

War on Kalulushi prostitutes[9]

Governor Mubanga declares war on prostitution[10]

The "wars" turn out to be one-sided verbal battles, in which self-appointed moral overseers of Zambian society announce that they are planning action in particular bars and hotels. The following story is typical of the genre:

UNIP of Ndola has declared war on three hotels which harbour prostitutes, the Youth Regional Secretary, Mr. Gilbert Yabe, said yesterday.

He said he knew of three hotels in the city where prostitutes loitered to make their "catch."

"We are now ready to declare war on these hotels. If they do not heed our warning, we shall hunt for these prostitutes and hand them over to the police," Mr. Yabe said.

UNIP would not tolerate this kind of thing to go on in Ndola. Prostitution would not be allowed to spoil Zambia's culture and customs.

Mr. Yabe said only accompanied women would be allowed in public places, and the party would demand proof of the genuineness of the men in their company.[11]

The Kalulushi UNIP Regional Secretary, Vincent Mulenga, in the article headed "War on Kalulushi prostitutes,"[12] outlined the problem of identifying prostitutes:

Some men moved in the company of girls at night pretending to be boyfriends while in fact they were their pimps.

In other news articles in the same vein, under the protection of their "pimps," Zambian women are reported to solicit white men, Somali men, and Senegalese men. In some articles, Zambian men are said to "smuggle" Zairean women over the border, or the women are reported to "smuggle" themselves. The women are variously reported to be working in hotels "at reasonable salaries," to be given "posh accommodation" in town, or to be living in African townships. Allegations are typically insubstantial:

> There were records . . . to show that a lot of married men were flocking to certain hotels . . . and some of them spend days with these prostitutes.[13]

The press serves as a forum for undisguised moral condemnation of prostitutes. In various articles, "prostitutes" are blamed for "spoiling stable marriages," and "breaking up families" and townspeople are described as "shocked and disgusted." The Reverend Ben Zulu, the Zambian head of the Copperbelt-based Marriage Guidance Bureau of Zambia, is a favored source of quotations on the subject. Says he:

> This is disgracing and degrading our high moral standards. Zambia cannot be a damping [sic] ground for foreign morality.[14]

> [The Rev. Zulu] called on the government to do anything it could in having the moral slide halted. "I am not going to be part and parcel of these sinister, sinful and abominable acts," he exclaimed with anger.[15]

In the early 1970s the Reverend Zulu was the main personality reported to be engaged in what he called "research" on prostitutes: he was a frequent visitor to bars and hotels in Lusaka and the Copperbelt. His "research" focused on a small number of women rather than on the crowds of drunken men, although prostitution was a far less widespread social problem in Zambia than was excessive drinking. But drinking was not widely considered degrading except by such teetotalers as President Kaunda. What could the government do to halt the "moral slide?" It is to this subject we now turn.

The unaccompanied woman   In April 1972 the campaign against townswomen crystallized with the coining of a new label: the "unaccompanied woman." Literally, she was any physically mature, urban-dwelling female who appeared outside her residence after dark without a male escort. It is very natural in thriving modern towns for women such as travelers and night-shift workers to be outdoors after dark. But for nearly a year when the campaign peaked, all unaccompanied women in town were assailed and harassed by the government, the ruling party, the media, and ordinary male citizens posing as plainclothes policemen. They were also subject to arrest by the police.

148

The label gave a focus to society's hatred and fear of the towns-woman. Her mysterious powers of sexual attraction could at last be confronted. But first the danger she represented had to be publicized. Sexual magnetism was said to be responsible for all manner of evil mischief in the towns, and all from the same basic cause. By making herself available, the she-devil drew men to her and made them lose their rational sensibilities. A man could not resist her. He either had to have sexual intercourse with her or kill her. One government official summed up the problem this way:

> It becomes dangerous for girls to loiter without an escort. In fact this is moral degradation at its worst. . . . Girls should not create situations for crimes like murder and rape and girls can help to curb this growing rate of rape in Zambia by stopping this aimless loitering at night.[16]

The mystique of the dangerous woman was considered a greater threat than the crime of rape by men. If a man raped a woman or, even worse, found her a willing partner he became her helpless victim, having "tasted" her.

> Many men spend their money wildly on the loose girls who patronize bars late at night. With girls cleared away from the streets, men would be encouraged to go home early and attend to their families.[17]

In addition to failing to attend to his family—by not spending time with them, by not giving them money for food, by not giving the children money for school uniforms—the victim neglected his work. He showed up late, with a hangover, or not at all. He therefore undermined Zambia's efficiency and productivity. Thus the she-devil's evil influence would ultimately destroy not only the institution of the family, but also the economy.

Now, by hindsight, the evil of the unaccompanied woman was seen to have infused society even before the threat was identified. Threatening themes had been running through urban Zambia for some time. Police and other moral agents had been unable (or unwilling) to control towns-women. Arrests of prostitutes and pimps were rare. And as a sign of the times, Afro wigs and miniskirts had not been banned. The parents of pregnant schoolgirls had not been punished. Contraceptives were being issued to trainees in various institutions. Crimes of violence were on the increase. A new abortion law had been passed in Parliament.[18] Hot pants were in vogue—and these were even more revealing than the miniskirts. Young women were speaking out defiantly:

> I know they look nice on me since I have got good legs for a Hot Pant [sic]. . . . A lot of people in Zambia think that makeup is not

good for African girls, as far as I am concerned they can go to hell.[19]

In the midst of these perceived threats, articles attacking women's liberation began appearing in the press. Members of the movement were likened to a cancerous growth on society. In sum, bits and pieces of scores of widely known and constantly discussed social problems were crystallized into the image of the unaccompanied woman, and in this form caught on and endured. The campaign against unaccompanied women identified the source of evil as the earlier reports of prostitution had not. Moreover, the new label included *all* women of the town, and whereas euphemisms for prostitute, such as "gay girl" and "pleasure girl," had suggested enjoyment, the new term, "unaccompanied woman," clearly connoted danger. Now that the source of all these problems could be readily identified—she was any woman in any part of Zambia's towns who was for any reason out of her home after dark—it was felt that the previously intractable problem of the wicked townswoman could be attacked in earnest.

The active campaign against the unaccompanied woman began early in April 1972. It was reported in the press immediately:

> Police have been ordered to declare war against good time girls found on the loose unaccompanied at night, according to instructions from Home Affairs Minister, Mr. Lewis Changufu. And legal sources immediately warned that the police have the power to arrest such girls as "common prostitutes," for which the sentence can be several years in jail.
> Mr. Changufu's statement says: "Police will be very tough with such girls if they are found loitering unaccompanied from now on." The order has been issued to police because of increased thuggery and rape at night, the statement says. . . .[20]

Thus a method was found to control women, to keep them at home, and assure that they would be less threatening: they were simply arrested. Over the next few months the newspapers occasionally printed stories of the hundreds of arrests that were being made, although by no means all arrests everywhere were reported. The following story is typical:

> Police yesterday arrested more than 100 women in a midnight raid on Lusaka's bars.
> Any woman who failed to produce an escort was held. Every female was questioned, a Zambezi bar customer said. "Some dashed to the toilets to hide, but were dragged out and joined their friends in the police truck."[21]

This story received prominence, being featured as the lead story, and was accompanied by a photograph of a bar owner, who was pictured holding her sleeping infant and weeping. The story continued with an interview with the woman:

> Mrs. Monteiro . . . claimed many women were dragged away from their husbands and friends.
> "Police stormed the bar and dragged all the women out, accompanied or not," she said. "Husbands and boyfriends made protests, but were told to keep out of the way."
> She claimed a mother of eight was arrested while her husband was in the toilet. He sped after the police truck. . . .
> Lusaka's Police Chief, Mr. Martin Tembo, said yesterday: "This war started in June this year. Anybody found loitering on the street without a good reason faces arrest."

From the outset the new order occasioned a heated public debate in the press. Most citizens were said to support the campaign, on the grounds that Zambia's morality would be improved. Objections came from bar owners who complained of a business slump, and from a few of their male patrons who claimed that drinking was "no longer interesting." A few married women who had faced the ordeal of arrest and shameful condemnation as prostitutes complained bitterly, but not in the press. Women who worked night shifts were particularly bitter, expressing their problem to the Hotel and Caterers Union, whose spokesman made a public appeal to the Home Affairs Minister.

Victimization of the innocent was a pattern found throughout the Zambian towns, and it became increasingly clear that the police were not the only men involved. In many situations, men pretending to be plainclothes policemen "arrested" and subsequently raped unaccompanied women, but only one such incident was reported in the press.[22] Other men attacked the women to steal their Afro wigs,[23] just as earlier they had stoned miniskirted women entering the vegetable markets. The "young hooligans" worked with impunity, selling the stolen wigs at "cut-rate prices to girls who need them badly."[24]

Women who were supposedly professional prostitutes did not complain. They were reported to be moving on to towns where police had not yet organized raids. The reactions of my unmarried, unaffianced informants received less publicity. To them, the threat of arrest was more of a nuisance than a danger, and a clear manifestation of male hostility.

Published responses by unmarried women, however, conveyed the impression that these women really were a menace to the state:

> Miss Lisie Musonda, of Chimwemwe Township, said: "The Minister is following the activities of the detained leader of the banned UPP, Mr. Simon Kapwepwe, who strongly preached against miniskirts, cosmetics, and wigs." Miss Musonda said the report surprised her because it had not mentioned white girls.[25]

In this instance the newspaper quoted what in a Zambian context was a deliberately inflammatory statement: Miss Musonda referred to the politician Kapwepwe and the banned UPP, a provocative act on her part. Kapwepwe was considered by the politicians in power to be a highly dangerous man, even after the banning of the party. It was audacious for Miss Musonda even to mention his name. But she not only mentioned him— she actually said that the current Minister was "following his activities" (i.e., that Changufu was under Kapwepwe's influence and carrying out his policies). This implies treason. The newspaper was "objectively" reporting the reaction of a member of the public, and could not be accused of criticizing the government's policy. Rather, by publicizing Miss Musonda's statement, it showed that the women had to be shut up.

Miss Musonda also hit a raw nerve by associating danger with women's fashion styles. The association had been made many times before and was to be made many times again during the course of the campaign. For example:

> In Chiliabombwe, Mrs. Mary Chisala, UNIP constituency
> chairman of the Women's Brigade, has said that the rounding up
> of unaccompanied girls will not be effective unless a law on
> decent dressing is introduced. . . .
> Mrs. Chisala said the number of rape cases has increased
> because women put on short dresses. It is this type of dressing
> which makes men think that every girl in a minidress is a
> prostitute, she said.[26]

Home Affairs Minister Changufu had not specified the methods the police should use in dealing with "aimless loiterers," where they should look for them, the circumstances under which women should be considered unaccompanied, or the penalties to which they should be subjected. Predictably, the police—many of whom were undisciplined under normal circumstances—went out of control in a manner rivaled only by bogus police pretending to be secret agents (CID), and thieves who were molesting women. Within days they had established a reign of terror, whereupon the Home Affairs Minister issued a statement qualifying his initial order:

> Home Affairs Minister, Mr. Lewis Changufu, said in Lusaka
> yesterday that he had instructed the police to assist people found
> helpless at night and explained that the measures he announced
> recently against loitering at night would not be carried out
> indiscriminately. . . . Specific instructions have been given to
> police to help all genuine cases of people moving around at night,
> he said. . . .
> "I announced these measures in the public interest and not
> to take people by surprise. It is very unfortunate to have people

branded prostitutes because of these measures. After all, the law allows us to take such measures," he said.[27]

Changufu's reassurance that "genuine cases" should be helped rather than prosecuted was as vague as earlier statements that women were accompanied by men who were really their pimps pretending to be boyfriends and that teenage girls were accompanied by married men who also pretended to be their boyfriends. In the case of the Changufu statement, the vagueness had a sinister element. His idea that the police should help stranded women was as impractical as his initial order. Were the police—already so well-known for using "lack of transport" as an excuse for failure to help in road accidents and in pursuing thieves—suddenly to become a taxi service? Changufu's proviso was not taken seriously, nor was his guideline of a night in jail ever consistently applied. The judiciary developed *ad hoc* punishments instead, and the occasional woman who refused to plead guilty and got a lawyer who then questioned the legality of the arrest was quietly freed. Meanwhile, the police excesses continued sporadically for months.

The order was never rescinded, for the government would never admit it had erred and would never allow the townswomen to be vindicated. By 1974 the campaign seemed to have quietly died. However, I was told that in 1975, while I was out of Zambia, Copperbelt police resurrected the campaign. Like other repressive measures, this one was not reported in the press. In April 1976, however, the campaign was publicly resurrected in Lusaka, under the State of Emergency regulations.

Ambivalence in the Media: Women as Folk Heroes

10

The press was not unrelentingly misogynist, as it reflected the ambivalence felt by the wider society toward modern young women. There were other compelling reasons as well. Female elites and subelites, like their male counterparts, symbolized successful national development. The government had made explicit its intention to involve qualified women in the modernization process, and this gave newspapers one easy opportunity to show uncritical support for government policy. Finally, Zambian social classes were still in a state of flux, and daughters of the masses could still aspire to subelite status. Newspapers were in a position to provide role models: examples of what right-thinking people could become. To do this, however, the image of Lusaka's young women had to be cleaned up.

Thus, while presenting the overpowering image of townswomen as a root cause of Zambia's social problems, news media also depicted women in very different, folk hero roles: as equal to men in their potential for contributing to national development, as Zambia's indigenous pin-ups, and as mothers of the nation.

THE IMAGE OF EQUALITY: IT'S UP TO US

A theme underlying many different types of articles was the image of equality between the sexes. In granting women political equality, Zambian leaders proudly pointed to the difference between Zambia and western democracies. Whereas western women had to fight long and hard to gain the right to vote, Zambian women were given this right immediately at independence. Similarly, the legal status of Zambian women "compares favorably" with that of western women, the leaders claimed. From this starting point, Zambian leaders reasoned, social and economic equality should logically follow as a chain reaction. It was up to women to achieve equality in these spheres. For the leaders, what *should* be already existed:

> Women in Zambia have not much to fight for on equality because the Party and Government have left the door open for them to show their worth. . . . [1]

If women lagged behind men socially and economically, they had only themselves to blame:

> It is not the wish of the government to build a nation of beggars. If this happens, it will be you, the mothers, to blame.[2]

In this view, the Zambian government and national institutions provided the basic framework and opportunities for women to catch up to men.

Newspapers fostered the image of equality in a number of different ways. One way was by straight reporting. Newspapers reported speeches by male and female politicians addressing women's groups, rallies, conferences, seminars. The politicians thanked and praised the government for not discriminating against women and for allowing women to participate in economic development. Women were asked to face the challenge, build the country, change their image. Headlines exhorted:

> Come on, women, play your part[3]

> Let's show what women can do for Zambia[4]

> Women urged to lead our progress[5]

> Women's role in nation building is a great pride[6]

> Help in building up your country, women urged[7]

> Women urged to face new challenges[8]

Another way the newspapers reflected the image of equality and the "it's up to us" ideology was by group success stories. In the three-year period in which I systematically collected articles, there were 15 reports of graduation ceremonies of women in community development centers and six articles on successful women's poultry and vegetable cooperatives.

There were also formal interviews of career women. The interview and photograph of the interviewee occupied a prominent place as a special feature, and sometimes occupied as much as half a page. In 1971, five top elite national leaders were interviewed; between 1971 and 1973, 13 local level leaders. Nineteen women who were the first Zambians to enter typically female western occupations and ten who were among the first Zambian women to enter typically male occupations were interviewed in this period. The folk hero treatment was given to all these women, some of whom were in modest occupations by western standards: receptionist, dressmaker, saleslady. Some of the interviewees in male occupations were in similarly modest positions: police officer, accounts clerk, news reporter. By interviewing women in male careers the message was that women could do anything they wanted if they underwent the relevant training. The ultimate folk hero in these interviews, however, emerged as the woman who mobilized her personal resources and became highly successful. She went to school, got a job or started a business, ran for political office, married, had many children and looked after them well. If she did none of these things, she had only herself to blame. This was a clear mimicking of government ideology by the press.

Interviews served an educative function for the reading public. The type of work, the work situation, the problems involved, the required training and how the interviewee acquired the training, the experience of occupational mobility, rising through the ranks, changing careers, taking further courses, seizing opportunities for further training, were all described in detail. The emphasis was on hard work rather than lucky breaks or family contacts: these were moral lessons. The interviewees' attitudes on various subjects such as men, children, fashion, and music were also detailed, with the intention of conveying to readers a vivid image of an unknown life style.

Between September 1971 and September 1974 there were 20 articles specifically describing the employment market for women, stressing either the existence of equal opportunity in employment or the existence of discriminatory practices that should be eliminated. Occasionally, and inconsistently, women were seen sympathetically as experiencing problems in gaining employment or in being promoted, and, as successful career women, beset with problems in their social lives.

Another newspaper technique used in portraying the image of equality was more subtle and indirect: sometimes a photograph showing a woman receiving an honor of some sort accompanied a story that disclosed both men and women had received the same award. Thus, while scores of males and females were graduated from the university, a photograph of a commencement exercise might show a woman receiving her certificate. In such cases, although a woman was singled out as the subject of the photograph, no special commentary was added about how unusual it was for a woman to be receiving such an award.

Far more rarely, there were news articles or features on the work of women's voluntary associations in training women for urban roles. Every so often an article appeared describing a club organized by elite Zambian women whose volunteer work was to train poor urban women in childcare, sewing, knitting, nutrition, and poultry-keeping. Reported were the Y.W.C.A.'s project to train female drop-outs, the Family Planning and Welfare Association's work on nutrition, the work of the Zambia Association of Women's Institutes to teach school-leavers unspecified skills. Also covered were speeches before the Catholic Women's League, the National Association of Business and Professional Women, the Girl Guides Association, and the Women's Council of Zambia.

Since women's position was supposed to be determined by women themselves, it was consistent for the newspapers to report on agitation for changes in women's legal status. Even those Zambians who were most insistent about the reality of equality of the sexes admitted that in some situations women were disadvantaged. One particular area was inheritance law. Under customary law a widow inherited nothing of her deceased husband's estate. Whereas under tribal conditions this brought about no undue hardship, under modern conditions the results have been disastrous. Relatives of a deceased husband take as much of his estate as they can get—which, more often than not, is all of it. But since a change in situation was "up to the women," all the newspapers felt they could do was passively report, rather than actively crusade. Between 1972 and 1974 nine news items or features appeared on agitation for legislation to improve the status of widows. In fact, stories and headlines were misleading, indicating imminent change—but up to August 1976 when I left Zambia, nothing had happened in Parliament.

THE INDIGENOUS PIN-UP

The second folk hero role designated to women was as indigenous pin-up. This arose from the promotion of local beauty contests. On October 23, 1972, the day before the eighth anniversary of independence, Zambia held its first Miss Independence Beauty Contest. Sponsored by the Cultural Services Department of the Ministry of Provincial and Local Government and Culture, the purpose of the beauty contest was to make Zambians "more conscious of independence," according to the then Lusaka District Governor, Justin Kabwe. The provincial capitals of all eight provinces were to organize their own beauty contests. An American "expert," Mrs. Emily Hightower, flown to Zambia by the Zambian Government especially for the event, visited each provincial capital for a few hours to review the contestants. Winners and runners-up in these local contests were to travel to Lusaka a week before the contest. They were to be accommodated in University of Zambia dormitories and to spend the week being trained by Mrs. Hightower in matters of dress, make-up, and stage presence.

The press conveyed the impression that Lusaka was doting on the contest, and that, indeed, it was among the epoch-making events in the country. From June through September, the *Zambia Daily Mail*, and, to a lesser extent, the *Times of Zambia*, interviewed and photographed the young women of Lusaka who were planning to enter the contest. The style of reporting combined the "hip" lingo of Zambia and the formula developed in the western world for interviewing movie stars. The women, transformed into instant celebrities, were asked their opinions on fashion, make-up, pop music, boyfriends, hobbies, and their own personal ambitions. Some confessed to dreaming of careers in entertainment or modeling:

> She digs fancy gear of any sort ranging from a miniskirt to a maxi. Musically, James Brown, Clarence Carter, Diana Ross, the Supremes and the Rolling Stones turn her on.[9]

In October, shortly after her arrival in Zambia, Mrs. Hightower herself was interviewed as a celebrity.[10] During the week that the participants were being trained, news stories and large photographs of their various activities were published almost daily. They were introduced as a group on October 18 (*Times of Zambia*), shown relaxing at a public park on October 19 (*Zambia Daily Mail*), and meeting President Kaunda at State House on October 20 (*Times of Zambia*). Both newspapers gave large amounts of space to photographic essays on the day of the contest.

In contrast to the passive treatment afforded equality, the newspapers actively promoted the indigenous pin-up from the beginning of preparations for the first beauty contest. A public relations job was needed to gain the support of a wider society that was in many ways hostile to the sexuality of the young townswomen. Public support was all the more necessary because the contestants were to be paraded in abbreviated costumes and Zambian men consider such dress highly erotic.[11] Most Zambians disapprove of women exposing themselves in public. Modest dress and a shy, eyes-downcast demeanor had always been highly valued attributes in young women, so that the dress, postures, and gestures required for participants were at extreme variance with long accepted codes.

The public had to be reassured that the participants were truly harmless. "Pretty Belinda has no time for the Lib"[12] informed readers that Belinda was anti-feminist. "When Edna had competition from a bottle"[13] told Edna's tale of woe over her alcoholic boyfriend: an ordinary tale of an ordinary girl.

A public relations job by the news media was also needed to encourage young women themselves to participate in the contest. "Zambian women have a long way to go. . . . Come on girls, don't be shy!" read one headline.[14] The press had to fight against the conservatism not only of the wider society, but of some of the young women themselves. Furthermore, some of Lusaka's most admired young women—the University of Zambia students—refused to participate and in fact actively campaigned against the beauty contest. Although their campaign was never reported in the press, their objection was based on a feminist stance. They did not want to parade their flesh and be evaluated as sex objects, they said. Against these currents, the press had to recommend and celebrate a personality and value change in young women:

> A beauty contest provides an opportunity for girls to put their looks on display. It also gives them a chance to take pride in themselves and their appearance.[15]

> In the pageant Joyce hopes to gain experience and self-confidence.[16]

Why the fuss over beauty contests? Before the Miss Independence Contest came into being, the only published pin-ups were of foreign models and film stars, and white women predominated in these. It is no accident that a well-known man-about-town, the dashing Justin Kabwe, should have said the beauty contest would make Zambians "more conscious of independence." The beauty contest itself, and its media treatment, were geared to elite and subelite Zambians. The "consciousness of independence" was an attempt to overcome their collective national self-image of inferiority. It was as if the media and the Cultural Services Department, which normally sponsored tribal dancing events, felt that the time had come to remedy this complex. This could only be done by creating a symbol of Zambian modernity and prosperity, a symbol of how far Zambia had come in eight years of independence. It therefore had to be according to terms set by western countries, in their own manner. Miss Independence was the perfect symbol. Reporters, editors, politicians, participants, readers, and foreign observers had to be convinced. Of the Miss Lusaka contest, reported under the headline "Black is beautiful—here's proof,"[17] readers were told:

> Zambia is full of beautiful girls. That's the verdict of the 500 people who attended the 1972 Miss Lusaka beauty contest at Charter Hall.
> Among the audience were Cabinet Ministers and members of the diplomatic corps. Before the show started, Minister of Home Affairs, Mr. Lewis Changufu, said he had been very impressed by the beauty of the girls taking part.
> "When I received the show programme with pictures of the contestants, I could not believe my eyes," he said. The minister noted that Zambian beauty had been hidden "for quite a long time," and urged the girls and beauty contest promoters to produce and project beauty. . . .

This from the very minister who ordered the arrest of unaccompanied women! Participants were drawn from the segment of the population that was supposed to be ruining the country.

A dilemma was posed by the contest's success. After the 1972 Miss Independence contest, small-scale beauty contests were being conducted in schools and colleges across the land. But they were not seen as fit material for newspaper coverage. The national contest was more or less a controlled event, with contestants inaccessible, on stage, under spotlights, following instructions, in identical two-piece playsuits, paraded as objects for passive delectation to be judged by Zambian and foreign men and women. The local contests were necessarily more free-wheeling, open, and amateurish. Lusaka had to set a new standard of control.

By 1974 a solution was found. The "woman in the news" was no longer to be an individual who had departed from tradition and actively sought to participate in a beauty contest. Long interviews of dreamy, ambitious, educated young contestants were replaced by more anonymous presentations of pin-ups. For its weekend edition, the *Zambia Daily Mail* magazine began featuring a full-page photograph of a different young woman every week, selected on the basis of her pretty face and fashionable outfit. The interview was replaced by a caption identifying the woman by name, town, and occupation. The focus became her unmarried status and good looks. Her photograph became important, not her ambitions or accomplishments. She became an idealized woman, a two-dimensional picture to be put up on a wall, to be appreciated in privacy, smiling for man's pleasure. Unattainable, unreal as flesh and blood, having no opinions, she posed no threat to men: an illusion of male control could be retained. The function of the pin-up, and even the beauty contest, was to channel sexuality into harmless reveries toward inaccessible fantasy figures. The press was thus able to extol the virtues of looking beautiful, while continuing to condemn the moral character of the women who chose to do so. The pin-up was only a partially cleansed and sanitized image of a devil.

THE UNIP WOMEN'S BRIGADE: TOWNSWOMEN AS MOTHERS

Beauty contests as symbolic representation of modernization, urbanization, and westernization were insufficient to satisfy either the city-dweller's personal experience of women in town or the government's commitment to development. Insufficient too were the women interviewed as an image of equality, for these remained isolated cases. There was a need to develop an alternative image of the townswoman. It had to be positive and strong, to provide comfort and security to a population confronted by rapid social change. Therefore it had to express the mistrust of modern townswomen that sterile pin-ups could not dispel.

160

Mother was needed. In other African countries, mother as an idealized female figure lived a pure, uncorrupted village life. But such idealization could not work in Zambia. Rural life holds no attraction to the Zambian reading public. Also, to extol the rural mother would have been contrary to government ideology, since rural women represented backwardness. In the press, therefore, mother had to migrate to town.

The women's branch of the ruling party, the UNIP Women's Brigade, gave the press the material it needed to develop this image. Most of the Brigade's support and publicity-receiving activities took place in Zambia's major urban centers. Most of its members were older townswomen who had little or no formal schooling.

The Brigade selected causes popular with the government and elements of the wider society. The causes were ones that no right-thinking people could really oppose, such as support for the ruling party, respect for tradition, morality, price control, and motherhood. Moreover, their position was usually that of the old-fashioned mother supporting traditional ways at the expense of bad new ones, and trying to forge a link between tradition and town life. They therefore expressed values shared by many female migrants to town whose rural way of life had changed much less than that of young educated women. They reinforced the conviction of many men and women that life had changed too fast for proper new values and social conventions to have emerged; the only good moral values were the old ones and they ought to be instilled in the young to keep modern town life from further deterioration. The Brigade's heated opposition to the immoral practices of young women furnished good news copy by appearing to reveal and foment a "war" between women, always a popular event with the male sex.

The Brigade's role of townswoman-as-mother was obvious in its publicized stand on non-political issues affecting town life. Life crisis situations—sickness and death—present townspeople with situations that cannot be solved in a completely traditional way. To fill the gap, early in 1972 Mrs. Chibesa Kankasa, the Director of the UNIP Women's Brigade, called on women regional secretaries to form district funeral committees to make arrangements for the dead and to help the bereaved.[18] Seventeen months later she was repeating the same call, adding that part of the work of the committees would be to visit the sick in hospitals.[19] It was obviously an idea whose time had not yet come, but it did project an appealing image.

Encouraged by their director, Brigade members also policed shops and markets checking on prices to eliminate "profiteering," since they felt the government price checkers were ineffective. It was Mrs. Kankasa's encouragement rather than the havoc her Brigade caused in markets that was publicized.[20] The Brigade's price checking proved ineffective and received no further publicity or encouragement from the press.

In contrast, however, repeated press attention was given to Brigade pronouncements and activities condemning young women—and sometimes their parents as well. In establishing their own image, the Brigade took the obvious step of condemning bad town mothers as well as their daughters. The press delighted in the "war" between the Brigade and other townswomen. For years the Brigade had been active in trying to get miniskirts and Afro wigs banned, in condemning young girls for getting pregnant before marriage, and in anti-abortion campaigns.

Young women were hostile to the Brigade. For example, in the "Women's Forum" one of the contributors wrote the following analysis of the miniskirt controversy:

> The furore about miniskirts is really an argument about the position of women in society. It is an issue where men, and even some governments, have taken a position which is demonstrably and laughably illogical. All they can say to support their arguments against miniskirts is that women should return to a more traditional mode of dress.
>
> Firstly they are caught in the double-talk about democracy and traditional society—democracy for themselves and traditional society for the women. Secondly they are caught because everybody knows that in traditional society women wore almost nothing!
>
> If it's traditional dress they want, where are the men in traditional dress? Nowadays they won't even wear chitenge shirts. The only men I see nowadays in chitenge shirts are expatriates— the Zambian men are all in suits.
>
> But of course the argument is not really about dress at all; what they want to say but can't is that women should assume a traditional role, not a traditional dress.
>
> They are frightened by the miniskirt and the Afro wig in the same way that the white racialists were frightened by the black shirt and the combed-up hairstyle.[21] The men were asserting their independence and their manhood, and so now are the women asserting their independence and their womanhood.
>
> By wearing a miniskirt a woman asserts her right to attract her own mate, not to have him chosen for her. She is an independent woman, who is not going to be sold off for lobola.
>
> And more than that, as an independent woman, she wants to be able to decide not only who she will marry, but where she will work and where she will live, and how many children she will have. She wants self-determination, and the men know it.
>
> That's why they don't like the miniskirt. . . [22]

This contributor, a graduate of the University of Zambia, was among Zambia's first African secondary school teachers, married, and a mother.

Her analysis was as serious as it was threatening to the views of the UNIP Women's Brigade. Soon after, the *Zambia Daily Mail* reported on Mrs. Kankasa's view:

> Mrs. Kankasa said that although Zambian men spoke against the use of minidresses and miniskirts [their attitudes] did not mean the same [as the] hate the colonial administrators had for men using black shirts during the struggle for freedom.
>
> But she added that these days men wanted Zambian women to keep their dignity in society by using respectable dresses other than minidresses. . . . [23]

Mrs. Kankasa was clearly referring to the "Forum" analysis without saying so.

Young townswomen, and sometimes their parents, found themselves opposing positions taken by the Women's Brigade time after time on issues concerning sex. For example, in July 1972 the Parent-Teacher Association of an Ndola secondary school called on the Ministry of Education to provide contraceptives to their daughters. Ignoring the seriousness of the problem that occasioned the group's plea, the Brigade pronounced its opposition, blaming the parents for their own loose morality and for encouraging their daughters' promiscuity in a theme that continued in the press for months. In Parliament two years later, an MP brought up the issue of contraceptives for schoolgirls because the problem of schoolgirl pregnancies had become so serious. He too was damned by the Brigade. The abortion controversy also continued on and off for years as an important press theme. Here again the UNIP Women's Brigade condemned women:

> Mrs. Chibesa Kankasa . . . condemned all those who resorted to abortion. She said that Zambia was a huge, rich country with a very small population.
>
> "Indeed, what right has a human being to kill another human being?" she asked. "Suppose the mothers of our leaders decided to abort them, what would Zambia be like today?"
>
> She suggested that to prevent unwanted pregnancies the Ministry responsible for culture should set up cultural committees from village to national levels whose duty it will be to teach young people, through initiation ceremonies, about how to behave before marriage.
>
> Being one of the traditionalists of our time, Mrs. Kankasa will always scoff at the idea of introducing sex education in schools and the use of contraceptives. To her the two suggestions are unacceptable.[24]

Mrs. Kankasa and other Brigade leaders identified themselves as "traditionalists." By taking this position and distorting the reality of African women's sex lives under both traditional and modern conditions, they undercut their own credibility.

Traditionally, women practiced magical means of birth control and also obtained abortions. The Botany Museum of the University of Zambia has a large collection of medicinal plants that were used as abortifacients under tribal conditions. Urban women, rich and poor, educated and uneducated, obtain abortions. Those who have access to modern contraceptives use them; several institutions and business firms have quietly introduced the birth control pill to their female employees. Schoolgirls get pregnant even in schools in which sex education has been introduced. Mrs. Kankasa's suggestion for confronting this problem—to organize cultural committees to hold initiation ceremonies—was not simply unfeasible, it was ludicrous. If this suggestion were implemented, who then would take the blame for the social problems that resulted from male-female relationships? Those who supervise initiation ceremonies and instruct the young initiates—the old women from the villages! But ridiculous as they were, the Brigade's condemnations were too valuable for the press to ignore. The value lay in a "divide and rule" tactic. By emphasizing the war between women, the press was in a stronger position to condemn them all.

The Brigade further hurt its image by participating in mass demonstrations in support of UNIP in August and September 1971. A new political party, UPP, had arisen, which UNIP took as a serious threat to its continued rule. UNIP politicians encouraged the belief that the new party, if allowed to exist, would cause bloodshed. Some of the UNIP women demonstrators, to show their fear of the impending bloodshed and disgust for Simon Kapwepwe, the leader of the UPP, stripped to the waist, threw themselves on the ground crying, and ululated in traditional vocal expression of extreme emotion. Two, three, and four column photographs of bare-breasted demonstrators appeared in the press, along with a great deal of publicity of the women's demonstrations. President Kaunda called it:

> A most touching, moving spectacle and demonstration of support.
> I understand the pain that leads you to such action. You as
> mothers feel the pain when you bring us into this world—that is
> why you now feel the pain.[25]

Thus encouraged, the demonstrations continued. Then, within days, the government's mood changed. Following a cue from President Kaunda, who remarked that the women were now creating a crisis,[26] the underlying contempt for the Brigade was revealed in a *Times of Zambia* editorial:[27]

> This is not the time to collect half-naked women and pack them
> on lorries for breast competitions.

164

The *Zambia Daily Mail* published satirical cartoons on the same theme. A Court Magistrate said:

> Women should leave politics to politicians. Mothers should stay home and look after children. . . . [28]

The political role of the Women's Brigade was eclipsed by subsequent events. The rival political party was banned and its leaders detained in prison. Mrs. Kankasa, however, found yet another role for her Brigade in February 1973 when the leaders were released from detention:

> We, as mothers, must look out for these misfits and watch their activities. It is easier for us to gather their views than it is for the men. [29]

Thus, Mrs. Kankasa suggested that their sexuality gave UNIP women an advantage in spying on the men to see that they remained loyal to UNIP, which by then had become the only legal political party in Zambia.

Thus press treatment of Zambian townswomen as folk heroes was very fragile. It could easily be turned around, to condemn women for the very modes of conduct and appearance it had advocated. Folk hero treatment in the newspaper was always ambivalent, reflecting the ambivalence felt by the wider society toward the women. If it was up to the women to change their position in society and at the same time to uphold morality, peace, and cultural traditions, then women could easily be blamed when the position of all but a few remained unchanged, when the state of morality was chaotic, when there was political unrest, and when cultural traditions became "contaminated" by western influence. Pin-ups were applauded—but girls in miniskirts were condemned. The Women's Brigade was lauded for its demonstrations—then told it was creating a crisis. Career women were praised for their initiative and independence —then condemned for being unmarried. These contradictions are more apparent than real, however, because the underlying motif is that women are folk devils: townswomen are out of control and hence to be feared, detested, attacked.

WOMEN AS SCAPEGOATS

The processes by which prejudices against certain groups develop in a society are speeded up in times of rapid social change. When a society's institutional structure is in a state of flux, members of the society may develop a sense of anomie. Their passions become less disciplined with the decline of traditional rules of conduct. The prejudices they feel against particular groups can lead to stigmatization of the group; stigmatization in turn leads to scapegoating.

Zambians had a great variety of prejudices, and some of these focused on groups that, over time, developed into scapegoats. For example, Rhodesian Africans resident in Zambia were victims of scapegoating. However, complex political factors involving Zambia's foreign policy with respect to Southern Africa made it impossible for the media even to report on, much less to exploit, the scapegoating of Rhodesian Africans. On the contrary, the news media had to play it down. Officially, Rhodesian Africans were the "brothers and sisters" of Zambian Africans. The news media therefore could not fan the flames of hatred against this group.

Young townswomen, in contrast, were very attractive targets for scapegoating, not only by society-at-large, but by the media.[30] Firstly, they were *safe* targets. They were few in number in proportion to the rest of the population. Their economic position, mainly as salaried workers in service industries, was relatively weak. They had limited access to the sources of production, an important source of power. While financially better off than most men and women, they were not nearly as wealthy as elite men.

The women were also attractive targets because their social position was highly vulnerable. It was easier for a member of Parliament to attack schoolgirls for becoming pregnant than it would have been to attack fellow members of Parliament for making the girls pregnant.

Another reason for social vulnerability was the inability of the women to unite in common cause. While under tribal conditions the sexual division of labor had enhanced and exaggerated distinctions and differences between the sexes, in-group solidarity among the men was paralleled by in-group solidarity among the women. In town, however, the in-group solidarity of the women disappeared even before education and career opportunities became available. As housewives in town, women had very limited reason or opportunity to cooperate with each other. The appearance of the new type of Zambian woman exaggerated the divisions that already existed, borne of housewifely isolation. Female solidarity is impossible when one group assumes the role of "townswoman-as-mother" and attacks the group that, by default, assumes the role of "townswoman-as-whore."

The fact that young educated townswomen were easily recognized and identified by their clothing and comportment also made them attractive targets for scapegoating. It is much more difficult to victimize people who do not stand out from the rest. In their miniskirts, Afro wigs, and, later on, their high platform shoes, the young townswomen stood out from women dressed in *chitenge* and headscarves, in flat-heeled shoes or barefoot.

Townswomen made attractive targets for scapegoating because they could be blamed for undermining all those core values of society which were associated with women's traditional roles. In this respect, scape-goating was not confined merely to educated women, but was extended to *all* townswomen: as we have seen, even the UNIP Women's Brigade was not exempt. Traditional values were associated with rural women. This association had roots in the colonial period of Zambian history, when most women remained in the rural areas while men migrated to the towns. By the time women began moving to the towns in large numbers, a social complexity had already developed there which virtually pre-cluded the general acceptance of any parochial tradition. Such forms as survived did not survive intact. The members of the UNIP Women's Bri-gade who bared their breasts to demonstrate their love of President Kaunda and their fear of the potential bloodshed that the rival political party would cause were supposedly expressing, in a traditional way, their maternal concern for the well-being of Zambian society. But despite their attempt to play up the maternal image of woman as guardian of tradition and symbol of fertility, theirs was a political, not a maternal act. In the end, they were humiliated. The mother-in-town was a new and disturbing image that could not be taken seriously as the guardian of old traditions. She was not supervising the initiation ceremonies of young girls as she once did; she was only calling for their reintroduction. She was not vis-iting the sick and forming burial societies: she was only suggesting these as good ideas. Her activities were either empty verbalizations or blatantly political statements, and she was the guardian of what Kaunda wanted to become: a tradition of unchallenged political rule. Thus she not only failed to provide a satisfying alternative to the core values associated with women's traditional roles, but despite propaganda to the contrary, she was also seen as eroding these roles.

Scapegoating becomes highly effective when society dehumanizes the victim. Then victims become psychologically expendable. It was not enough to dehumanize townswomen by labelling them all prostitutes. The older, "respectable" Brigade members certainly could not be so dis-missed. The new label of "unaccompanied woman" served the purpose far more effectively. Here was woman at her most dangerous, alone after dark. But if she was at her most dangerous, she was also at her most vul-nerable. So here is where she was most easily victimized, under the guise of social control. Here the press, the police, and society-at-large operated in common interest, and hate could be channeled into safe and respectable activity.

Stereotyping precedes scapegoating, and stereotypes do not arise in a vacuum. A stereotype must have some kernel of truth in it, and this truth later becomes inflated into more imaginary distinctions that justify the ill-treatment that comes with scapegoating. One of the stereotyped im-ages of young Zambian townswomen had to do with the clothes they wore and the way they wore them. On one level, it could be argued that Zambian women were no more fond of western-style miniskirts and tight, provocative trousers than Zambian men were of fashionable European men's clothes. Neither men nor women wore traditional dress. But on another level, miniskirted women did sometimes cultivate a sexy ambience. They did not adapt to their miniskirts by taking care when they bent over, or by sitting close-legged in chairs: knowingly, they provoked men. Their skirts were often not simply a few inches above the knee, but barely covered their panties. It amused them to observe male reactions, although they sometimes became hostile and angry when men responded by demanding sex. It was also true that unmarried women were rarely reluctant to have sexual intercourse with married men, and if one of their lovers had a high-paying job they were not averse to actively urging him to divorce his wife. The women were also "expensive," in that they were highly class-conscious.

In theory, Zambian men could as easily have been stereotyped. Men dressed in platform shoes and tight trousers to be sexy; married men told their girlfriends they would divorce their wives; men were as class-conscious as women. But because they had a monopoly of political, economic, military, and social power, men could not in fact be scapegoated so easily. And, since men controlled the media, there was no opportunity for counterstereotyping to develop.

The victims of stereotyping and subsequent scapegoating almost inevitably develop certain distinctive personality traits in response to their treatment in the hands of the wider society. In *Coppertown: Changing Africa*, a study of life in the Copperbelt towns of the 1950s, Hortense Powdermaker found that schoolgirls dreamed of being men. What they were doing was unconsciously denying their membership in a victimized and powerless group, a very straightforward and understandable psychological response. When sex is the basis for victimization, "passing," or denying membership, can only be done at the fantasy level, of course. Other reactions to victimization are more realistic for women. Among the most common are withdrawal and passivity, slyness and cunning, and aggression against one's own group. In Zambia, these traits were not only the private defenses of individuals, but were socially encouraged. They were all negative traits, developed as tactics for survival. They were certainly not adaptive for individual enrichment.

Positive personality traits that sometimes result from victimization are sympathy, militancy, enhanced achievement motivation, and symbolic status striving. These too were supposed to be socially approved in Zambia. But few women became particularly sympathetic types of people, and those who adopted the other supposedly positive traits found themselves condemned as "too proud" and thereby dismissed.

Were they "too proud?" Perhaps it would seem that some were. But all human interaction is by definition reciprocal. There is a strong element of the self-fulfilling prophesy in the stereotyping of these women. What people thought of them was bound to some degree to fashion what they became. It was a vicious circle.

The Future

11

With the young women of Zambia suffering in their new-found "emancipation" and the wider society deeply ambivalent, the question naturally arises: how permanent will be the change in the social status of women? Do the opportunities for education and career created by Zambia's political independence herald a time when the women will achieve equality in all spheres, as envisioned by some of their leaders? Considering the Zambian scene as a whole, there are legitimate grounds for pessimism.

Disadvantages for women begin early in life. The vast majority of children do not go beyond the primary school level and the drop-out rate for girls is much higher than for boys at succeeding levels of schooling. Women therefore continue to lag behind men in education. Social conditions are largely responsible for the underachievement in the girls' intellectual and creative potential. Young girls who live with relatives while attending day school are expected to do housework, serve adults, and care for babies as a matter of priority. Adolescents and women just out of their teens leave secondary school or training programs because they get pregnant and are expelled.

Women lag behind men in economic activity. The percentage of women directly participating in the modern economic sector is small, both absolutely and in proportion to the number of men. To an extent this is unavoidable, because mining is the backbone of the industrial economy. The job market is considerably narrower for women than for men. Although the government emphasizes the development of *all* its human resources, the main areas in which it aims at recruiting women are in the classic women's occupations in the west. There are many more places for women in nursing, clerical work and teaching than in industrial technology.

Women's new educational and occupational status is partly an artifact of the Zambianization of the labor force. Zambian women *must* replace foreign women in specific professions: this is government policy. At the same time, old prejudices against women are still very much alive and new ones are rapidly developing. Whenever they can get away with it, employers tend to prefer hiring foreign women. Often Zambian women are as much window dressing as are the black Zambian Personnel Managers hired by the mines to demonstrate to the government the sincerity of their desire to Zambianize. Yet since the trend in the immediate future is to replace foreigners with local citizens, this prejudice against hiring Zambian women is probably a passing phase that will soon be corrected. Most jobs will eventually be filled by Zambians.

The long-term future seems bleak, however. As long as the process of Zambianizing jobs continues, there will be additional places for women in the modern economic sector, and it will appear that women are making progress. But what will happen after all the foreigners are replaced?

The government has so far published three five-year plans to expand, diversify, and continue to develop Zambia's modern economy. Few of the goals set forth in the plans have been achieved. In fact, in 1975 the economy appeared to be moving steadily backward rather than forward.

Even if the economy of Zambia grows in the future, it cannot keep pace with population growth. There will be fewer positions opening in the modern economic sector relative to the size of Zambia's exploding population. Even now the income gap between rich and poor Zambians steadily widens. An economist at the University of Zambia estimates that the gap in 1976 was about 300 to one—that is, the rich enjoyed an income 300 times larger than that of the poor. Socioeconomic class lines are hardening now even more than in the colonial era. The social and economic conditions of Zambia's masses appear to be steadily worsening. And the population keeps growing.

Women may discover that their initial economic success and enhanced status were an ephemeral product of Zambia's achievement of political independence. In the coming inevitable stiff competition for school places and jobs, it seems to me that females will be particularly disadvantaged. The recognized male offspring of elite men will have a competitive advantage over females and poor people. The results of competition and sex prejudice under conditions of scarcity are already obvious in Lusaka's primary schools. There are many more children living in town than there are school places. On registration day parents queue up for hours to register their children—theoretically on a first-come-first-served basis. Teachers registering children have begun demanding bribes, calling them "registration fees." As word of the need for registration fees gets around the shantytowns, parents are tending to use the little money they have to register their sons rather than their daughters—if they can get a child in to school at all. On the Copperbelt of the 1950s, it used to be said that education was wasted on girls. This attitude changed with the flush of independence and an era of rising expectations. But with the flush and its attendant optimism gone, old attitudes are beginning to reappear.

There will continue to be a small number of places opening for women in the modern sector. Women employed at present will retire; the economy may recover and grow. But these will almost certainly be insufficient, and there are other grounds for concern. If the male children of elite men cannot be placed in men's jobs, they may well begin cutting into the job market for women. Even now some business firms, frustrated by the drop-out rate of female trainees due to pregnancy, have announced they are recruiting males for typing courses. The teaching profession is already mixed; men may well come to dominate. Perhaps women will create new opportunities for themselves in farming and business; perhaps professional prostitution will increase; perhaps a category of bourgeois housewives will arise. But it does not seem to me that in the future women will participate in the formal wage-earning modern economic sector with the same vigor that they do today.

A few years after independence, a small group of women came together to agitate for the introduction of legislation in Parliament to improve the position of women. Customary law, modern law, and western-inherited custom were all sex-prejudiced, especially rules governing marriage and divorce. Both single and married women were discriminated against. For example, married females were not eligible for housing and single pregnant teachers were not given maternity leave. On marrying, women in government service were forced to "retire" and were rehired on probation. Wives were sometimes not eligible for loans or their husband's signature was required although they were working. To get contraception at the government hospital required a husband's written permission. Wives were taxed at a higher rate than husbands, which produced hardship in cases of separation. Widows whose husbands died intestate surrendered their husbands' property to his relatives.

In 1970, a conference of 33 Zambian African and three non-African women leaders, educated and uneducated, was held at the Mindolo Ecumenical Foundation, a mission-backed institution on the Copperbelt. The issue was women's rights. Recommendations were passed by the conference and presented to the Attorney General. The Foreword to the *Report of the Proceedings* stated:

> Women's rights in Africa today present a particularly urgent challenge because of the existence of two legal systems: customary law and statutory law. The upheaval in family life and sexual ethics, inherent in the process of rapid industrialisation and urbanisation, has brought confusion and unhappiness, as well as an increase in the divorce rate. . . .
>
> It was hoped that the consultation would achieve two main effects:
>
> a) the impetus for a nation-wide campaign to educate women concerning their rights, and
> b) the initial step toward legislative reform.

The recommendations included a request for a unitary law of marriage embodying the best in both custom and statutory law. Also requested was a unitary law of divorce, an end to forced purification (a traditional ritual of many of Zambia's tribes in which a widow was required to have sexual intercourse with a successor of the deceased husband in order to be cleansed and released from the marriage bond), decisions on custody of children with the childrens' interest at heart, and child support and alimony for divorcees who are awarded custody of their children.

The recommendations of 1970 were repeated in a paper presented by a leading elite Zambian woman in early 1973 before another conference. Later that year she once again read her paper to a meeting of the Lusaka Young Women's Christian Association I attended. There were similarities to a revival meeting as women spoke out against their own bitter experiences and the need for reform. Over the years articles appeared in the newspapers: features describing the necessity of legislative reform to benefit women, news articles reporting results of women's seminars, resolutions, and speeches on behalf of women's rights by male and female politicians.

Despite this agitation, there was no change in the law. Some people felt this was because there were only two women in Parliament, and that if their number increased reform would be possible. One of these female MPs had told me, for example, that over the years she had received a number of secret messages of support from her male colleagues for her speeches on behalf of women's rights. Wishing to avoid the problems in their personal lives and ridicule sure to follow from their other male colleagues, the men said, they could only rarely support her openly. This woman's sometimes emotional speeches in Parliament did in fact evoke laughter at times.

Women's enthusiasm and some publicity were generated at the time of the December 1973 elections. At that time 523 candidates contested 124 seats; 13 contestants were women and six were elected. Of the six, one, the country's first female Ph.D., was named Minister of Health; another, its first female lawyer, was named Solicitor General. Although collectively considering themselves firmly committed to women's rights and equality of opportunity, most of the new token force of female parliamentarians proved ultimately as conservative as the leaders of the UNIP Women's Brigade. They fell into the trap of the war between women. The "radicals" were swamped. Yet again reform was not forthcoming.

The lack of progress is not surprising. Women seriously dedicated to working for women's rights were a minority of a minority. Their views were pitted against those of conservative women who were determined to make the situation comfortable for men. Speeches like the one given at the Mindolo conference by the President's wife, Betty Kaunda, had a decidedly repressive effect:

> I feel it necessary at the outset to clarify our goals in this consultation. The question of women's rights is a controversial issue in our day. When we talk about women's rights, we run the risk of antagonising the men—our husbands, our fathers, our brothers, our colleagues. We have no desire to offend them.
>
> Our Zambian men fear the question of women's rights. They are afraid of three things: they fear we want to overthrow tradition, to do away with our old customs; they fear we shall neglect our duties in the home, our role in the family as wives and mothers; and they fear that we women want to take away their authority and power. Indeed they fear indiscipline in the home. Even now with this Consultation following closely the Preparatory Meeting of the Women's Organisation . . . some think we are becoming a Civil Rights Movement or a Liberation Organisation.
>
> My fellow women, we must take these doubts seriously. We Zambian women respect our menfolk. . . . We are not seeking to overthrow tradition. To the contrary. . . . Further, by way of reassurance to our menfolk, *we do not want to neglect our duties in the home.* To the contrary. . . . Our Zambian brothers, *we do not want to take away your authority and power.* We talk about woman-power, but we do not mean it as a threat to man-power! . . . We do not want development at the cost of moral decay. Broken homes and unhappy marriages are too high a price to pay for progress. I see a new role for women, a new task for woman-power: we must be the custodians of happiness and security in the home, the watchdogs of morality in our society. . . . We must unite our talents and energies to work towards stabilising the position of women in our society. . . . Perhaps the biggest obstacle to the achievement of full rights for women is women themselves. There is not only the problem of attitudes and prejudices of men towards women but also of women towards themselves. Many women are taught from childhood that they are second-class

174

human beings. . . . Every woman can do something—starting from herself. . . .

Lacking the gift of prophesy, I cannot be certain of women's future role in Zambia. However, it seems to me that as long as there is a war between married and unmarried women, as long as barriers separate the educated and the uneducated, and female political leaders play more to a male than a female audience, the status and rights of Zambian women will be less than those of Zambian men. I do not see these basic weaknesses of the women's position changing. One can only hope that they will, however, as one hopes that the institutional and demographic structures of the country will change to provide a climate in which the oppression of women will cease.

As unlikely as it would seem in this decade, the institutional and demographic structures of Zambia may possibly change to provide a climate for the enhancement of women's position. The lesson of the colonial experience is germane. In the 1950s, it seemed to most Northern Rhodesians that colonial rule would last forever. Yet within a decade, Zambia was free. A few individuals born in the right time and place helped in this achievement, leading the African citizens to make conditions so uncomfortable for Britain that in the end Britain willingly handed over political power. Then, it seemed, Britain would never relinquish its economic hold over its former colony. The colony was politically free but it seemed forever economically enslaved to Britain. In a few short years, that too changed: the Americans, Germans, Italians, Yugoslavs, Russians, and Chinese came to overshadow British involvement.

Perhaps a parallel group of a few educated young women of Lusaka will soon write their own scenario for the future and will not accept reversals. This is their time and their place to come forward. Perhaps these individuals will refuse to give up their gains and will work to expand them for all Zambia's women to pass on a tradition of achievement to the next generation.

Appendix:
The Survey Questions

(SUBELITE SAMPLE)

I. *Childhood data obtained from all interviewees*

1. What is your home area?
2. What is your place of birth?
3. What is your birth date? (or approximate year of birth)
4. What languages do you speak? Where did you learn these?
5. Where did you live before starting primary school? With whom? (relationship to ego [i.e., interviewee]; occupation of host—tribe and occupation of host's spouse; other children in household)
6. Where did you attend lower primary school? (other questions as above)
7. Where did you attend upper primary school? (other questions as above)
8. What other places have you lived? (other questions as above) Question repeated later in interview for accuracy check: Did anyone besides your parents (sister, brother, etc.) help raise you?
9. What was your father's job? (occupational history) Did he go to church? (details) Did he go to political meetings? (details)
10. Did your mother ever earn any money herself? Did she go to church? (details) Did she go to political meetings? (details) Did she go to a homecraft center? (details)
11. Marital history, tribes of parents, number of children, dead and alive, of mother and father. (Sample question: Are your parents: still mar-

ried/widowed: mo. dead fa. dead/remarried/divorced: mo. fa. remarried/monogamous/polygamous)
12. Occupations of parents' male and female friends and neighbors.
13. Have any members of either your mother's or father's families especially influenced you? When you were growing up, were there any older women or girls you especially admired? Who? Why?
14. Since so many girls from your early school days did not become as successful as yourself, can you say that your family was somehow "different" from other families you knew as a child? How?
15. Siblings data: age, education, occupation, marital status, number of children, tribe and occupation of spouse, place of residence.

Additional childhood data obtained for female university students

16. Parents' education, social activities, mother's age at time of marriage.
17. Did you ever feel a sense of conflict over traditional and modern values at home? (details)
18. What household chores did you learn to do as a child?
19. Did you ever have any illnesses? How were these treated?
20. Do you remember a time when your family was hungry? What about other children you knew?
21. Primary school: name, location, language of instruction, nationality of teachers and students, coeducational or girls school, age of attendance, like or dislike.
    Did you like your teachers?
    Did they encourage you?
    Did you do better in school than your schoolmates?
    What were the attitudes of your schoolmates toward your performance?

II. *Data on adolescence obtained from all interviewees*

1. Secondary school: name, location, coeducational or girls, government or mission, boarding or day, form completed.
2. Did you like school?
3. Did you belong to any teams or clubs? Were you a prefect? (detail)
4. Did any teachers seem especially interested in you? (detail)
5. Did you or anyone in your family want you to take a job or marry instead of continuing in school?
6. Casual employment history (e.g., on school holidays, between leaving school and being accepted in the next training program).

7. Did you ever want to leave secondary school? Why did you stay?
8. Did anyone ever help you with school work? Who? When?
9. Did you ever feel you were competing with boys?
10. What was the attitude of the boys toward your academic performance?
11. When did you decide to apply to UNZA (i.e., the University of Zambia)? Whose idea was it?

Additional data on adolescence from working women and nursing students

12. Who supported you during adolescence? In training?
13. Did you want to do any kind of work other than office work/nursing?
14. For nurses: When did you decide to become a nurse? Did you know any nurses before you decided to become a nurse? Was nursing your first choice? Why did you choose nursing?

III. *Attitude data for nurses, office workers, student nurses*

1. Would you raise your female children differently from the way you were raised? (examples: to speak more freely; to be close to the father)
2. Life for women in Zambia has changed rapidly since grandmother's day and even more since independence. Do you think Zambian women have any special problems as a result of these changes?
3. Are there any traditional practices you would like to keep?

Attitude data for university women

1. The President's wife, Mrs. Betty Kaunda, has said that as Zambian girls grow up they are not given as much chance to express themselves *at home* as their brothers are. Do you agree or disagree?
2. Mrs. Kaunda says that girls are expected to obey their parents and also their older brothers and sisters. Agree or disagree?
3. Do you feel you worked harder at household chores than your brothers did?
4. Did your brothers have more leisure time?
5. Do you feel your brothers were more free to come and go as they pleased?
6. Were your brothers expected to speak up—to argue—more than you were? Were they permitted to speak up?
7. Mrs. Kaunda says that because of the type of upbringing a Zambian girl has, she becomes very shy and unsure of her intelligence and

abilities. Do you think this is *generally* true? Is it true of yourself? Do you see this kind of upbringing as being a social problem in Zambia?

8. Do you ever feel frustrated or dissatisfied with the situation or do you basically accept it for yourself?
9. Would you try to raise your own daughter to believe or behave differently?
10. Would you criticize more aggressive women or would you (openly or secretly) support them?
11. Have you ever thought about these things before?

IV. *Data on present life style: for university women*

A. Studies

1. Year, degree program
2. What career are you being trained for? Is this your first choice? What was your first choice? Are you satisfied with your present program? Do you think you will change careers? What would you change to? Is there something you would rather be doing other than attending UNZA?
3. Do you enjoy your courses?
4. How do UNZA men feel about having women in the classroom? How do UNZA women feel about having men in the classroom?

B. Leisure

1. What do you enjoy doing when not studying?
2. Do you belong to any clubs?
3. Do you enjoy your life at the university?
4. How do you like having men around the campus? How do the men like having women around the campus?
5. Do you have a steady boyfriend? (Would you like to have one?)
6. Boyfriend: occupation, place of residence, length of relationship. Do you hope to marry him? When?
7. Do you think most university women marry men they met on campus? If not students, what sort of men are the university women's boyfriends? Where do they meet these men?

Data on present life style: single working women

A. Work and daily life

1. Type of work, company, how long had job, how got job, like or dislike present job.

180

2. Would you like to change jobs? What would you rather do?
3. How do you get to work? (Bus, taxi, walk, car: whose car?)
4. How do you normally spend lunch hour? (with girlfriends, boyfriend, eat in restaurants, in office, shop)
5. Do you see your girlfriends daily? What do they do? (where they work, type of jobs)
6. How do you spend your hours after work? (If with boyfriend: do you cook for him?)
7. Are your girlfriends mainly from your own language group? Did you meet them after you started working? Are they mainly from your secondary school? What sort of things do you do together?
8. How do you spend weekends?

B. Leisure

1. Hobbies and interests.
   Do you like: parties/dances/films/nightclubs-bars-discos/music (own record player? radio?)/sewing (own machine?)/clubs/church (which, how often)/reading/sport/other/courses now taking.
2. Boyfriend: occupation, location of work, of residence.
   How long have you been with him?
   What is his language group?
   What was his education?
   Does he sometimes buy you presents? What? (details)
   Does he have a car?
   What things do you like or dislike about him?
   Would you like to marry him? (If not, why not; if yes, why)
   Are you on the pill?

C. Income Management

1. Salary.
2. Do you keep a budget?
3. What do you spend your money on? (how much for: food, rent, clothing, cosmetics, hire-purchase, water, electricity, debts, transport, support of relatives: regularly, irregularly; savings)
4. Who can you *borrow* money from when you run short of cash?
5. Who *gives* you money when you run short of cash?
6. Relationship to ego of those she supports. Amount of support.
7. Favorite shops (Lusaka, Copperbelt).

D. Household Structure

1. How long have you lived in this flat/house? (description of residence, including possessions)

2. Who lives with you? (how long, relationship, occupation, if shares expenses, other details).
3. Has anyone else stayed with you? (who, how long, when).

E. Relatives in Lusaka

Who are they, where do they live, how often do you visit them: any information interviewee can provide including marital status, occupations, number of children, tribes of relatives and spouses.

Data on present life style: student nurses

NB: Same questions asked as for working women, IV. B., C., E. as above. A. not necessary (work routinized; observed at hospital) and D. irrelevant (live in dormitories).

1. Do you still have friends from your school days? Where are they? How often do you see them?
2. Do you have other girlfriends in Lusaka? Where do they work? Are they married?
3. Are most of your girlfriends student nurses?
4. When do you manage to get to town? (weekday evenings, weekends) How?
5. How do you spend your time after work? Weekends?
6. Would you rather live away from the hospital? Why do you live in the dormitory? Have you ever had your own flat?

Data on present life style: married working women

NB: Same questions asked as for single working women, IV. A. 1, 2; B.1; C; D; E. (to E. added husband's relatives).

C. Income Management: Additional Data

1. Husband's occupation, salary.
2. Do you keep your own salary separate or do you combine salaries?
3. If separate: what do you pay for? What does he pay for?
4. Amount spent monthly on: (to C. as above, add the following:) car, servants, insurance, own relatives, husband's relatives, (who, how often, how much), reasons for saving money.
5. Who decides on special purchases? If you want something that your husband doesn't want, do you buy it with your own money?

D. Household Structure

Additional question: Is this the first house you've lived in since getting married? If not, where did you live before?

F. The Marriage Relationship

1. How long are you married?
2. Did you choose your husband?
3. Did your family approve?
4. Is he of your tribe? (If not: what tribe is he?)
5. Was it a church/boma/customary marriage?
6. How much was *lobola*? Has he finished paying?
7. How long did you go steady with him before marrying him?
8. Were you married before this? Was he?
9. Did you have other boyfriends before you went steady with him?
10. Are you happy with the marriage? Are there any special problems with it?
11. Do you have children? Who cares for them while you work?
12. How many (more) would you like to have? Does your husband agree?
13. Leisure activities: as for B.1, single working women, but add if ego does this alone or with husband, and detailed data on visits to own relatives and husband's relatives alone or together; friends visited alone or together.

Additional autobiographical data on single and married working women

Full employment histories: type of work, dates, location, how obtained, who lived with.

V. Aspirations data obtained from all unmarried interviewees

1. When would you like to marry?
2. What type of man would make an ideal husband? (detail) (own marital history data obtained here: have you ever been married; if yes, reasons for divorce; own childbearing history here: did you want to marry the father of your child(ren); why/why not.) Would you marry a man your family disapproved of?
3. Should you marry a man from your own tribe? (Why/why not)
4. How many children would you like to have? (If already has children: where are they living?)
5. Would you work after the children are born? Why?
6. Would you like to stay in Lusaka? Where would you rather go?
7. Other future plans, hopes.

Aspirations data for married women: 6, 7 above.

Additional aspirations data for UNZA students

8. If you were given K10,000 tomorrow—no strings attached—what would you do?
9. Is there something—besides working—you would really love to do after graduating from university?

*   *   *

Order of the interviews

Interviews began with a discussion of the woman's present life style: the life on campus, at the job, leisure, friendships with women and boyfriends, income management, household structure, and relatives in Lusaka. (For married interviewees, read husband for boyfriend.)

Next came questions about the future aspirations and plans. It was felt that by opening the discussion with present and future, a woman would be more likely to relax and "open up" to the more difficult task of remembering the past. Potentially embarrassing or painful questions (divorce, illegitimate children, for example) were "snuck into" other topics, or were casually mentioned during the course of the interview.

Interviews gradually worked back into the past: training, secondary schooling, primary schooling, preschool, family background, and, finally, attitudes.

Interviewees were encouraged to digress whenever they felt like it, or to decline to answer any questions they wished. They were also encouraged to ask the interviewer why certain questions were raised.

Notes

Chapter 1

1. Not all interviewees knew their year of birth. My general interest was in women under the age of thirty. I was able to establish approximate age by asking them when, in relation to Zambia's attainment of political independence in 1964, they experienced their first menses. Both of these are unforgettable events in the lives of Zambian women.

2. It was the native language of many of the peoples who migrated to Lusaka, and was adopted by others as the language of communication.

3. For providing me with various materials I wish to thank Bernice Ezeilo, Margie Hall, Gwen Konie, Ilse Mwanza, and Namposha Serpell.

Chapter 2

1. The *Colonial Office Report* No. 145 relates how commercial exploitation of lead, zinc, and vanadium in Kabwe (Broken Hill) began in 1904. The extension of the railway from Bulawayo in Southern Rhodesia to Livingstone began by 1905. It reached Broken Hill by 1906, and Ndola, an old African-Arab trade center, by 1909. Sawmilling developed in Livingstone for the railroads and eventually the mines; in 1907 it became the territorial capital.

The British South Africa Company was successful in its attempts to establish rubber and sisal plantations. But by 1936 there were 343 European permits of occupation in the fertile area along the line of rail. Cattle and trading figured prominently here before World War One, and maize and cattle thereafter.

Small European towns grew up in what are now Southern and Central Provinces: Mazabuka, Choma, Kalomo, and Lusaka, all south of Broken Hill. In Eastern Province around Chipata (Fort Jameson), a quarter century after British troops conquered Ngoniland, a slump forced 107 families to quit their tobacco farms in 1926–27, leaving 54 settlers who were assisted by the colonial government to remain. There were also 12 coffee estates at Mbala (Abercorn), extremely small scale even today.

2. Between 1940 and 1963, the proportion of laborers migrating to the Copperbelt from Western, Central and Southern Provinces remained constant. Northern, Eastern, and Copperbelt Provinces varied upwards or downwards between two and five percent. Migration from the Luapula Province declined because a lucrative fish trade to the Copperbelt developed between 1940 and 1950, and Luapulans created urban-like conditions there. Migrations from Northwestern Province also declined because Northwesterners were recruited to work in the South African gold mines.

3. There are three parastatal corporations in Zambia. These are basically holding companies in which the government owns the controlling shares. They cover the mining (MINDECO), industrial (INDECO) and financial (FINDECO) development of the country. Managing directors are appointed by the President of Zambia, Kenneth Kaunda.

4. The 1969 census records Lusaka's population as 262,425. But by then the city had more than doubled since the previous census six and a half years before, and in the mid 1970s the municipal boundaries were extended to include outlying suburbs and additional thousands of residents. It is one of the fastest growing cities in the world.

5. The low-income site and service scheme was the Zambian government's answer to the problem of accommodating the burgeoning urban population. A site and service scheme is an area authorized by the government for housing development. The government surveys and grades the area, designating plots and sometimes digging pit latrines. Piped water is provided, sometimes to every house, sometimes to every few houses. Plots are allocated to individuals who are then required to build their own houses out of approved materials and to an approved design, and are given a loan of K120.00 (K1.00=$1.50 in 1972) to do so.

6. "Coloured" is a distinct, named group, designating persons of mixed white-African ancestry. The usage in Zambia is the same as in South Africa and Rhodesia.

Chapter 3

1. No accurate statistics can be compiled from other sources—not even from the school records if these could be obtained. Girls who find they are pregnant often quietly leave school rather than face the public humiliation of expulsion. Nevertheless, news articles yield some insight into the extent of the problem.

For example, ten of fifteen trainee air hostesses had to leave the program

("More pregnant airgirls quit training," *Zambia Daily Mail,* October 19, 1971); "more than twenty" trainee typists quit a mining company program ("Pregnant typists hand over to men," *Zambia Daily Mail,* September 23, 1971); five student nurses were expelled from a hospital ("Five girls expelled," *Zambia Daily Mail,* September 10, 1973); two from secondary school ("Girls out," *Times of Zambia,* January 9, 1973); 65 from two other secondary schools ("Don't write off these pregnant school girls, pleads teacher," *Times of Zambia,* July 5, 1972). One article ("Pregnancies: let the guilty pay," *Zambia Daily Mail,* July 10, 1972) reported that more than 200 girls are expelled from secondary schools each year because of pregnancy.

Chapter 4

1. In 1953, 21 girls were enrolled in lower secondary school, and senior secondary school was made available. A new technical training program was launched five years later by the Mindolo Girls Boarding School, which had been founded in 1942. The program was a one-year course, either in dressmaking or in cooking, and cost 16 pounds. Thirty girls were enrolled the first year.

Figures for enrollment in homecraft training programs in 1960 show 411 female primary school graduates and 166 wives of students at teacher training colleges. In addition, 183 women were enrolled in primary teacher training programs, and 135 were enrolled in other homecraft or health education courses. Three women were studying at the University College of Rhodesia and Nyasaland in Salisbury, Rhodesia. Two women were studying domestic science in England.

On the eve of independence only six or seven women were qualified to teach secondary school, perhaps 1,000 were primary school teachers, some others were domestic science instructors, and a few were nurses. Zambia's first state registered nurse had only finished training in South Africa in 1958.

2. Urban secondary school students are cynical about certain aspects of their "Zambianized" curriculum. Their history and civics classes teach the official government ideology of a society based on the philosophy of "humanism"—a democracy in which the worth of the individual and the value of work on the land are respected. But there is a discrepancy between the official policy presented to school children and what they experience. For example, Zambian teachers punish children by forcing them to work in school gardens. The author of their civics text, a white university lecturer, was deported by the government after being imprisoned without charge. Their mothers are forced to buy membership cards in the only legal political party in Zambia in order to enter the vegetable market; their fathers must produce these cards in order to board a bus. Political repression and class privilege are obvious to urban secondary school children.

3. *Phillips Report,* quoted in "Aims of Education for Girls in Nyasaland," *African Women,* IV, 4 (1962), 91–92.

4. *African Women,* V, 2 (1962), 10.

5. Foreword to first edition of *African Women,* I, 1 (1954), 3.

6. *African Women,* II, 4 (1958), 76.

7. In the mid 1970s, the Zambian government began requiring students to enter National Service camps in the rural areas. The description of adolescent years in the text is relevant to the times before these camps were established.

8. Friendships among Zambia's top elite women seem to confirm the enduring nature of high school relationships. One group attended Chipembi Secondary School. After leaving Chipembi, they tended to leave Zambia for a time to study for advanced degrees, returning as "firsts" in a variety of fields. Some see each other socially and are close friends. They work together on committees and in clubs. In 1971 none were in politics; by 1974 seven were in top government posts.

Chapter 5

1. When the interviews were conducted in 1972–73, it was my hope to interview all the Zambian African women who were working in the offices of the most important business firms in Lusaka, and all the Zambian African women who were fully employed as State Registered Nurses at the bigger of Lusaka's two hospitals: the University Teaching Hospital. The aim was thus to interview a total population of professional career women in offices and in nursing.

Since in those early years after independence female staff in both offices and hospitals was almost entirely foreign, total population sampling seemed to be a realistic technique. There were no statistics available on the citizenship of female personnel, however, or even on the number of personnel according to sex.

The method I used in locating interviewees was to introduce myself to the Personnel Managers of the major business firms, explain the project, and ask permission to make contact with staff. In the case of the hospital interviews, I asked the permission of the Matron. The Matron and the Personnel Managers were most cooperative in making initial introductions, and then the women themselves continued introducing me to their workmates, distinguishing between Zambian African and non-Zambian African employees.

The office women who were the subjects of interviews worked at the headquarters of the three parastatal corporations of the Zambian government: INDECO, the industrial development corporation, FINDECO, the financial development corporation, and MINDECO, the mining development corporation. I also interviewed office staff in the Lusaka headquarters of the major private mining companies in Zambia: the Anglo-American Corporation and the Roan Consolidated Trust, as well as some of the spin-off companies of INDECO.

Nearly all the single women I approached agreed to interviews. In fact, nearly all of them expressed both shock and excitement that someone would be willing to talk to them about their lives and were pleased when I said I would be writing a book about them.

The technique used was to make an appointment with a woman for some time after work, either on a weekend or a weekday evening. The woman chose if she wanted to be interviewed at her home or if she wanted me to pick her up from her home or workplace and drive her to my home for the interview and then back to her home.

As with all sociological surveys, more women made appointments than kept them. Over time I developed a set of guidelines regarding broken appointments, allowing a maximum of four before I stopped pursuing an interviewee. In the end, 48 women were interviewed.

The spin-off informal observations that were made in homes, the neighborhoods, and in the night life of Lusaka over the years seemed to me to make up for the absence of clear-cut sampling techniques. The few simple statistics I use are to provide examples of possible trends.

2. "Mpika in transition," *Zambian Daily Mail*, September 24, 1974.

3. Editorial, *Zambia Daily Mail*, February 18, 1976.

4. "Moving up and down," like "movious" are Zambian-English slang expressions. A "movious" person "moves up and down." That is, he or she leads a gay life after dark of drinking, dancing, and having casual sexual encounters. "Movious" people bar-hop, starting their drinking after work at a downtown bar and later driving to a nightclub or party away from the downtown area.

5. *Viva*, I, 8:20.

6. Zambian currency consists of the *Kwacha* (K) and the *ngwee* (n). One *kwacha* equals 100 *ngwee*. K1.00 was equal to $1.50 in 1972–73, the time these data were collected.

7. Over the years, imported clothes became scarcer due to import restrictions. Ultimately the import of clothes was banned altogether. Among the subelites, used imported clothes bought from foreigners—in 1976 the only way to obtain imported clothes—had higher prestige value than expensive new locally manufactured clothes. People wear locally made clothes as a last resort and beg acquaintances going abroad to buy them clothes, for which they are willing to pay double or triple the price of locally made clothes.

Chapter 6

1. *UZ* (the student newspaper), III, 2.

2. *UZ*, III, 14.

3. *UZ*, III, 4.

4. The night life activities described in the text were true only for the years up to 1974. In 1975 night life was virtually ended under a State of Emergency regulation.

5. Zambia's infant mortality rate, according to the Zambian newspapers, is the highest in Africa. While this is certainly open to question, it is true that children do seem to die so often that it is a rare extended family which can report all the children born to it growing up. The major causes of death in infancy seem to be gastroenteritis and malaria. Malnutrition is increasingly becoming a cause among bottle-fed babies whose mothers or nannies dilute the powdered milk with too much water, to save money. Malnutrition is a major killer after weaning.

6. Interview with a tourist guide: "Why John feels cocky and sweet to be alive," *Zambia Daily Mail*, November 8, 1974.

7. A. Kardiner and L. Ovesey, *The Mark of Oppression: Explorations in the Personality of the American Negro* (1951), p. 385.

Chapter 7

1. Subhead to an article, "Are engagement parties necessary in our society?" *Zambia Daily Mail*, January 9, 1975.

2. The nature of an interviewee's relationships with men was considered an open issue requiring discussion and clarification. Marital status was not a criterion for selecting interviewees, and of 48 women, only twelve considered themselves married at the time of the interview. Others were engaged, or had been married and divorced, or had histories of having lived in consensual (*mapoto*) unions in the past.

Married women were more reluctant interviewees than were single women. Some refused immediately. Others consented but later declined, explaining their husbands refused to allow it. The majority would not agree without first obtaining their husbands' permission. Only one wife among the scores I approached not only agreed but did not inform her husband until I arrived in her home. Few husbands would agree to having their wives interviewed unless they could be present, but I myself would not agree to this condition.

Men were particularly eager to express their views after hearing that I was "writing a book about women." Wives, they said, would not give me a realistic impression. Married men were highly cooperative in helping me learn about male attitudes toward and experience with marriage. I spent many hours in informal discussions with them.

Married men were subtle in their discussions about marriage. For example, they rarely admitted to having personal difficulties. They preferred discussing marriage in the abstract, and blamed interference from relatives and the Women's Liberation Movement as the main causes of marital discord.

From the mistresses of married men I learned what men told them about the problems they had with their wives. Mistresses "understood" them; wives did not. Mistresses "excited" them; wives bored them. Wives "nagged" and "got too emotional." Wives grew "ugly and demanding."

Whenever possible I confronted married men with their girlfriends' assessments of their marriages. This was a useful but potentially compromising technique, for I could not, in conscience, expose my sources of information.

In articulating what I came to understand as the attitudes of wives, I was often accused by Zambian men of imposing personal (or American) values on Zambian society. This seemed to me a device to deny a voice to the women and to deny that their own behavior had anything to do with their wives' misery. For example, two university professors I knew well beat their wives regularly. Neither knew I had access to their wives. The men spoke to me freely about how much they loved their wives, never wanting to divorce them, admitting only that their wives had to be "disciplined" on occasion, being inclined to "foolishness." Their wives had quite different views and lived in a state of terror, not without reason. One had been twice hospitalized from beatings. Perhaps educated men would not admit their marriages were unsatisfactory because it would indicate they could not control their wives, or that African women were perhaps not quite as satisfied as men would like foreigners to believe.

Some older, prosperous businessmen and politicians I knew praised their old "bush" wives who had borne them many children and stood by them through years of economic vicissitude. I never met their wives and wondered if the women were serene or were perhaps jealous and insecure. It was so common for these old men to divorce "bush" wives that in 1966 President Kaunda publicly condemned the practice.

It was very difficult to obtain data from both partners in a marriage. This in itself is data: one can rarely befriend both a husband and wife, instead being forced to choose sides. There is little sharing between spouses, and one cannot observe the relationship with any degree of easy intimacy. If one knows the wife first, the husband is suspicious, and vice versa.

3. "Personality plus spells Cicewa," *Times of Zambia*, June 13, 1971.

4. A *Zambia Daily Mail* feature, "Would you let your husband take a holiday all on his own?" (February 6, 1973) says:

> Women are a deceitful sex. You may think that your wife loves you "above everything else in this world," but give her the liberty to go and enjoy herself wherever she wants, and you may lose her forever. . . . Ours are women in whom you cannot put your full trust; they are so prone to temptation. . . . If you allow your wife to take a holiday on her own, she may while there fancy another gentleman who is, both financially and materially, far better off than yourself and probably moving in a plush, high-powered limousine.

5. The quote is from W. T. McClain, "The legal position of women and children under Zambia's customary laws" in a mimeographed volume entitled *Women's Rights in Zambia: Report of a Consultation* (Kitwe, Zambia: Mindolo Ecumenical Foundation, 1970), p. 76.

Chapter 8

1. The divorce rates are evidently increasing in Zambia. In 1969, 8,671 divorces were granted in local courts. In 1970, 13,259 divorces were granted. See "Divorce: the one for the road can wreck a home," *Zambia Daily Mail*, February 4, 1972. Psychiatrists and physicians indicate that mental breakdowns and suicides are also increasing.

2. The usual jail sentence for theft of livestock is seven years plus ten strokes of the cane (cf. "He stole a cow—7 years jail," *Times of Zambia*, August 17, 1971; cf. also *Times of Zambia*, December 19, 1971, November 29, 1972, January 20, 1973 for further cases of theft of cows; *Zambia Daily Mail*, September 2, 1972 for theft of sheep; September 9, 1971 for theft of goat).

A man who stole nine head of cattle from four different villagers over a period of a year was sentenced to thirty-one years plus ten strokes ("Cattle thief gets 31 years," *Zambia Daily Mail*, March 16, 1972).

In 1971–72 the jail sentences for manslaughter of a wife, as reported in the *Times of Zambia*, averaged five years (N=13). The range was from twelve years to an absolute discharge to an old villager who beat his old wife to death when she accused him of impotency during a drunken fight. Men involved included villagers, and townsmen of various socioeconomic classes. A former District Governor got two years ("Wife killing: Ex DG jailed," *Times of Zambia*, July 15, 1971).

3. "Divorces: the one for the road can wreck a home," *Zambia Daily Mail*, February 4, 1972.

4. Edwin Smith and Andrew Murray Dale, *The Ila-Speaking Peoples of Northern Rhodesia*, Vol. 2 (New York: University Books, 1968 ed.), p. 35.

5. *UZ*, III, 16. (*UZ* is the student newspaper of the University of Zambia.)

6. "How perseverance paid dividends for Esther Antonio," *Zambia Daily Mail*, September 24, 1974.

Chapter 9

1. Stanley Cohen, *Folk Devils and Moral Panics* (Harmondsworth, Eng.: Penguin, 1973), pp. 9–10. Cohen analyzes the role of the media in Great Britain in inducing a state of moral panic in society over the Mods and Rockers phenomenon of the 1960s. The Mods and Rockers were Britain's folk devils. My analysis of the Zambian material is a modification of Cohen's approach.

2. June 13, 1972.

3. "Ban 'danger' women," *Times of Zambia*, March 3, 1972.

4. "Hey, lover boy, you're being watched," *Zambia Daily Mail*, March 10, 1972.

5. "How pleasure girls look like—and what they do," *Zambia Daily Mail*, November 9, 1973.

6. *Zambia Daily Mail*, December 27, 1973.

7. *Times of Zambia*, May 10, 1972.

8. *Zambia Daily Mail*, October 19, 1972.

9. *Zambia Daily Mail*, January 16, 1973.

10. *Zambia Daily Mail*, January 29, 1973.

11. "It's full scale war on prostitute hotels," *Times of Zambia*, May 19, 1972.

12. *Zambia Daily Mail*, January 16, 1973.

13. "Prostitutes smuggled over the border," *Zambia Daily Mail*, August 1, 1972.

14. "Whores: they money spinners," *Zambia Daily Mail*, October 4, 1972.

15. "Will prostitution ever be erased from our society?," *Zambia Daily Mail*, December 27, 1973.

16. Shadrack Soko, Minister of State for National Guidance, quoted in "Police to round up the good time girls," *Zambia Daily Mail*, April 5, 1972.

17. Mrs. Rosemary Phiri of Ndeke Township, quoted in "Good-time girls under fire again," *Zambia Daily Mail*, April 7, 1972.

18. The new abortion law was actually more restrictive than the old law. However, this was not widely understood by most people, who assumed it would be more liberal.

19. "Why be modest when it comes to hot pants? 'They look good on me,' says Pezo." Interview with Miss Pezo Njolomba, a student at the University of Zambia, *Zambia Daily Mail*, October 27, 1971.

20. "Police round up the good-time girls," *Zambia Daily Mail*, April 5, 1972.

21. "100 women arrested in midnight swoop on bars," *Times of Zambia*, September 23, 1972.

22. "Bogus police on sex prowl," *Zambia Daily Mail*, May 2, 1972.

23. "Lone girls in Chingola face wig snatchers," *Times of Zambia*, April 19, 1972.

24. "Help . . . wig snatchers at large," *Zambia Daily Mail*, April 19, 1972.

25. "Good-time girls under fire again," *Zambia Daily Mail*, April 7, 1972.

26. "Night prowlers will get police help—Changufu," *Zambia Daily Mail*, April 17, 1972.

27. Ibid.

Chapter 10

1. "Don't sit back and watch, women told," *Times of Zambia*, March 2, 1975.

2. "It's up to you, women told," *Times of Zambia*, September 6, 1971.

3. *Zambia Daily Mail*, November 18, 1971.

4. *Times of Zambia*, January 17, 1972.

5. *Times of Zambia*, March 21, 1972.

6. *Zambia Daily Mail*, September 22, 1972.

7. *Times of Zambia*, January 16, 1973.

8. *Zambia Daily Mail*, December 20, 1973.

9. *Zambia Daily Mail*, interview, June 22, 1972.

10. "Make a date with a bevy of beauties," *Zambia Daily Mail*, October 13, 1972.

11. Men claimed that the sight of women's thighs made it impossible for them to concentrate on anything but sex. University students, for example, said the presence of miniskirted coeds on campus was inconducive to serious studying. A man could not read in the library or listen to a classroom lecture, they said, if there were coeds in miniskirts in the room. Student newspapers frequently referred to the problem, and it was the subject of satire by columnist Kapelwa Musonda of the *Times of Zambia*.

12. *Zambia Daily Mail*, June 22, 1972.

13. *Zambia Daily Mail*, June 29, 1972.

14. *Zambia Daily Mail*, December 31, 1971.

15. "Lovely Rita wants more contests," *Zambia Daily Mail*, December 22, 1972.

16. "The girl who hates desk work," *Zambia Daily Mail*, July 12, 1972.

17. *Times of Zambia*, August 28, 1972.

18. "Party forms burial groups," *Zambia Daily Mail*, February 14, 1972.

19. "Mrs. Kankasa calls for increase in women MPs," *Times of Zambia*, July 26, 1973.

20. "UNIP want women to take over the markets," *Times of Zambia*, February 12, 1973.

21. The black shirts and combed-up hair style were used by African men organizing opposition to colonial rule.

22. "We're still used as beasts of burden," Women's Forum, *Times of Zambia*, August 29, 1972.

23. "Women's role in nation building is a great pride," *Zambia Daily Mail*, September 12, 1972.

24. "Traditionalists clash with intellectuals on abortions," *Zambia Daily Mail*, August 19, 1971.

25. "Racists and UPP: KK can prove it," *Zambia Daily Mail*, September 6, 1971.

26. "KK hints at big changes," *Zambia Daily Mail*, September 7, 1971.

27. September 6, 1971.

28. "Keep out of politics, UNIP mums warned," *Times of Zambia*, October 3, 1971.

29. "Kankasa tells women to be spies," *Times of Zambia*, February 14, 1973.

30. In "African women, fashion and scapegoating" (*Canadian Journal of African Studies*, VII, 2 [1972], 329–49), Audrey Wipper analyzes how the fashionable mini-skirt was a trigger for the scapegoating of East African townswomen. Her analysis is a model for the Zambian material.

194

Zambian Glossary

apamwamba   the elite of modern Zambian urban society

banachimbusa   elderly female instructors at a girl's initiation

Bantu   a group of related African languages spoken by widely dispersed peoples with a common origin, probably in West Africa

Bemba   a Zambian tribe from the Northern Province

Boma   an administrative center of government originating in the colonial period

bwana   Mr., sir

Chibemba   the language of the Bemba people

Chikankata   a mission school in Southern Province

Chinyanja   an Eastern Province language which became the dominant language of Lusaka

chisungu   the traditional female initiation ceremony undergone at puberty

chitenge   brightly printed cotton cloth

dis-as-ter-ous   Zambian urban slang for a young townswoman with no sex appeal (Zambian-English slang)

kapenta   a small popular fish, also an old fashioned slang term for a dolly girl

kwacha   unit of Zambian currency equivalent to U.S. $1.50 in 1972–73.

Lenje   a Zambian tribe from the Central Province
lobola   a South African word for bride-price widely used in urban Zambia
madoilies   crocheted antimacassars
Mambwe   a Zambian tribe from the Northern Province
Ngoni   a Zambian tribe from the Eastern Province
ngwee   unit of Zambian currency equal to 1/100 of a kwacha
Nsenga   a Zambian tribe from the Eastern Province
nshima   the boiled corn meal staple of the Zambian diet
Nyanja   see Chinyanja
Tonga   a Zambian tribe from the Southern Province
toughu   an attractive, appealing townswoman (Zambian-English slang)
Xhosa   a South African tribe

Glossary of Anthropological Terms

bride-price   in modern times, the cash payment made by a groom to his bride's father at the time of their marriage as compensation for the expenses he incurred in raising and educating her.

classificatory daughter   a female addressed and/or referred to by the word "daughter" according to the kinship terminology of the vernacular of a tribe, who is not a biological daughter.

elite   in a stratified society, the top-most members.

extended family   relatives of the husband and wife of a nuclear family.

matrikin   relatives on the mother's side of the family.

matrilateral extended family   the matrikin.

polygyny   the marriage of a man to more than one woman simultaneously.

subelite   in a stratified society, those members who rank beneath elites.

uxorilocal societies   societies in which the groom resides in the locality of his bride's parents.

witchdoctor   a healer who uses magical and herbal means to cure illnesses of both physical and psychological nature.

Bibliography

STUDIES OF ZAMBIAN SOCIETY: A SAMPLING

Barnes, J. A.
1951   *Marriage in a Changing Society.* Rhodes Livingstone Papers No. 20.
Colonial Office
1938   *Report of the Commission Appointed to Enquire into the Financial and Economic Position of Northern Rhodesia.* Colonial Office Report No. 145. London: Her Majesty's Stationery Office.
Colson, Elizabeth
1958   *Marriage and Family Among the Plateau Tonga of Northern Rhodesia.* Manchester University Press.
Cunnison, Ian
1959   *The Luapula Peoples of Northern Rhodesia.* Manchester University Press.
Doke, Clement
1931   *The Lambas of Northern Rhodesia: A Study of Their Customs and Beliefs.* London: George Harrap & Co., Ltd.
Epstein, A. L.
1958   *Politics in an Urban African Community.* Manchester University Press.
Gluckman, Max
1950   Kinship and marriage among the Lozi of Northern Rhodesia and the Zulu of Natal. A. R. Radcliffe-Brown and C. D. Forde (eds.), *African Systems of Kinship and Marriage.* London: Oxford University Press.

199

Heisler, Helmuth
    1974   *Urbanisation and the Government of Migration: The Inter-Relation of Urban and Rural Life in Zambia.* London: C. Hurst & Co.

Long, Norman
    1968   *Social Change and the Individual.* Manchester University Press.

Mindolo Ecumenical Foundation
    1970   *Women's Rights in Zambia: Report of a Consultation.* Katwe, Zambia.

Mitchell, J. Clyde
    1957   Aspects of African marriage on the Copperbelt of Northern Rhodesia. *Rhodes Livingstone Journal* No. 22.

    1969   (ed.). *Social Networks in Urban Situations.* Manchester University Press.

Mitchell, J. C. and A. L. Epstein
    1959   Occupational prestige and social status among urban Africans in Northern Rhodesia. *Africa,* XXIX, 22–39.

Mwanakatwe, J. M.
    1968   *The Growth of Education in Zambia Since Independence.* Lusaka: Oxford University Press.

Powdermaker, Hortense
    1962   *Coppertown: Changing Africa.* New York: Harper & Row.

Republic of Zambia, Central Statistical Office
    1969 Census, Final Report, Vol. I. Lusaka: Government Printer.

Richards, Audrey
    1940   *Bemba Marriage and Modern Economic Conditions.* Rhodes Livingstone Papers No. 3.

    1956   *Chisungu: A Girl's Initiation Ceremony Among the Bemba of Northern Rhodesia.* London: Faber & Faber.

Smith, Edwin and Andrew Murray Dale
    1920, 1968 ed. *The Ila-Speaking Peoples of Northern Rhodesia.* New York: University Books.

Stefaniszyn, Bronislaw
    1964   *Social and Ritual Life of the Ambo of Northern Rhodesia.* London: Oxford University Press.

Turner, Victor
    1957   *Schism and Continuity in an African Society: A Study of Ndembu Village Life.* Manchester University Press.

    1968   *The Drums of Affliction: A Study of Religious Processes Among the Ndembu of Zambia.* Oxford: Clarendon Press.

Viva Magazine
    1975   I, 8 (August 1975). Nairobi: Trend Publishers, Ltd. *See:* Intermarriage: The husbands how they feel; Special report: the new African woman.

White, C. M. N.
    1959   *Preliminary Survey of Luvale Rural Economy.* Rhodes Livingstone Papers No. 25.

    1962   *Tradition and Change in Luvale Marriage.* Rhodes Livingstone Papers No. 34.

Wilson, Godfrey
1941   *An Essay on the Economics of Detribalisation in Northern Rhodesia.*
        Part I. Rhodes Livingstone Papers No. 5.
1942   Part II, Rhodes Livingstone Papers No. 6.

SOME STUDIES OF WOMEN

Albert, Ethel
1963   The status of women in Burundi. Denise Paulme (ed.), *Women of
        Tropical Africa.* London: Routledge & Kegan Paul.
Boserup, Ester
1970   *Woman's Role in Economic Development.* London: Allen & Unwin.
Evans, David R.
1972   Image and reality: career goals of educated Ugandan women. *Canadian
        Journal of African Studies*, VI, 2, 213–32.
Evans-Pritchard, E. E.
1965   *The Position of Women in Primitive Societies and Other Essays in Social
        Anthropology.* London: Faber & Faber.
Gough, Kathleen
1961   The modern disintegration of matrilineal descent groups. D. Schneider
        and Kathleen Gough (eds.), *Matrilineal Kinship.* Berkeley: University
        of California Press.
Gugler, Joseph
1972   The second sex in town. *Canadian Journal of African Studies*, VI, 2,
        289–301.
Hellman, Ellen
1935   Native life in a Johannesburg slum yard. *Africa*, VIII, 34–62.
Hoffer, Carol P.
1972   Mende and Sherbro women in high office. *Canadian Journal of African
        Studies*, VI, 2, 151–64.
Kratochvil, Laura and Shauna Shaw
1974   *African Women: A Select Bibliography.* Cambridge: African Studies
        Centre (England).
Kuper, Hilda
1965   Nurses. Leo Kuper, *An African Bourgeoisie: Race, Class and Politics
        in South Africa.* Clinton: Colonial Press, Inc.
Le Vine, Robert A.
1966   Sex roles and economic change in Africa. *Ethnology*, V, 2, 186–93.
Leith-Ross, Sylvia
1939   *African Women: A Study of the Ibo of Nigeria.* London: Routledge &
        Kegan Paul.
Little, Kenneth
1973   *African Women in Towns: An Aspect of Africa's Social Revolution.* Cam-
        bridge University Press.

Lloyd, Peter C.
   1968   Divorce among the Yoruba. *American Anthropologist*, 70, 1, 67–81.

Longmore, Laura
   1959   *The Dispossessed: A Study of the Sex Life of Bantu Women In and Around Johannesburg*. London: Jonathan Cape.

Marris, Peter
   1961   *Family and Social Change in an African City: A Study of Rehousing in Lagos*. London: Routledge & Kegan Paul.

Oppong, Christine
   1974   *Marriage Among a Matrilineal Elite: A Family Study of Ghanaian Senior Civil Servants*. Cambridge University Press.

Ottenburg, Phoebe
   1959   The changing economic position of women among the Afikpo Ibo. William Bascom and Melville Herskovitz (eds.), *Continuity and Change in African Cultures*. Chicago University Press.

Pool, Janet
   1972   A cross-comparative study of aspects of conjugal behaviour among women of three West African countries. *Canadian Journal of African Studies*, VI, 2, 233–59.

Simons, H. J.
   1968   *African Women: Their Legal Status in South Africa*. London: C. Hurst & Co.

Southall, Aiden and P. C. W. Gutkind
   1957   *Townsmen in the Making*. East African Institute for Social Research.

Wipper, Audrey
   1972   African women, fashion, and scapegoating. *Canadian Journal of African Studies*, VI, 2, 329–49.

OF THEORETICAL INTEREST

Allport, Gordon
   1954   *The Nature of Prejudice*. Reading, Pa.: Addison-Wesley Publishing Co.

Andreski, Stanislav
   1968   *The African Predicament: A Study in the Pathology of Modernization*. London: Michael Joseph, Ltd.

Benedict, Ruth
   1938   Continuities and discontinuities in cultural conditioning. *Psychiatry*, I, 161–67.

Cohen, Stanley
   1973   *Folk Devils and Moral Panics: The Creation of the Mods and Rockers*. St. Albans: Paladin.

Douglas, Mary
   1966   *Purity and Danger: An Analysis of Concepts of Pollution and Taboo*. New York: Praeger.

Fromm, Erich
 1944   Individual and social origins of neurosis. *American Sociological Review*,
         IX, 380–84.
 1956   *The Sane Society*. London: Routledge & Kegan Paul.
Kardiner, Abram and Lionel Ovesey
 1951   *The Mark of Oppression: Explorations in the Personality of the American
         Negro*. New York: World Publishing Co.
Komarovsky, Mirra
 1946   Cultural contradictions and sex roles. *American Journal of Sociology*,
         52, 3, 184–89.
Laing, R. D.
 1961   *Self and Others*. London: Tavistock.
Weston, Peter J. and Martha T. Mednick
 1970   Race, social class, and the motive to avoid success in women. *Journal
         of Cross-Cultural Psychology*, I, 3, 284–91.

Index

Abortion, 47, 94, 149, 163, 164
Age mates, 109
Alienation, 64, 80, 84, 101, 123, 130–31
Alimony, 136, 173
Ambition, career, 73, 139, 183
Authority: figures of, 65; male, 37, 67, 68, 105, 174; submission to, 121

Banachimbusa, 44, 45, 195
Bars, 25, 83, 87, 89, 91, 99, 118, 122, 147, 149, 189; owners of, 151
Beating, of women, 93–94, 99, 114, 117, 126–27, 130
Beauty contests: organization of, 157; participants in, 158–59, 160; public reception of, 158–59; symbol of, 160
Birth control, 46–47, 149, 163, 164; pill, 11, 92, 119, 164, 181
Bottle feeding, 35
Boyfriend-girlfriend relations, 93, 99, 181
Boys: alienation in, 64; in family, 36–37; in school, 55, 62, 172
Bride price, 32, 40, 128, 196, 197
British South Africa Company, 14, 15
Brutalization, 93

Budget: of married couples, 118, 120, 182; of unmarried women, 80–81, 181. *See also* Surplus

Changufu, Lewis, 150, 152, 159
Chastity, 20, 42, 45, 61
Childbearing, 101, 110, 112
Childhood: early, of interviewees, 35–37, 177, 178; of modern couples, 125
Child rearing, 28, 35–37, 111, 112, 136, 137, 143, 170
Children, of elites, subelites, 125, 172
Chisungu. See Initiation, female
Christianity: ideals, 20; ministers, 146; missionaries, 161; missions, 21, 29. *See also* Morality
Clothing, 80, 85, 112, 114, 115, 121, 136, 143, 146, 167–68, 189
Coeducation, 55–56
Cohen, Stanley, 140, 192
Conflict: employer-employee, 69–70; marital, 14–15, 109, 117, 123, 127, 129, 132–33; of career and mother-craft, 113; of cultures, 32–33, 60, 64; of values, 114; parent-child, 43; sexual, 14, 74, 75, 89, 91, 109, 131, 192–93; with relatives, 114

Housing: eligibility for, 172; of divorcees, 137; of married couples, 105–06; shortage of, 75–76; types of, 76–77, 186
Husband: allocation of income, 113; attitude toward wife's work, 116; control of income, 119; data on, 190–91; death of, 115–16, 173; employment of, 105–06; help with housework, 110; transporting wives, 112

Illegitimacy, 45
Illness, 32–34, 67, 100, 135, 145, 161, 197
Independence: financial, 66, 81, 102, 103; of men, 66, 67–68; of women, 65, 77, 81, 101, 162; Zambian, 10, 21, 29, 157, 159, 171, 172, 185, 187
Inefficiency, 70–71
Infancy, 35
Inferiority: of female, 23, 68; feelings of, 62, 64, 159, 174–75
Infidelity, 94, 99, 113, 115, 116, 117, 124
Inheritance, 157
Initiation, female, 44, 45, 51, 164, 167, 195
Intermarriage, 128
Isolation, social, 100, 124

Jealousy, 74, 93, 101, 116, 123
Job market, 171

Kankasa, Chibesa, 161, 163, 165, 193, 194
Kapwepwe, Simon, 151–52, 164
Kaunda, Dr. Kenneth, 101, 107, 122, 144, 148, 164, 167, 194
King, Dr. Felicity Savage, 6, 7

Labor: division of, 166; migration, 15–16, 18–19, 20; in schools, 59. See also Housework
Law: customary, 157, 172; labor, 19–20; systems of, 173
Love medicine, 34
Luxury, 113; of offices, 73–74, 92

Magic, 33, 60. See also Love medicine; Witchcraft
Male-female relations, 19, 27, 85, 86, 89, 91, 100, 126, 137–39, 144
Malnutrition, 35, 36, 125
Market women, 6, 32, 67
Marriage, 8, 62, 182–83; as defective institution, 139; as process, 104–05; as value, 31, 44; as goal, 79, 183; companionship in, 111; companionate activity in, 123, 124; financial aspects of, 113–14, 118–19, 172; instability of, 14, 31, 68, 126; interference in, by relatives, 129; laws of, 173; pathology of, 130; rural features in town, 132; traditional behavior in, 133–34; types of, 105, 133; westernization in, 109. See also Conflict, marital
Maternal role, of career women, 75
Maternity leave, 71, 172
Matriliny, 13–14, 101, 114, 119
Media, importance of, 141
Misogyny, 20, 143, 154
Mobility: residential, 32, 39, 40, 49, 68, 116; social, 72
Modernity, symbols of, 159
Modernization, 154, 160
Morality, 20, 56–57, 122; education in, 44; improvement of, 151; lack of, 21, 163, 165, 174; overseers of, 21, 147; supervision of, 56; traditional, 21
Mother: as ideal, 161; attitude toward employment, 71; -daughter relations, 40, 90; -infant relations, 35; of educated women, 31, 32, 35, 38; support of, 82, 115; UNIP Women's Brigade as, 161
Murder, 149; of wives, 127, 191

Neighborhood, as status marker, 25, 106
Neighbors, relations of, 8, 84, 85, 86, 124
Networks, 5, 8, 77, 90
Nurses, 6, 10, 46, 47, 52, 73, 113, 179, 182

Orgasm, 131

Parties, 87, 123, 127
Patriliny, 13–14, 115, 119
Peers, female, 48
Pimps, 148, 149, 153
Pin-up, lack of threat of, 160
Police, 86, 148, 149, 150, 152, 153, 167;
    lack of control of, 152
Politicians, 100–01, 107, 108, 146, 155,
    165, 166, 173–74
Polygyny, 95, 105, 114, 115, 197
Pregnancy, 43, 44, 45, 46, 47, 48, 69,
    71, 76, 92, 109, 115, 117, 131, 163,
    164, 166, 170, 172, 186–87
Prejudice: in employment, 171; in law,
    172; occupational, 54; race, 20, 29.
    See also Misogyny
Prestige, 98, 103, 106, 133; system,
    urban, 98–99; traditional woman's,
    112
Prostitutes, 5, 67, 89, 121, 122, 192;
    branding as, 146, 153; condemna-
    tion of, 148; labels for, 145; profes-
    sional, 151, 172; research on, 148;
    war on, 147–48
Prostitution, 108, 172, 192

Questionnaires, in fieldwork, 6–7

Rape, 149, 150, 151, 152; fear of, 76
Reciprocity, 85, 99
Relatives: and pregnancy, 47–48; at
    death, 157; conflict with, 42–43,
    114; emotional distance from, 39,
    43, 49–50; greed of, 116; of women,
    95; support by, 41, 48; support of,
    114, 115; visits to, 40, 42–43, 86
Remarriage, 115, 132, 137–38
Residence, rules of, 107, 108
Respect, shown by girl, 37–38
Revenge, 117, 135
Role models, 28, 60, 140, 154; educated
    women as, 1; family members as, 28
Role playing: maternal, 75; sexual, 116
Role segregation, 110
Roles, traditional, rejection of, 101
Roommates, 79

Savings, 81, 122–23
Scapegoats: Rhodesians as, 166; role of
    media in creating, 140; women as
    targets for, 166
School, 177, 178, 179; activities in,
    58–59, 62; and social mobility, 61,
    171; boarding, 40; colonial, 52, 187;
    daily life in, 58; expenses, 82; per-
    formance in, 113; primary, 37, 51,
    54, 55; registration for, 172; sec-
    ondary, 55–56, 144, 170
School system, 54–55, 56; staffing of,
    58
Self-esteem, 66
Servants, 110, 112, 117, 121
Servility, of women, 95
Sex: attitudes toward, 131; fear of, 44,
    76, 116, 117; interest in, 45, 46, 131
Sexual advances, 69–70, 76, 116
Sexual availability, 74, 90, 94, 127, 149
Sexual intercourse, 35, 45, 76, 86, 89,
    91, 96, 149, 168; abstinence from,
    129; ritual, 129
Sexual interest, 45, 131
Sexual tension, 109, 131, 193
Shame, as control, 65, 132
Shanty towns, 25, 76, 172
Social change, 1, 5, 21, 28, 130, 144,
    160, 165, 179
Social control, 65, 102, 132, 167. See
    also Control: of women
Socialization: in family, 35–37, 51; in
    school, 52, 60, 64–65
Socially patterned defect, 3, 27, 50, 132
Solidarity, female, 39
Status: legal, 157, 171; markers of,
    106; social, change of women's, 2,
    5, 22, 170. See also Law; Women's
    rights
Stereotyping, dichotomous, 140; of
    townswomen, 145; tribal, 128;
    truth in, 167–68
Superstition, 31, 33, 34, 129
Surplus, income, 68, 80–81, 118–19; of
    women, 115
Suspicion, in society, 8, 66, 103, 131,
    139
"Sweet talk," 8, 63, 74

Teachers, 55, 56, 77; relations with students, 59–60, 178
Toddlers, 35
Townswoman, as temptress, 145
Tradition: attitudes toward, 10, 44; beliefs in, 129; departure from, 160; threat to, 145; tribal, 128–29; values of, 167
Training programs, 55–56, 68, 72–73, 109, 170
Transiency, of workers, 68–69, 71

UNIP Women's Brigade, 144, 152; as ideal mother, 161; condemning women, 162–63; credibility of, 164; political role of, 164–65; position of, 161
University of Zambia, 6, 10, 157, 179, 180, 184
University Teaching Hospital, 6, 10, 46, 121, 188

Vacations, from school, 58, 76, 80, 109
Victimization, 149, 151
Virginity, 44, 45
Visiting, 112; of men to hostels, 91; to households, 106, 109. *See also* Hosting
Voluntary associations, 58, 86, 156–57

Wage labor, male, 15, 18, 19, 186
Weaning, 35, 36

Wedding, white, 92–93, 108, 133, 144
Westernization, 160; in boarding schools, 62–64; in dining habits, 38; of couples, 109, 133; of newspapers, 142
Widows, 157, 172, 173
Wife: as interviewee, 190; control of, 116, 133; dependency of, 132; discrimination against, 172; murder of, 127; neglect of, 115, 127; role of, 31; support of, 114
Witchcraft, 32–33, 60, 94, 108, 116, 135
Witchdoctor, 32, 34, 197
Women: arrest of, 150–51, 153; beliefs about, 10, 145; control of, 10, 20, 132, 149, 150; danger of, 10, 145; disadvantages for, 170–71; envy of, 146; fear of, 165, 174; fieldwork with, 4, 5; lack of unity of, 166, 174–75; leisure of, 86; literature on, 5; migration of, 19; opportunities for, 22, 155; lack of, 21; in future, 172; position of, 1–2, 172; relative to men, 1–2, 20, 22; vulnerability of, 166; successful, 156; threat of, 160; western, 155. *See also* Friendship; Status
Women's liberation movement, 4, 102, 111, 124, 140, 150, 174
Women's rights, 111, 172–75, 191
Workplace, functions of, 74

Zambianization, 21, 115, 171